U-BOATS OF THE SECOND WORLD WAR
THEIR LONGEST VOYAGES

Two ocean-going U-boats on the high seas.

U-BOATS OF THE SECOND WORLD WAR

THEIR LONGEST VOYAGES

JAK P. MALLMANN SHOWELL

FONTHILL

Learn more about Fonthill Media. Join our mailing list to find out about our latest titles and special offers at: www.fonthillmedia.com

Fonthill Media Limited
Fonthill Media LLC
www.fonthillmedia.com
office@fonthillmedia.com

First published in the United Kingdom in hardback 2013
This paperback edition published 2017

British Library Cataloguing in Publication Data:
A catalogue record for this book is available from the British Library

Copyright © Jak P. Mallmann Showell 2013, 2017

ISBN 978-1-78155-102-8 (hardback)
ISBN 978-1-78155-634-4 (paperback)

Typeset in 10/13 Sabon LT
Printed and bound by CPI Group (UK) Ltd, Croydon, CR0 4YY

Connect with us
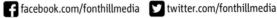 facebook.com/fonthillmedia twitter.com/fonthillmedia

Contents

Introduction

There are a number of good books describing U-boat battles in far-off waters, but hardly any of them tell us how it was done. U-boats were small, they lacked the majority of mod cons of their age, and men were squeezed in with hardly room to move. So how did they manage to live, fight and maintain their complicated machinery for such incredibly long periods?

The research to answer that question began a long time ago in 1980, and I must thank Lionel Leventhal and David Gibbons of the original Arms and Armour Press for providing the impetus to start this project. Their encouragement led me to make contact with many people who had direct connections with far-distant waters, and I am most grateful to everybody who helped. The list is so long that it would be difficult to mention everyone, especially as some boxes containing notes and letters disappeared during a house move.

This original project was lying dormant when I stumbled upon some incredible documents left in the German U-boat Museum by the war correspondent Walter Schöppe. He was remarkable inasmuch that although many war correspondents were given honorary officer ranks, Schöppe was already a fully fledged naval artillery officer when he became a war correspondent and he accompanied U178 on its journey to the Far East and back. After the war he made a detailed study of several exciting topics, collecting first-hand information from men who had taken part in very long range U-boat operations, and his incredible study generated the spark to go ahead with this book.

Searching through the U-boat Museum's documents produced a number of other interesting files. This material was digested and sorted with the help of the museum's library, and I am especially grateful to Werner Kraus (U-Boat Engineer Officer of U123 under Reinhard Hardegen) who left much of his library to the museum. This has been useful in giving a flavour of those times.

Walter Schöppe, the officer and war correspondent who did much of the research for this book, tries out chopsticks in the Far East.

U178, a very long range Type IXD2, approaching Bordeaux in France.

All this material would never have been assimilated had it not been for the untiring help from the founder and director of the museum, Horst Bredow. I must also thank all the other museum volunteers for doing so much to make this a place of research excellence.

Walter Schöppe's massive collection contains considerable material compiled by Jochen Brennecke for his book about U-boat operations in the Far East. Also of great use was *War in the Southern Oceans 1939–45*, the South African Government's official history. I used the preliminary draft manuscript of *U-boat Operations in South African Waters*, a copy of which is in the museum.

The material from the British Government's Code and Cypher School, which is Crown Copyright and has been reproduced by kind permission of the National Archives at Kew (London), was supplied by Bletchley Park, and I am grateful to John Gallehawk and the other archivists for helping with access to this valuable cache. This material was compiled by Lt Cdrs L. A. Griffiths RNVR and K. W. McMahan USNR.

The papers, photographs and information from the German U-boat Museum (www.dubm.de) on which this book is based were contributed by the following: Franz Berger (U195), 'Ajax' Bleichrodt (U67 and U109), Jochen Brennecke (author, historian, and war correspondent), Matthias Brünig (U195), Otto Giese (*Anneliese Essberger* and U181), Reinhard Hardegen and his crew (U123), Wolfgang Hirschfeld (U67 and U109), Konrad Hoppe (Far Eastern bases), Jost Metzler (U69 and U847), Fritz Müller (U171), Werner Musenberg (U180 commander), Günther Neumann (U195), Friedrich Peitl (U862), Albert Schirrmann (U862), Max Schley (U861), Rudolf Schneider (U160), Dr Armin Wandel (U-boat medical officer), Paul Weidlich (U518 chief engineer), and Hermann Wien (U180).

CHAPTER 1

Very Long Range Ocean-going U-boats

Although the Type VII U-boat was so successful that it became the biggest submarine class ever to have been built, the linchpin of Germany's early development was the slightly larger Type IA. This had a displacement of 1,200 tons submerged, while the Type VII was originally rated at just over 900 tons. Only two Type IA boats were ever built, but this class was developed on paper to produce several specialised versions at a time when Germany was not allowed to build or own submarines. This secret preparatory work was thwarted rather unexpectedly in June 1935, two years after Hitler had come to power, when the Anglo-German Naval Agreement was signed. This generous treaty allowed Germany to build up its new submarine strength to one third of the Royal Navy's tonnage. Being keen to keep within these restrictions, the U-boat Office within the Supreme Naval Command in Berlin abandoned earlier plans for specialised craft and concentrated on general-purpose vessels.

One of the favourite discussion points at this time was the development of a submarine capable of reaching potential hotspots in the eastern Mediterranean, to operate there for some time, and then to return home to Germany. Britain, with its powerful base at Gibraltar, was not considered as a potential enemy. Today it is in vogue to give the impression that Germany was preparing for a war against the United Kingdom, which is far from the truth. As far as the Mediterranean was concerned, it was the unstable situation in the Balkans and in the Middle East, not British colonial power, that gave great cause for concern. Both the IA and VII could get there and back, but neither could carry enough provisions, fuel and ammunition to make such a long journey worthwhile. With specialist boats already out of the planning process, many people argued that this was a good opportunity for developing a long distance, multi-purpose submarine to act as torpedo and/or mine carrier and also serve as reconnaissance craft.

One of the early long distance boats with its characteristic wide upper (outside) deck and a rescue buoy in the foreground. These contained a flashing light that illuminated automatically when triggered by the crew and it was possible to blow the contraption out of its holder with a depth charge. These aids were therefore removed once the war started.

In addition to this, they wanted a dedicated communications boat for an on-the-spot commander at sea. Although many history books tell us that Karl Dönitz, the U-boat Chief, introduced U-boat patrol lines or wolf packs in 1939, attempts to assemble such groups had already been made during the First World War. The stumbling block was that radios were not advanced enough and many messages just did not get through to the boats at sea. By 1935, this part of technology had advanced so dramatically that a special communications submarine was under serious scrutiny. Such a boat, with additional radio equipment, could act as a base for a group commander at sea or work as a spy submarine to transmit intelligence information back to base.

Now that the technical boffins had the requirements for the new large boat, all they had to do was to fit everything together and it did not take them long to calculate that there was no way in which all of this could be packed into a Type I hull. Something bigger was definitely called for. The initial concept for such an enlarged version, identified as the Type IX, had already been committed to paper before 1935. It was based on U81 of 1915 and had a double hull, similar to the Type IA, meaning a set of tanks were wrapped around the pressure hull, enabling it to store considerably more fuel than the single hull of the Type VII. In order to carry the additional armament, the shape of the outside casing was merely widened at the top to provide space for a series of pressure-resisting containers, two of them side by side, for holding torpedoes or mines. Since these had to be as light as possible, it was necessary to dispense with the heavy firing mechanism and leave them as simple storage tubes. The idea was to extract the torpedoes and lower them into the boat once there was enough space there to accommodate them. The original Type IA had a capacity for fourteen torpedoes or a maximum of about forty-two mines. (The three types of special torpedo mines being developed were either one third or half as long as a torpedo.) The larger Type IX was a considerable improvement on this, carrying twenty-two torpedoes or a maximum of sixty-six mines.

Meeting the demand to provide a range of 10,000 nautical miles was a good deal easier than achieving a cruising speed of 14 knots. At first it was thought that an extra cylinder on the Type IA engine plus some boosters or superchargers might get near this figure, but this was the area where technology came unstuck. Right from the outset it was clear that some compromise was going to be necessary. The engines were going to be so heavy that they would need all the space aft of the central control room. This was most disappointing because both the IA and the VII had a room there for petty officers' bunks. These fitted snugly between the noisy engines and the central control room. The cruising speed of 14 knots remained pie in the sky, and despite a great deal of optimism it quickly became clear that this would not be achievable in the foreseeable future.

Artillery enthusiasts fared a little better inasmuch that the enlarged upper deck provided a good platform for some impressive guns and the boat had enough reserve buoyancy to carry this additional weight up top. To the astonishment of many people, the additional size did not have too much detrimental influence on the other critical factor of the period: the diving time was only about 10 seconds longer than the smaller Type VII. So the first Type IXA boats made a good impression. They had four bow and two stern torpedo tubes, and carried a 105 mm and a 37 mm quick firing deck gun, plus what was thought to be a reasonable anti-aircraft armament. The consensus of opinion was that aircraft could not hurt submarines, as a crow could not hurt a mole. With such a fast diving time the submarine would vanish long before an aircraft came close enough to attack it. It has often been claimed that this hitting power was the ultimate in submarine design, but it is strange that many other countries were already building comparable boats with six bow torpedo tubes and with considerably superior accommodation for the crew. One wonders what might have happened if the 'aces' of autumn 1940 had attacked convoys with six instead of four bow tubes.

Yet, despite all the positive points, there were enough minor niggles to push the designers into starting to plan an improved version even before the first Type IXA boats were launched. Thus the Type IXB followed about a year later without having benefited from extensive trials. The first IXB, U64, was launched a few days after the outbreak of the Second World War. The already

One of the early long distance boats, showing the effectiveness of the 'V'-shaped water deflector at deck level, protecting the feet of the gun crew. The gun is a 105 mm quick firing deck gun for use against surface targets.

operational Type IXA boats had by that time taken up waiting positions in lonely parts of the Atlantic, and since they had the longest endurance they were allocated the furthest away, off Spain and Portugal. Unfortunately, these long range ocean-going boats did not have a happy start to the war. Three of the nine boats lost during the autumn of 1939 were Types IXA.

Although Germany had a comparatively successful 1940 and controlled much of the coast from Norway's North Cape as far as Spain, things started to look decisively gloomy in 1941. Eight supply ships were lost during one swoop around the time of the *Bismarck*'s breakout, and keeping other surface raiders at sea was becoming increasingly more difficult. The majority had had their heyday by the end of that year. One of the major contributing factors to this state of affairs was that Britain enlarged its back-up staff to such an extent that it was possible to use the incoming intelligence to forecast what the Germans were likely to be doing. On the other side of the North Sea exactly the opposite happened. Thinking there were leaks in security, staffs were reduced to the barest minimum, meaning less and less intelligence trickled into the Operational Command.

Not wanting to accept that Britain was reading much of the German naval radio code, the German High Command was under the impression that the Royal Navy was powerful enough to stretch its forces over the entire Atlantic. Therefore the Naval High Command took the decision to order the U-boat

Command to send submarines into distant waters to draw British hunting forces far away from the North Atlantic convoy routes. This move then gave more priority to the concept of the new very long range submarine. The major snag was that the Type IX (of which the 'C' version was already in production) had been designed to go to the eastern Mediterranean, and the admirals were now thinking of sending them into the Indian Ocean and south beyond the Caribbean. (Japan had not yet entered the conflict and was therefore not included in these early plans.)

The prospects, however, for building this new type of very long range boat did not look too gloomy. Amazing progress had been made with marine diesel engines and with electric motors since the First World War and by 1939 it was no longer a secret that so-called diesel-electric propulsion provided the most economical system. This was quite simple. One diesel engine was connected to an electric motor to generate electricity and this was fed to the other motor on the opposite shaft, which then propelled the boat while one diesel engine was shut down to save fuel. The principle was so successful that merchant ships were built with powerful diesel generators that did nothing other than generate power for a set of electric motors driving the propellers. The attractive part of this equation was that these electricity generators could be a good deal smaller than an engine driving the propellers. Of course, the downside was that this system did not go anywhere near as fast as the pure diesel drive, but it did produce impressively long ranges. So, with this in mind, the designers came up with the proposition of fitting this new very long range boat with a double set of diesels: one for economical cruising and another, bigger, set for when high speeds were called for.

For some strange reason, Germany never seriously experimented with diesel-electric drive until after the start of the war and therefore did not have anyone capable of making suggestions as to the best way of doing this. One would have thought that the navy might have conducted some long range, fuel-saving tests but this was not the case and once the war started, submarine chief engineers were left to their own devices to work out the best way of cruising at the most economical speeds. The system eventually recommended was to connect one diesel engine running at half speed to its electric motor to charge the batteries. The other diesel engine was then switched off and the propeller on that shaft was turned by the electric motor running at somewhere from slow to half speed. This produced a maximum speed of about 7 knots and proved to be the most economical way of cruising. Fuel was not so critical for boats operating in the convoy routes of the North Atlantic and they therefore continued running on diesel engines at cruising speed, producing about 10 knots. By the beginning of 1943, the opposition in the North Atlantic had become so fierce that even the long range boats crossed those waters at the slightly faster cruising speed.

One of the first choices for this new submarine type, with a set of two different diesel engines, was to modify the submarine cruiser of the Type XI, which was due to have been built by Deschimag AG Weser in Bremen but was abandoned shortly after the start of the war. It was proposed to remove its heavy artillery, fit more torpedo tubes and then convert the 3,140/4,650 tons into an especially very long range boat. The problem was that the initial plans for this Type XI had got only as far as a discussion with the builders, and no one could say for certain whether the massive hull would live up to the expectations put upon it. After all, it was three times as big as the Type IXC and four times as big as the VIIC. Ideas for modifying other existing plans already on the drawing board were deemed unsuitable for the same reason, the Naval High Command preferring a simpler proposal of converting something that had already proved its worth. As a result, the choice fell to using the Type IXC hull and providing it with another set of economical cruising engines. However, things were not always quite so simple, and this suggestion triggered off another set of heated discussions. One side wanted something impressive, like six high-speed diesel engines for the new motor torpedo boats. There appears to have been more gold braid on the diesel-electric side because only a couple of the high-speed powerplants were authorised. So the high-speed diesel engine idea went into production as Type IXD1 and the other as IXD2. In the end it was too difficult to get powerplants in the Type IXD1 to perform satisfactorily and the IXD2 version emerged as the winner.

The hull for both these versions was identical to a standard Type IX, except that an additional section was added aft of the conning tower to accommodate the cruising engines, this weight being balanced with a similar section further forward. The lower half of this forward section was filled with heavy batteries and the upper half provided additional accommodation for the men. The drawback was that virtually all other gear was identical to the existing Type IXB and C. This did not have too much of a detrimental effect on the cruising speed as new the variant could manage a comfortable 10 knots, although this was considerably slower than the original demand for 14 knots. However, it did make the larger, new version considerably more sluggish when manoeuvring and there was no way that such a craft could be employed in areas with determined opposition. Submerged attacks were also more or less out of the question and could only be attempted in exceptional circumstances. The reason for this was that both hydroplanes and periscopes were identical to the smaller Type IXC and the additional length made it exceedingly difficult to hold the boat just below the surface without the bow and stern breaking through the waves. On calm days, when it might be possible to keep all of the extremities below the surface, the water in which these boats operated was often so clear that lookouts on surface ships could spot the submerged submarine below the waves.

Right: U67, an ordinary ocean-going Type IXC with 105 mm quick firing deck gun in front of the conning tower. The 'T'-shaped structure on the top of the conning tower is a detachable metal loop held up by two upright poles to support another lookout slightly higher than the rest of the duty watch.

Below: A close-up of U67's conning tower with its 'T'-shaped lookout support. The commander's flagpole is in position and two machine guns can be seen pointing upwards.

The only two IXD1 boats, U180 and U195, were commissioned in May and September 1942, the first IXD2, U178, being launched on 28 October 1941 and commissioned on 14 February 1942. After that there followed another twenty-eight IXD2 boats with the following dimensions:

Note: in this table ↑ = on the surface, ↓ = submerged.

	Type VIIC	Type IXC	Type IXD2
Displacement	769/1,070 tons	1,120/1,540 tons	1,610/2,150 tons
Length (Overall)	66.5 m	76.4 m	87.6 m
Length of Pressure Hull	50.5 m	58.8 m	68.5 m
Beam	6.2 m	6.8 m	7.5 m
Depth	4.7 m	4.7 m	5.4 m
↑ Speed Max	17.7 kt	18.3 kt	19 kt
↓ Speed Max	7.6 kt	7.3 kt	6.9 kt
↑ Range Max Speed	17 kt/3,250 nm	18 kt/5,000 nm	19 kt/8,500 nm
↑ Range Cruising Speed	10 kt/8,500 nm	10 kt/13,450 nm	10 kt/31,500 nm
↑ Range Diesel-Electric	10 kt/9,500 nm	10 kt/16,300 nm	10 kt/32,300 nm
↓ Range	4 kt/80 nm	4 kt/63 nm	4 kt/57 nm
Torpedo Tubes Bow	4	4	4
Torpedo Tubes Stern	1	2	2
Torpedoes/Mines carried	14 T/39 M	22 T/66 M	24 T/72 M
Artillery	1 x 88 mm Variable AA	1 x 110 mm 1 x 37 mm Variable AA	1 x 110 mm 1 x 37 mm Variable AA
Crew	44-56	44-56	44-56

- The Type VIIC carried two torpedoes and the larger boats four or more in storage tubes outside the pressure hull. These had to be transferred into the pressure hull before they could be discharged.
- The guns were all quick firing deck guns, shells being inserted singly into the barrels. The anti-aircraft (AA) armament was semi or fully automatic and variable but hardly strong enough to cope with fast flying, front-armoured aircraft.
- The crew usually consisted of the commander, chief engineer, first watch officer (1WO, pronounced One W-O), second watch officer, several warrant officers and petty officers and the lower ranks. The long range boats also had a medical officer (a qualified doctor) rather

than a first-aider on board.

- The basic designs were improved during the war to give rise to Types VIIC/41 and IXC/40. The main difference was a stronger and therefore heavier pressure hull for deeper diving, as well as several other minor modifications. However, the general specifications remained roughly the same as their predecessors.

When considering the significance of the distances in nautical miles (nm) quoted in the above table, one should bear in mind that the cruising speed of 10 knots was usually maintained only in European waters or when operating in the North Atlantic; the majority of long distance boats travelled with diesel-electric propulsion at 6 or 7 knots and often at less than 5 in headwinds.

U-boats followed a variety of routes, some of them with considerable detours to avoid known anti-submarine patrols. The following table gives the shortest (peacetime) distances. The time taken for covering each distance has been calculated at the diesel-electric cruising speed of 7 knots.

U802 under Helmut Schmoeckel in Loch Eriboll shortly after the end of the war. This was an ocean-going Type IXC/40.

Kiel–Bordeaux: (via the North Atlantic)	2,820 nm	16 days
Bordeaux–Freetown	2,670 nm	16 days
Freetown–Cape Town	3,220 nm	19 days
Bordeaux–Cape Town	5,890 nm	35 days
Cape Town–Penang	5,340 nm	32 days
Bordeaux–Penang	11,230 nm	67 days
Bordeaux–New York	3,170 nm	19 days

(One nautical mile equals 1.15 land miles or 1.85 kilometres. A knot is one sea mile per hour. The diesel-electric cruising speed to distant waters was therefore 8 mph or 13 kph, slower than the average cyclist.)

A walk through a Type IXD2 U-boat

[The numbers at the beginning of each paragraph are marked on the diagram of a long range U-boat.]

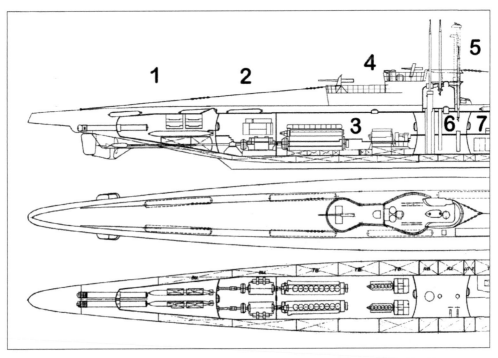

The back half of a Type IXD2 U-boat.

1. *The rear torpedo compartment with two torpedo tubes*

Underneath the torpedo tubes was a pit with a hand wheel, depth gauge and position indicator for an emergency (manual) control of the stern hydroplanes. Immediately in front of them was an emergency steering wheel that could be swung sideways to move it out of the way when not required. This compartment also had a most noisy air compressor, some spare torpedoes, a lavatory and accommodation for the crew in bunks and hammocks. There was a torpedo loading hatch in the ceiling and below the floor were a pair of trimming tanks for balancing the boat and a torpedo tank for filling with seawater when torpedoes were discharged, to compensate for the change in weight. Two pipes connected this pair of trimming tanks to another set in the bow. Each tank was usually about half full so that water could be moved from one end to the other through taps in the central control room. A curved water- and pressure-resisting bulkhead separated this compartment from the next one. This out-of-the-way area was connected to the central control room by a telephone and there was also a voice pipe, but that could be used only during submerged attacks when the incredibly noisy diesel engines did not drown out speech.

2. *The electric motor room with control panel above the electric motors*

The largest parts of these two motors were located below floor level. A flat, sound-muffling wall separated this compartment from the diesel engine room.

3. *The diesel compartment*

The propeller shaft ran through the electric motor to a large clutch between it and the main diesel engine. A large tank above the engines contained the ready-to-use fuel, and there were vents in the ceiling for supplying fresh air. The smaller diesel engines for diesel-electric drive were forward of the main engines, each of which had an electricity generator in front of it. There was also a ladder leading up to a hatch, but this was not opened when the boat was at sea because it was dangerously near the surface of the water, even when all the diving tanks were fully blown. A curved water- and pressure-resisting bulkhead separated the engine room from the central control room. There was a huge clutch on each shaft immediately behind the electric motor and another one immediately forward. This made it possible to use the diesel engine to turn the motor for generating electricity without rotating the propeller and when dived, the electric motor could turn the propeller without engaging the diesel engine. The small cruising engine for diesel-electric drive was not connected directly to the propeller shaft. The electricity this generated was fed directly to the electro-motors or it could be used for charging batteries. Spare parts for machinery that was known to wear out, such as piston rings, were usually carried in specially labelled wooden boxes. In addition to ready-made spares, this compartment also had some rudimentary metal working facilities, and each boat carried a set of metal bars for making any other parts that might fail during the voyage. Long distance boats also carried welding gear and specialised tools for the majority of maintenance jobs. The diesel room was so noisy that it was impossible to hold a conversation; neither shouting nor the emergency dive bells could be heard while the engines were running. In view of this, the lights flashed whenever the alarm button was pressed.

4. *The bridge or top of the conning tower with anti-aircraft guns*

Two periscopes, one with a small head lens for attacking and another with a larger lens for navigation or checking for aircraft, terminated inside the commander's control room inside the conning tower. Towards the end of the war, some of the long distance boats were fitted with a folding snorkel. This hinged at the bottom of the conning tower and could be lowered to lie between the upper (outside) deck grating and the pressure hull. The snorkel was raised and lowered hydraulically and was held in position by a bracket at the top of the conning tower. At the beginning of the war, boats were provided with a single 20 mm anti-aircraft gun, but from 1942 onwards this was increased to two twin 20 mm guns and usually one single or one double 37 mm semi-automatic gun. There were also a number of water- and pressure-resisting containers for storing ready-to-use ammunition. Earlier models, without the

The stern of a long range boat with 37 mm quick firing deck gun in the foreground.

enlarged gun platforms, had a 37 mm quick firing deck gun on the upper deck just aft of the conning tower. This differed from the semi-automatic AA gun by the need for shells to be fed singly into the breech and was not intended for use against flying targets.

5. The commander's control room inside the conning tower for submerged attacks

Long range boats had a duplicate set of rudder controls and a torpedo calculator inside this small space. The hatch at the bottom had a special water- and pressure-resisting lid strong enough to prevent the pressure hull from flooding even when the main hatch remained open and the conning tower was completely filled with water. The jumping wires running from the top of the conning tower to the bow and to the stern were originally fitted to help boats slide under nets, and early submarines also had a net cutter on the bows. These thick wires doubled up as an anchor for attaching safety harnesses for when men were working on the upper (outside) deck in rough conditions and were also used as radio aerials. The vast majority of boats had a single wire running to the bow and two running down to the stern, but some later boats had two wires at the front so that the signals from a rigid radar set could be sent out in between the two. The part of the conning tower wall where the lookouts

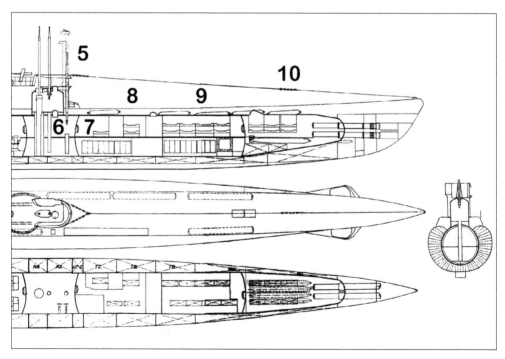

The front half of a Type IXD2 U-boat.

stood was wide enough to accommodate openings for airshafts leading down to the engine room, a circular radio direction finder aerial and radar detector aerials. Later in the war the wall was thickened to include some armour and a variety of other gear.

6. *The central control room*
The floor level was halfway up this compartment, and the crew had no access to a variety of tanks in the lower section. A number of 'wells' were sunk through these tanks for accommodating periscopes and a periscopic radio aerial. The large hump on the outside, at the forward base of the conning tower fairing, contained a magnetic compass that could be viewed by the helmsman through an illuminated periscope, but most of the time he would have steered by using the gyrocompass. There were also two hydroplane operators and a large panel with many wheels for trimming or balancing the submerged submarine. In addition to these main controls, there was a main navigation desk with a chart, a large ballast pump and a condensing still for making distilled water. A curved water- and pressure-resisting bulkhead separated the central control room from the forward part of the vessel.

7. *The commander's 'cabin'*
This was located on the left or port side of the corridor, the radio room being on the right or starboard side. Another special room for detecting noises picked up by sensitive hydrophones was located forward of the radio room. The floor was about halfway up the pressure hull. Underneath was space for batteries, and ammunition was stored under the radio room. Some of the boats had a 105 mm quick firing deck gun above this compartment. The majority of these were removed from late 1942 onwards, although some long distance boats kept theirs for much longer than boats operating in the Atlantic. The commander's 'cabin' was nothing more than a small corner that could be shut off from the corridor by a heavy curtain. He was provided with a small desk and several lockable cupboards for secret materials.

8. *The Officers' accommodation with forward galley*
There was a hatch in the ceiling of the galley. This was kept closed once at sea but formed the main way in and out when in port. Although more luxurious than the other accommodation areas, the beds or bunks were not terribly long and tall men could not stretch out in them. The lower bunks doubled up as seats during the day.

9. *The warrant and petty officers' accommodation*
The various areas in this section were separated from each other by flat sound-muffling walls, and a curved water- and pressure-resistant bulkhead

was located at the front, before the bow torpedo compartment. Some boats had two lavatories in this area, one at the forward end of the officers' mess and the other by the forward bulkhead, but the one towards the rear was not fitted to all boats. The floor ran about halfway up the pressure hull and there were batteries, food storage areas and a deep freeze in the lower section. There was just enough space above the batteries for a trolley to slide along on a small wheel-and-rail system so that a man lying on top could inspect the lead/acid batteries and top them up with distilled water when necessary. Batteries when charging and discharging gave off both hydrogen and oxygen, a highly explosive mixture, and this vented into the accommodation areas. Therefore all forms of naked lights were prohibited inside the submarine and men were allowed to smoke only on the bridge during daylight or inside the well-ventilated commander's control room inside the conning tower when it was dark. Going to the top of the conning tower for a smoke was often the only reason for allowing extra men up top, and there were cases of non-smokers taking up the habit in order to see the sky and to breathe fresh air.

10. *The forward torpedo compartment*

There were four torpedo tubes with emergency hydroplane controls in a pit under the floor immediately below the tubes. Below the floor was space for four torpedoes and above it were a set of bunks on both sides and a torpedo-loading hatch in the ceiling. The base of this compartment was occupied by a torpedo compensation tank, mentioned in the paragraph dealing with the stern compartment. Next to it, towards the front, was a pair of bow trim tanks for balancing the boat. Like the rear compartment, this section was connected

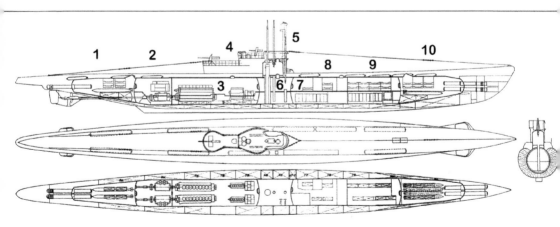

A Type IXD2 U-boat.

to the central control room by telephone and voice pipe. Voice pipes also terminated in other compartments and were usually left open during action to enable the men to hear what was going on. All these pipes had taps to shut them off where they passed through bulkheads.

The space between the top of the pressure hull and the grating for the upper (outside) deck accommodated a number of steel compressed air bottles and some water- and pressure-resisting storage containers. The space between the strong pressure hull and the more flimsy outside contained a vast number of small tanks. These were used for storing fuel, water and oil, or as diving tanks. The main diving tank was situated below the central control room, and there were a number of other diving tanks along the length of the hull.

CHAPTER 2

Very Long Distance U-boat Voyages – A Summary of Operations

The days at sea in this chapter must be taken as an approximation because without checking every logbook it is difficult to determine whether the first and last days should be included. The category 'Attacked' refers to ships, not aircraft, and these figures can also be somewhat dubious in places. There are cases where U-boat lookouts watched ships sinking, yet there are no records from the other side that a ship of considerable size was lost on the day given in the log. In addition to this, even reliable published sources of information about shipping losses are somewhat inconsistent. As far as possible, the lists have been presented in the order of leaving port.

1. The first exploratory move to Freetown (Sierra Leone, Africa): summer 1940

The first long distance operation started on 6 June 1940 when UA (*Kapitänleutnant* [KL] Hans Cohausz) left Kiel to accompany the auxiliary cruiser *Pinguin* into the Central Atlantic. The idea was to act as escort on the way out, to be refuelled and then operate in distant waters before returning home. Whilst this was reasonably successful, the event was marred by engine trouble and by a faulty torpedo turning round to almost hit the U-boat instead of the target. UA, a massive boat of 1,128/1,284 tons, had been built for export to Turkey but the war started before it could be handed over, so it was commissioned into the German Navy.

The next boat to head into far-off waters, U65 (KL Hans-Gerrit von Stockhausen), also went to the Freetown area of Africa, stopping some 600 miles north of the Equator. Although relatively successful, both these voyages were regarded as unsatisfactory in terms of the number of ships sunk per days at sea, and it was thought that more could have been achieved if they had operated nearer home, thus cutting out the long voyages to and from the operations area. UA was at sea for eighty-five days, sinking seven ships, and U65 for eighty-seven days, sinking nine ships, but other U-boats were achieving similar or better figures much closer to home. Therefore there was no great urge within the U-boat Command to continue with long distance operations.

2. The second wave to the Freetown area: early 1941

The name 'Freetown' continued to crop up so frequently in naval intelligence reports that despite the U-boat Command's reticence to go there, planning continued unabated. It stood out as a thorn in the flesh because it was the only port in the Central Atlantic area where ships could wait for assembly into northbound convoys. At the same time it was thought that the area served as a dispersal point for southbound groups. So with this information confirmed by naval intelligence, planning started early in 1941 for operations aimed specifically at this location, and the first group to travel that far consisted of the following boats, all of which left from and returned to Lorient during 1941:

U105 (KL Georg Schewe)	Type:	IXB
	Left:	22.02.1941
	Arrived:	13.06.1941
	Days at sea:	111
	Attacked:	12
U124 (KL Wilhelm Schulz)	Type:	IXB
	Left:	23.02.1941
	Arrived:	01.05.1941
	Days at sea:	66
	Attacked:	12
U106 (KL Jürgen Oesten)	Type:	IXB
	Left:	26.02.1941
	Arrived:	17.06.1941
	Days at sea:	111
	Attacked:	10
U107 (KK Günter Hessler)	Type:	IXB
	Left:	29.03.1941
	Arrived:	02.07.1941
	Days at sea:	95
	Attacked:	14
	(This was the most successful single voyage of the whole war.)	

U103 (KL Viktor Schütze)	Type:	IXB
	Left:	01.04.1941
	Arrived:	12.07.1941
	Days at sea:	102
	Attacked:	12
U38 (KL Heinrich Liebe)	Type:	IXA
	Left:	09.04.1941
	Arrived:	26.06.1941
	Days at sea:	61
	Attacked:	8
UA (KK Hans Eckermann)	Type:	ex-Turkish *Batiray*
	Left:	03.05.1941
	Arrived:	30.07.1941
	Days at sea:	88
	Attacked:	0
U69 (KL Jost Metzler)	Type:	VIIC
	Left:	05.05.1941
	Arrived:	08.07.1941
	Days at sea:	64
	Attacked:	6 plus the results from a mine-laying operation
U123 (KL Reinhard Hardegen)	Type:	IXB
	Left:	15.06.1941
	Arrived:	23.08.941
	Days at sea:	69
	Attacked:	5

The tail-end of this wave to southern waters ran out of luck and it was only thorough planning that prevented a disaster of unprecedented proportions. U38, U107, U69 and U103 had just been replenished from the tankers *Egerland* and *Lothringen* when these were sunk, forcing the U-boats to break off their operations to return home. There was no way of supplying them with enough fuel for prolonged operations. Even the long trek back to France presented some enormous problems, and U69 had no choice but to visit the highly secret refuelling base 'Culebra' during the early hours of 27 June 1941. 'Culebra' remained an enigma for a long time after the war, with only a few people knowing its exact location and identity. It turned out that this was the motor tanker *Charlotte Schliemann*, which had taken refuge in Las Palmas in the Canary Islands a couple of days before the outbreak of the war. By the time she helped U69, her crew had supplied enough submarines for British authorities to lodge an official complaint with the Spanish Government, therefore bringing the clandestine activities to an end. U123, refuelled from

U123, one of the successful long range boats of Type IXB, with both the attack (towards the rear) and sky or navigation periscopes (towards the front) raised slightly. The outside section, containing a variety of storage tubes, is clearly visible along the sides of the upper or outside deck.

the *Charlotte Schliemann* three days before U69, had enough fuel to continued hunting in those southern waters for some time, but generally the lack of supply facilities brought an end to long distance U-boat operations.

3. The loss of supply ships in the North, Central and South Atlantic: June 1941 – around the time of the battleship *Bismarck*'s breakout

The background to the sudden loss of supply ships is most interesting. It came about as a direct result of Britain capturing a working Enigma machine from U110 (KL Fritz-Julius Lemp) on 9 May 1941. This made it possible for the Royal Navy to put an end to eight supply ships sent out primarily to help the battleship *Bismarck*. The U-boat arm took advantage of this move by asking permission to use the same ships to extend the operations areas of U-boats. Luckily for them, the U-boats were not under time pressure to achieve quick results and were therefore refuelled *before* rather than *after* their offensive. As a result, all the boats stranded at sea in June 1941 managed to return home. (Later, shortly after the United States entered into the war, Admiral Karl Dönitz, the U-boat Chief, took a gamble and refuelled boats in American waters after the start of their action.)

When considering these early long distance operations, it is important to remember that Germany did not allow U-boats into the western Atlantic, where the United States had created the so-called Pan American Neutrality Zone. So there were no opportunities of heading west until after the beginning of 1942. (Germany declared war on the United States on 11 December 1941.)

The abovementioned supply ship saga of May and June 1941 created many serious repercussions for Germany and left a number of ships and submarines stranded in far-off waters. The recovery period lasted until September, by which time a number of new supply ships were kitted out. In late summer, before these were ready for action, the Supreme Naval Command came up with the idea of using the auxiliary cruiser *Atlantis*, then on her way home, as a stopgap measure before the hurriedly converted submarine supply tankers *Python* and *Kota Penang* could reach the southern oceans. *Kapitän zur See* (KzS) Kurt Weyer (the commander of the auxiliary cruiser *Orion* from December 1939 to September 1941, who had taken up a position at the Supreme Naval Command), protested most bitterly on behalf of the men aboard the surface raider, saying that they had done enough and should be allowed home without having such an extra burden placed upon them. However, the deskbound admirals did not listen. They knew that the *Atlantis* was carrying spare torpedoes and had plenty of fuel and provisions. What they apparently did not know was that these torpedoes were so old that they could not be discharged from U-boats.

This move to use the *Atlantis* as a submarine supply ship gave the cryptanalysts at Bletchley Park a field day. The Royal Navy was delighted. The auxiliary cruiser or surface raider code had been used so infrequently that there was no way in which it could be cracked, but now some of the information was being repeated in U-boat code when the positions of the supply ships were broadcast to submarines at sea. Since Britain could read this code, it was a straightforward matter of dispatching a cruiser to sink the *Atlantis* and then another cruiser to deal with the supply ship *Python*. To make this even more awkward for the Germans, the survivors from the *Atlantis* were first picked up by the submarine being refuelled (U126 under KL Ernst Bauer) and were passed on to the *Python*, giving the survivors the double-whammy of being shipwrecked. Yet despite this disaster, some of the survivors got home for Christmas 1941, the rest managing to get back for the New Year celebrations.

This rescue operation was a terrific achievement by all concerned. Men were brought home over a distance of 5,000 miles, and none of this would have been possible had the Italian submarines *Torelli* (*Capitano di Corvetta* [CC] Giacomo), *Finzi* (CC Giudice), *Tazzoli* (CC Fecia di Cossato) and *Calvi* (CC Olivieri) not joined in to help with the vast undertaking. The U-boats involved with the rescue were UA (*Korvettenkapitän* [KK] Hans Eckermann), U68 (KK Karl-Friedrich Merten), U124 (KL Johann Mohr), U126 (KL Ernst Bauer) and U129 (KL Nicolai Clausen).

4. The Central and South Atlantic and beyond: autumn 1941

These operations started towards the end of August, when the supply ships *Kota Penang* and *Python* were made ready, and included the following U-boats:

U111 (KL Wilhelm Kleinschmidt)	Type:	IXB
	Destination:	west of the Azores
	Left:	14.08.1941
	Sunk:	04.10.1941
	Days at sea:	51
	Attacked:	2
U107 (KK Günter Hessler)	Type:	IXB
	Destination:	Freetown area
	Left:	06.09.1941
	Arrived:	11.11.1941
	Days at sea:	67
	Attacked:	3
U103 (KL Werner Winter)	Type:	IXB
	Destination:	Freetown area
	Left:	10.09.1941
	Arrived:	09.11.1941
	Days at sea:	60
	Attacked:	2
U68 (KK Karl-Friedrich Merten)	Type:	IXC
	Destination:	Freetown area
	Left:	11.09.1941
	Arrived:	25.12.1941
	Days at sea:	105
	Attacked:	4
U67 (KL Günther Müller-Stöckheim)	Type:	IXC
	Destination:	Freetown area
	Left:	14.09.1941
	Arrived:	16.10.1941
	Days at sea:	32
	Attacked:	1
U126 (KL Ernst Bauer)	Type:	IXC
	Destination:	Freetown area
	Left:	24.09.1941
	Arrived:	13.12.1941
	Days at sea:	80
	Attacked:	4

U129 (KL Nicolai Clausen)	Type:	IXC
	Destination:	Cape Town
	Left:	21.10.1941
	Arrived:	28.12.1941
	Days at sea:	68
	Attacked:	1
UA (KK Hans Eckermann)	Type:	ex-Turkish *Batiray*
	Destination:	Central Atlantic
	Left:	21.10.1941
	Arrived:	25.12.1941
	Days at sea:	65
U124 (KL Johann Mohr)	Type:	IXB
	Destination:	Cape Town
	Left:	30.10.1941
	Arrived:	29.12.1941
	Days at sea:	60
	Attacked:	2

U67 coming into port.

5. Moving west to the Caribbean – Operation *Westindien*: January–February 1942

The first thrust into the Caribbean was an emergency response to capitalise on any opportunities created by America's entry into the war. So many books have covered Operation *Paukenschlag*, the first U-boat thrust against the United States, early in 1942, that it should not be necessary to mention it here. Yet the fact that this move brought about a change in thinking is often omitted and there are a couple of points that should be considered. First, thus far the main theatre of operations had been the shipping lanes of the North Atlantic, and the long distance voyages had been sideshows. The U-boat Command was not unduly perturbed if the long distance boats expended some of their torpedoes while on their way to the designated operations area and the majority of the boats travelled at a reasonably fast cruising speed. With sinkings in American waters reaching astronomical levels, creating the so-called 'Second Happy Time' for U-boats, it was important for them to remain there for as long possible, and that involved a new approach to the process of reaching distant waters. Fuel economy suddenly took on a new meaning.

At the same time, it was discovered that the smaller Type VIIC boats, sent across the shorter northern routes to Canada, were considerably more economical than had previously been imagined. In fact, they used so little fuel that it proved practical to employ them along the eastern seaboard of the United States if there was a tanker there to support them. The new specialist supply submarines of Type XIV were not quite ready to start operations, so UA was sent over to act as a stopgap supply submarine. A hastily converted mine-layer of Type XB followed her before the purpose-built submarine tankers took over the main burden of supplying boats in American waters.

February 1942, around the time of the first thrust against the United States and the first thrust into the Caribbean, also saw the introduction of a new U-boat radio code. This was done by adding a fourth wheel to the naval version of the Enigma machine and meant that Bletchley Park in England was shut out until the end of the year when such a machine, with the supporting codebooks, was recovered from U559 under KL Hans Heidtmann. The change in the code meant that throughout 1942 neither Britain nor the United States had any means of discovering the secret refuelling locations in remote areas and therefore German supply operations continued without any serious disruption from Allied forces.

The fiasco in American waters with U-boats achieving high success with hardly any opposition was still in full swing when the U-boat Command made plans to send U-boats further south into the Caribbean and the Gulf of Mexico. The first thrust into the Caribbean was planned for the new-moon period of February 1942, meaning when the nights were especially

U515, an ordinary Type IXC under Werner Henke, coming into port.

dark because there was no moon at all. The plan was to send two boats to Trinidad and three other Type IXCs to Aruba, Curaçao, and north-west of the Paranagua peninsula.

The boats of this group, codenamed 'Neuland', (all of which left from and returned to Lorient in January–March 1942) were as follows:

U67 (KL Heinrich Bleichrodt)	Type:	IXC
	Left:	19.01.1942
	Arrived:	30.03.1942
	Days at sea:	70
	Attacked:	3
U156 (KK Werner Hartenstein)	Type:	IXC
	Left:	19.01.1942
	Arrived:	17.03.1942
	Days at sea:	57
	Attacked:	7
U502 (KL Jürgen von Rosenstiel)	Type:	IXC
	Left:	19.01.1942
	Arrived:	16.03.1942
	Days at sea:	56
	Attacked:	6

U161 (KL Albrecht Achilles)	Type:	IXC
	Left:	24.01.1942
	Arrived:	02.04.1942
	Days at sea:	68
	Attacked:	9
U129 (KL Nicolai Clausen)	Type:	IXC
	Left:	25.01.1942
	Arrived:	05.04.1942
	Days at sea:	70
	Attacked:	7
U126 (KL Ernst Bauer)	Type:	IXC
	Left:	02.02.1942
	Arrived:	29.03.1942
	Days at sea:	55
	Attacked:	10

At this stage it was not yet possible for Germany to support any long distance operations with a submarine tanker; these boats therefore made the long voyages without refuelling support.

6. Return to African waters in the Freetown area: February 1942

The U-boat Command abandoned operations in the Freetown area of Africa during October 1941 because of the problem with supply ships mentioned earlier, and also due to dwindling successes in those waters. It was thought that the British traffic was being routed through the Pan American Neutrality Zone rather than running along the African coast. This line of thought needed to be reconsidered once America joined the war, especially when naval intelligence found evidence that ships were running through the eastern Atlantic again. U68 and U505 were immediately diverted from crossing the ocean and ordered to proceed south with a view to carrying out a thorough reconnaissance of the Freetown area. U68 discovered that the traffic around the Canary Islands was especially heavy, and the successes gained there were better than the sinkings achieved during earlier voyages to those waters. Yet calculating the statistics on the basis of the number of ships sunk per U-boat at sea, the American waters were still yielding better results, making the U-boat Command somewhat reticent in sending more boats into African waters. However, the bonanza in American waters did not last and it was not long before the eastern Atlantic became another hotspot for U-boats (all of which left from and returned to Lorient):

U68 (KK Karl-Friedrich Merten)	Type:	IXC
	Left:	11.02.1942
	Arrived:	13.04.1942
	Days at sea:	61
	Attacked:	7
U505 (KK Axel-Olaf Loewe)	Type:	IXC
	Left:	11.02.1942
	Arrived:	07.05.1942
	Days at sea:	85
	Attacked:	4

7. Renewed operations in the Caribbean: March–May 1942

The German Naval High Command did not have any forewarning of Japan's intention to attack the US Pacific Fleet in its anchorage at Pearl Harbor and therefore had not prepared any plans for operating in the Western Atlantic. Following the dispatch of the first wave of U-boats, considerable arguments raged about which targets should be attacked in this new war zone. As a result, several weeks passed before the next set of orders were prepared. Three boats were ready in March and at least one of them had orders to attack oil installations on land. At the same time the U-boat Command juggled with what was already in the Western Atlantic and ordered two boats, which had been supplied by the tanker U459, to proceed to the Caribbean. Another set of boats being made ready in French ports were then directed to the Caribbean as well, all of them with slightly different operations areas. Once at sea, these boats were ordered to commence their attack simultaneously on 10 May 1942. By this time the United States was already making a concerted effort to attack U-boats off its eastern seaboard, and the boats in southern waters found the conditions considerably better. Obviously the surprise element of their onslaught had worked well, with hardly any retaliation. So while activity along the eastern seaboard of America decreased, activity in the Caribbean and the Gulf of Mexico increased dramatically.

The boats of the spring 1942 wave consisted of the following:

U154 (KK Walther Kölle)	Type:	IXC
	Destination:	Haiti area
	Left:	11.03.1942
	Arrived:	09.05.1942
	Days at sea:	60
	Attacked:	5

U66 (KK Richard Zapp)	Type:	IXC
	Destination:	Trinidad area
	Left:	Lorient 21.03.1942
	Arrived:	Lorient 25.05.1942
	Days at sea:	65
	Attacked:	7
U130 (KK Ernst Kals)	Type:	IXC
	Destination:	Curaçao
	Left:	Lorient 24.03.1942
	Arrived:	Lorient 06.06.1942
	Days at sea:	75
	Attacked:	2
U108 (KK Klaus Scholtz)	Type:	IXB
	Destination:	Bahamas Channel/ Windward Passage
	Left:	Lorient 30.03.1942
	Refuelled:	from U459 on 22.04.1942
	Arrived:	Lorient 01.06.1942
	Days at sea:	62
	Attacked:	5
U507 (KK Harro Schacht)	Type:	IXC
	Destination:	Gulf of Mexico
	Left:	Lorient 04.04.1942
	Arrived:	Lorient 04.06.1942
	Days at sea:	61
	Attacked:	9
U125 (KL Ulrich Folkers)	Type:	IXC
	Destination:	Cuba-Yucatan Strait
	Left:	Lorient 04.04.1942
	Arrived:	Lorient 13.06.1942
	Days at sea:	70
	Attacked:	9
U506 (KL Erich Würdemann)	Type:	IXC
	Destination:	Gulf of Mexico
	Left:	Lorient 06.04.1942
	Arrived:	Lorient 15.06.1942
	Days at sea:	70
	Attacked:	11
U162 (FK Jürgen Wattenberg)	Type:	IXC
	Destination:	Trinidad-Guiana
	Left:	Lorient 07.04.1942

	Arrived:	Lorient 08.06.1942
	Days at sea:	65
	Attacked:	9
U69 (KL Ulrich Gräf)	Type:	VIIC
	Destination:	Curaçao-Aruba
	Left:	St Nazaire 12.04.1942
	Refuelled:	from U459 01.05.1942
	Arrived:	St Nazaire 25.06.1942
	Days at sea:	75
	Attacked:	5
U502 (KL Jürgen von Rosenstiel)	Type:	IXC
	Destination:	Curaçao-Aruba
	Left:	Lorient 22.04.1942
	Refuelled:	by U459
	Sunk:	05.07.1942
		(This was the first boat to be sunk with the use of a Leigh Light)
	Days at sea:	74
	Attacked:	10
U155 (KK Adolf Piening)	Type:	IXC
	Destination:	Panama Canal area
	Left:	Lorient 24.04.1942
	Arrived:	Lorient 14.06.1942
	Days at sea:	51
	Attacked:	8
U156 (KK Werner Hartenstein)	Type:	IXC
	Destination:	Panama Canal area
	Left:	Lorient 22.04.1942
	Arrived:	Lorient 07.07.1942
	Days at sea:	67
	Attacked:	7

8. Increased Caribbean U-boat operations: summer 1942

With the availability in 1942 of three submarine tankers (U459, U460, and U116) it was possible for sea-going boats as well as the long range types to operate in the Caribbean. These boats did not go terribly far south but supplied fuel, oil and food so that operational boats could extend their operations area and later return home without further support. This made it possible to send three boats as far as Brazil and to make the Gulf of Mexico and the Caribbean briefly the main theatre for U-boat operations. The number of boats operating in the western Atlantic increased sufficiently to make listing every boat somewhat impractical. The length of time these boats remained at sea was roughly the same as the boats listed above. By the middle of June 1942 it was possible to reach the vital traffic bottleneck created at the eastern end of the Panama Canal. However, the bonanza lasted for a period of only a few weeks before retaliation in some areas became so vicious that U-boats had to withdraw.

It was very difficult for the U-boat Command to draw definite conclusions of what was going on. For example, in May, U156 found itself having to remain submerged for 140 hours in a period of seven days while lying off Port de France. (This equates to about 20 hours per day – an incredible torture for the crew in such hot conditions.) Yet the following month, when there were fewer U-boats in the area, they were sinking considerably more shipping. So the question as to what was actually going on remained a huge enigma in the U-boat Command. Successes declined rapidly during the late summer of 1942 to the extent that operations were reduced to occasional lone ventures, and even these ceased in 1943 when it was no longer possible to use supply submarines in distant waters close to enemy bases.

9. South American waters: summer 1942

On 27 January 1942, Brazil broke off diplomatic relations with Germany, sparking off new plans of sending U-boats into a previously prohibited area. Shortly after this it was discovered that Chile and Argentina were arming their merchant ships, which resulted in U-boats being given permission to attack them from the middle of May 1942 onwards. However, sending U-boats to Brazilian waters could only be done by weakening operations in other areas. As a result, a frenzied debate about future developments continued for some time. Plans to send a dozen or so boats into South American waters were not finalised until summer of 1942, when a supply boat of Type XIV was due to support a new group in that area. However, all this fell foul of political moves and the pack was eventually recalled before reaching the operations area and boats diverted into other areas, especially into the Caribbean, where activities continued unabated.

The first boats to make for Brazil, all leaving from and returning to Lorient, were:

U126 (KL Ernst Bauer)	Type:	IXC
	Left:	25.04.1942
	Arrived:	25.07.1942
	Days at sea:	91
	Attacked:	8

U128 (KL Ulrich Heyse)	Type:	IXC
	Left:	25.04.1942
	Arrived:	22.07.1942
	Days at sea:	88
	Attacked:	6
U161 (KL Albrecht Achilles)	Type:	IXC
	Left:	28.04.1942
	Arrived:	07.08.1942
	Days at sea:	100
	Attacked:	5

10. Back to Freetown: autumn 1942

The Freetown area came under close scrutiny again during the summer of 1942, when the successes in American waters had dwindled considerably. Once the boats were off Freetown again it was discovered that their results were not only disappointing but also highly disheartening due to the fierce opposition. The U-boat Command was especially frustrated because reports from informers had suggested there was a considerable volume of traffic moving through those waters. The mouth of the Congo River produced equally disappointing results: U161 and U126, both with experienced commanders, found powerful opposition rather than lucrative targets.

The following boats left from and returned to Lorient:

U128 (KL Ulrich Heyse)	Type:	IXC
	Left:	14.09.1942
	Arrived:	via Brazil 15.01.1943
	Days at sea:	118
	Attacked:	4
U126 (KL Ernst Bauer)	Type:	IXC
	Left:	19.09.1942
	Arrived:	07.01.1943
	Days at sea:	110
	Attacked:	3
U161 (KL Albrecht Achilles)	Type:	IXC
	Left:	19.09.1942
	Arrived:	09.01.1943
	Days at sea:	112
	Attacked:	5

11. South African waters: autumn 1942

Boats of the first wave travelling further south to Cape Town found the opposition somewhat easier. The plan, based on information from agents, was to launch a surprise attack against ships anchored off the port. Apparently there were up to fifty ships there at any one time. The boats for this wave left Europe a short while before Britain was able to read the U-boat code again and, being somewhat suspicious, the U-boat Command ordered strict radio silence for everything other than essential messages. On top of this, the boats were allowed to attack only large targets such as aircraft carriers, large troop transports or other valuable warships while *en route* to South Africa. Consequently Britain was taken by surprise, allowing U-boats to reap a worthwhile bonanza around South Africa until storms, rather than enemy activity, caused the action to be broken off. Some of the boats had orders to sail further around the Cape of Good Hope to hit other South African ports in the Indian Ocean as well.

The following boats set out for South African waters during the summer/autumn of 1942. They left Lorient unless otherwise stated, and a few remained at sea until January 1943:

U172 in the distance with U152 in the foreground. Both were standard long range boats of Type IXC.

Group Eisbär 1 (Polar Bear 1)

U172 (KL Carl Emmermann)	Type:	IXC
	Left:	19.08.1942
	Arrived:	27.12.1942
	Days at sea:	130
	Attacked:	8
U504 (KK Fritz Poske)	Type:	IXC
	Left:	19.08.1942
	Arrived:	11.12.1942
	Days at sea:	114
	Attacked:	6
U68 (KK Karl-Friedrich Merten)	Type:	IXC
	Left:	20.08.1942
	Arrived:	06.12.1942
	Days at sea:	109
	Attacked:	9
U156 (KK Werner Hartenstein)	Type:	IXC
	Left:	20.08.1942
	Arrived:	16.11.1942
	(Returned with survivors from the Laconia rescue)	
U159 (KL Helmut Witte)	Type:	IXC
	Left:	24.08.1942
	Arrived:	05.01.1943
	Days at sea:	134
	Attacked:	11

Group Eisbär 2 (Polar Bear 2)
Kap U-boote (Cape U-boats)

U179 (KK Ernst Sobe)	Type:	IXD2
	Left:	Kiel 15.08.1942
	Sunk:	08.10.1942
	Days at sea:	54
	Attacked:	1
U178 (KS Hans Ibbeken)	Type:	IXD2
	Left:	Kiel 08.09.1942
	Arrived:	Bordeaux 09.01.43
	Days at sea:	123
	Attacked:	7
U181 (KK Wolfgang Lüth)	Type:	IXD2
	Left:	Kiel 12.09.1942
	Arrived:	Bordeaux 18.01.1943

	Days at sea:	128
	Attacked:	12
U177 (KK Robert Gysae)	Type:	IXD2
	Left:	Kiel 17.09.1942
	Arrived:	Bordeaux 22.01.1943
	Days at sea:	127
	Attacked:	8

Supply boat for Group Eisbär

U459 (von Wilamowitz-Moellendorf)	Type:	XIV Special supply U-boat
	Left:	St Nazaire 18.08.1942
	Arrived:	St Nazaire 04.11.1942
	Days at sea:	78
	Attacked:	0 (no armament)

Group Seehund 1 (Seal 1)

U160 (KL Georg Lassen)	Type:	IXC
	Left:	Lorient 06.01.1943
	Arrived:	Lorient 10.05.1943
	Days at sea:	124
	Attacked:	9
U506 (KL Erich Würdemann)	Type:	IXC
	Left:	06.07.1943
	Sunk:	12.07.1943

Group Seehund 2 (Seal 2)

U198 (KS Werner Hartmann)	Type:	IXD2
	Left:	Kiel 09.03.1943
	Arrived:	Bordeaux 24.09.1943
	Days at sea:	199
	Attacked:	7
U196 (KK Eitel-Friedrich Kentrat)	Type:	IXD2
	Left:	Norway 13.03.1943
	Arrived:	Bordeaux 23.10.1943
	Days at sea:	224
	Attacked:	1
U197 (KL Robert Bartels)	Type:	IXD2
	Left:	Kiel 03.04.1943
	Sunk:	20.08.1943
	Days at sea:	139
	Attacked:	4

U510 (KL Alfred Eick)	Type:	IXC
	Left:	Lorient 03.11.1943
	Arrived:	Penang 05.04.1944
	Days at sea:	153
	Attacked:	8
U516 (KK Gerhard Wiebe)	Type:	IXC
	Left:	Lorient 23.12.1942
	Arrived:	Lorient 04.05.1943
	Days at sea:	128
	Attacked:	4

Transport U-boats

U182 (KL Nicolai Clausen)	Type:	IXD1
	Left:	Horten 09.12.1942
	Sunk:	16.05.1943
	Days at sea:	159
	Attacked:	5
U180 (FK Werner Musenberg)	Type:	IXD2
	Left:	Kiel 09.02.1943
	Arrived:	Bordeaux 02.07.1943
	Days at sea:	143
	Attacked:	2
	(Met Japanese submarine in the Indian Ocean – exchanged passengers and cargo)	
U195 (KK Heinz Buchholz)	Type:	IXD1
	Left:	Kiel 20.03.1943
	Arrived:	Bordeaux 23.07.1943
	Days at sea:	125
	Attacked:	2

12. The Indian Ocean: summer 1943

Around the time of this first thrust to South Africa, Japan offered Penang as a German base and asked Germany to send U-boats into the Indian Ocean. The problem with such a move was that there was no basic infrastructure for keeping boats operational and an advance guard needed to be sent out to ensure that the necessary provisions were in the right places. This happened so quickly, without a great deal of advance warning, that there was not even time to send a specially prepared boat from Germany, and U178 (KL Wilhelm Dommes), already in the Indian Ocean, was diverted to Penang.

U178 with one of the external torpedo storage containers raised for gaining access to the screwed-down cover and extracting the contents.

The Japanese were also keen on having two German U-boats so that these could be copied. The U-boat Command did not like this proposal, arguing that it would take too long for Japan to build boats and they would never construct them in the quantities required to make a significant impression on the war. The arguments dragged on from March until May 1943, and, in any case, this was not a good time to leave Europe if the destination was the Indian Ocean. Boats doing so would arrive there during the monsoon, when the stormy weather would make life more than difficult.

This wrangling within the German Naval High Command came to a dramatic climax during the spring of 1943, when Hitler ordered the navy to send a couple of U-boats to the Far East with a view to giving them to Japan. He was under the impression that raw rubber and other scarce commodities would be handed over in return, but payments were hardly forthcoming and the one boat that survived the journey became a gift rather than part of an exchange. The final result in this chain of events was that U511, under KL Fritz Schneewind, left Lorient on 10 May 1943 with a small number of passengers and was later handed over to the Japanese Navy to become RO 500. The other boat, U1224, was sunk *en route*. The handing over of the U-boat to Japan took place with great ceremony, marked by an extraordinary exchange of friendship messages passing through the ether and also by providing a personal gift for the Japanese Emperor.

The Fifth U-Flotilla's guest book page by U1224, which was dispatched to the Far East as a gift from Hitler to become RO501. The boat did not make it all the way. She was sunk with all hands by the US destroyer *Francis M. Robertson* near the Cape Verde Islands on 13 May 1944, having been handed over on 28 February 1944, with a crew of forty-four Japanese on board plus a German commander, KL Georg Preuss, and had left Germany on 16 April.

The arguments about moving into the Indian Ocean started to heat up in March 1943, when the largest convoy battle of all times took place and the debate was still in full swing during May, when the offensive in the North Atlantic collapsed most dramatically. More than forty U-boats were sunk in a period of about thirty days. This meant it was necessary to vacate the danger areas of the North Atlantic for the time being. As a result, the U-boat Command looked upon long distance operations in a new light and was less reticent in sending a force into distant waters.

The first boats of Group *Monsun*, destined for bases in Japanese-controlled territory and accompanied by the tanker U462 (KL Bruno Vowe), left Europe towards the middle of June 1943, shortly after U511. The idea was that U462 should refuel the boats before reaching the Equator so that they could move on to meet a surface tanker from the Far East somewhere to the south of Mauritius. The plan failed because the submarine tanker did not break through the tight blockade around the Bay of Biscay. It returned to port with serious damage, and it was obvious that the tanker would remain in dock for some time. To make life awkward, the other operational boats from this group were already some distance ahead. U487 (KL Helmut Metz), a U-tanker of Type XIV and already at sea, was set to supply the group with enough fuel to reach Penang, if the surface supply ship failed to put in an appearance.

To make this thrust into the Far East possible, the U-boat Command diverted a few boats that had originally been sent out to operate around South

Africa. They were already at sea by the time the *Monsun* question arose. Thus technically, although the *Monsun* boats were the first to leave Europe with the option of going on to the Far East, they were not the first ones to arrive there.

Losses were severe and only seven of this first wave reached the Indian Ocean. One boat, a Type IXC, U516 under KL Hans-Rutger Tillessen, was chosen by the U-boat Command to share a large proportion of its fuel with other boats and then return to Europe. This happened while it was still a long way north of the Equator and made the difference between the entire group being able to reach a destination rather than being stranded in mid-ocean. This refuelling issue also dominated boats heading for the western reaches of the Atlantic. The reason it became so critical at this time was that Bletchley Park had got back into cracking the U-boat code. At the same time, the voyages to operations areas were becoming so long that boats were sent out towards a general area and then had detailed instructions radioed to them once they were at sea.

The Allies had a good number of auxiliary aircraft carriers at sea to make the destruction of supply submarines a fairly efficient operation. The few boats that did manage to find targets in American waters also discovered that the determination of the anti-submarine forces had become considerably fiercer and some boats such as U516 only just managed to extract itself from the most serious chase. This was the time when the Allies introduced the so-called hunter-killer groups, sent out especially to hunt U-boats to destruction rather

The *Bachstelze* or gliding helicopter that was used by some U-boats in the Far East to increase the field of vision of their lookouts.

U178 meets the supply ship
Charlotte Schliemann on
the high seas.

than turn them away from convoys. This began to take a serious toll of long range U-boats.

The tanker *Charlotte Schliemann* refuelled U-cruisers operating in the Indian Ocean during the middle of June 1943 and they then separated again for their individual operations areas. All these boats achieved moderate success and U177 used its *Bachstelze* (Wagtail), a gliding helicopter towed by the submarine, to raise an observer for increasing his field of vision. The Greek freighter *Efthalia Mari* was sighted on 6 August, to become what was probably the one and only sinking achieved by this primitive aid.

The big opportunity for Britain as far as the U-cruisers were concerned was that decrypts from Bletchley Park combined with accurate forecasts by the Admiralty's secret Submarine Tracking Room under the direction of Rodger Winn in London made it possible to forecast what was likely to happen. It was therefore a relatively easy task of keeping one step ahead of the U-boats by putting the hunting forces in place at around the same time as the Germans wanted to make a definite impression in the Indian Ocean. The calmer weather conditions, providing smoother seas than the North Atlantic, and the often brilliant visibility combined with the good use of high-frequency radio direction finders and radar were ideal for aircraft. So the Allied air forces became a big thorn in the flesh of German undertakings. As a result, German achievements were so disappointing that the U-boat Command had to rethink its strategy.

The six boats of this U-cruiser group, refuelled from the tanker *Charlotte Schliemann* to join the *Monsun* undertaking, were as follows:

U198 (KS Werner Hartmann)	Type:	IXD2
	Left:	Kiel 09.03.1943
	Arrived:	Bordeaux 24.09.1943
	Days at sea:	199
	Attacked:	7

U196 (KK Eitel-Friedrich Kentrat)	Type:	IXD2
	Left:	Bordeaux 16.03.1943
	Arrived:	Penang 10.08.1943
	Days at sea:	147
	Attacked:	2
	(Part of Group Monsun 2)	

U178 (KL Wilhelm Dommes)	Type:	IXD2
	Left:	Bordeaux 28.03.1943
	Arrived:	Penang 27.08.1943
	Days at sea:	153
	Attacked:	5
	(Part of Group Monsun 1)	

U181 (KS Kurt Freiwald)	Type:	IXD2
	Left:	Kiel 12.09.1942
	Arrived:	Bordeaux 18.01.1943
	Days at sea:	128
	Left:	Bordeaux 23.03.1943
	Arrived:	Bordeaux 14.10.1943
	Days at sea:	206
	Left:	16.03.1944
	Arrived:	Penang 08.08.1944
	Days at sea:	145
	Attacked:	14
	(Part of Group Monsun 1)	

U197 (KL Robert Bartels)	Type:	IXD2
	Left:	Kiel 03.04.1943
	Sunk:	20.08.1943
	Days at sea:	139
	Attacked:	4

U177 (KK Robert Gysae)	Type:	IXD2
	Left:	02.01.1944
	Sunk:	06.01.1944
	Days at sea:	4

U178 became the first U-cruiser to reach the Far East, although U511 had already got there a few weeks earlier. This boat had undertaken the voyage with a view to being handed over to the Japanese authorities.

13. Indian Ocean: after the summer of 1943 (the *Monsun* operations)

The first thrusts into the Indian Ocean moved into the area not too far from the South African coast, The operations area was then enlarged and later reinforced by the following boats:

U511 (KL Fritz Schneewind)	Type:	IXC
(Handed over to Japanese Navy)	Left:	Lorient 10.05.1943
	Arrived:	Penang 07.08.1943
	Days at sea:	90
	Attacked:	3
U200 (KL Heinrich Schonder)	Type:	IXD2
	Left:	Kiel 12.06.1943
	Sunk:	24.06.1943
	Days at sea:	12
	Attacked:	0
U188 (KL Siegfried Lüdden)	Type:	IXC/40
	Left:	Lorient 30.06.1943
	Arrived:	Penang 30.10.1943
	Days at sea:	122
	Attacked:	2
U514 (KL H.-J. Auffermann)	Type:	IXC
	Left:	Lorient 01.07.1943
	Sunk:	08.07.1943
	Days at sea:	7
	Attacked:	0
U532 (FK Ottoheinrich Junker)	Type:	IXC/40
	Left:	Lorient 03.07.1943
	Arrived:	Penang 30.10.1943
	Days at sea:	119
	Attacked:	5
U168 (KL Helmuth Pich)	Type:	IXC/40
	Left:	Lorient 03.07.1943
	Arrived:	Penang 11.11.1943
	Days at sea:	131
	Attacked:	7
U509 (KL Werner Witte)	Type:	IXC
	Left:	03.07.1943
	Sunk:	15.07.1943
	Days at sea:	12
	Attacked:	0

U183 (KK Heinrich Schäfer	Type:	IXC/40
KL Fritz Schneewind)	Left:	Lorient 03.07.1943
	Arrived:	Penang 30.10.1943
	Days at sea:	119
	Attacked:	1
U533 (KL Helmut Hennig)	Type:	IXC/40
	Left:	Lorient 05.07.1943
	Sunk:	16.10.1943, one survivor
	Days at sea:	103
	Attacked:	0
U847 (KL Herbert Kuppisch)	Type:	IXD2
	Left:	Kiel 06.07.1943
	(Returned to Bergen due to ice damage)	
	Left:	Bergen 29.07.1943
	Sunk:	19.08.1943
U506 (KL Erich Würdemann)	Type:	IXC
	Left:	Lorient 06.07.1943
	Sunk:	12.07.1943
U516 (KL Hans-Rutger Tillessen)	Type:	IXC
	Left:	Lorient 08.07.1943
	Arrived:	Lorient 23.08.1943
	Days at sea:	46
	Attacked:	0
	(Acted as emergency supply boat, returned to France)	
U523 (KL Werner Pietzsch)	Type:	IXC
	Left:	Lorient 16.08.1943
	Sunk:	25.08.1943
U848 (KL Wilhelm Rollmann)	Type:	IXD2
	Left:	Kiel 18.09.1943
	Sunk:	05.11.1943
U849 (KL Heinz-Otto Schultze)	Type:	IXD2
	Left:	02.10.1943
	Sunk:	25.11.1943
U850 (FK Klaus Ewerth)	Type:	IXD2
	Left:	Kiel 18.11.1943
	Sunk:	20.12.1943
U172 (OL Hermann Hoffmann)	Type:	IXC
	Left:	Lorient 22.11.1943
	Sunk:	13.11.1943

U196 (OL Werner Striegler)	Type:	IXD2
	Left:	Bordeaux 11.03.1944
	(Put into La Pallice on 13th and left again on 16th)	
	Arrived:	Penang 10.08.1944
	Days at sea:	153
	Attacked:	1
U219 (KK Walter Burghagen)	Type:	XB (mine-layer used as transporter)
	Left:	Bordeaux 23.08.1944
	Arrived:	Batavia 11.12.1944
	Days at sea:	110
U195 (OL Friedrich Steinfeld)	Type:	IXD1 (transporter)
	Left:	Bordeaux 24.08.1944
	Arrived:	Batavia 28.12.1944
	Days at sea:	126

The following belonged to Group Monsun 2:

U510 (KL Alfred Eick)	Type:	IXC
	Left:	Lorient 03.11.1943
	Arrived:	Penang 05.04.1944
	Days at sea:	154
	Attacked:	6
U177 (KK Heinz Buchholz)	Type:	IXD2
	Left:	Bordeaux 23.12.1943
	Arrived:	La Pallice 26.12.1943
	Left:	La Pallice 02.01.1944
	Sunk:	06.02.1944
U1062 (OLzS Karl Albrecht)	Type:	VIIF (torpedo transporter)
	Left:	Bergen 03.01.1944
	Arrived:	Penang 19.04.1944
	Days at sea:	107
U852 (KL Heinz-Wilhelm Eck)	Type:	IXD2
	Left:	Kiel 18.01.1944
	Sunk:	03.05.1944
	Days at sea:	107
	Attacked:	2

U1059 (OL Günter Leupold)	Type:	VIIF (torpedo transporter)
	Left:	Kiel 04.02.1944
	Sunk:	19.03.1944
U843 (KL Oskar Herwartz)	Type:	IXC/40
	Left:	Lorient 19.02.1944
	Arrived:	Batavia 11.06.1944
	Days at sea:	123
	Attacked:	1
U851 (KK Hannes Weingaertner)	Type:	IXD2
	Left:	Kiel 26.02.1944
	Sunk:	Lost – unknown cause
U196 (OL Werner Striegler)	Type:	IXD2
	Left:	La Pallice 16.03.1944
	Arrived:	Penang 10.08.1944
	Days at sea:	148
	Ships sunk:	1
U181 (KS Kurt Freiwald)	Type:	IXD2
	Left:	Bordeaux 16.03.1944
	Arrived:	Penang 08.08.1944
	Days at sea:	146
	Ships sunk:	4
U537 (KL Peter Schrewe)	Type:	IXC/40
	Left:	Lorient 25.03.1944
	Arrived:	Batavia 02.08.1944
	Days at sea:	130
	Attacked:	0
U859 (KL Johann Jebsen)	Type:	IXD2
	Left:	Kiel 04.04.1944
	Sunk:	near Penang 23.09.1944
	Days at sea:	172
	Attacked:	3
U860 (FK Paul Büchel)	Type:	IXD2
	Left:	Kiel 11.04.1944
	Sunk:	15.06.1944
U861 (KK Jürgen Oesten)	Type:	IXD2
	Left:	20.04.1944
	Arrived:	Penang 23.09.1944
	Days at sea:	156
	Attacked:	5

U198 (OL B. Heusinger von Waldegg)	Type:	IXD2
	Left:	Bordeaux 20.04.1944
	Sunk:	10.08.1944
	Days at sea:	113
	Attacked:	4
U490 (OL Wilhelm Gerlach)	Type:	XIV (tanker)
	Left:	Kiel 04.05.1944
	Sunk:	12.06.1944
U862 (KK Heinrich Timm)	Type:	IXD2
	Left:	Kiel 20.05.1944
	Left	Left Narvik 03.06.1944
	Arrived:	Penang 09.09.1944
	Days at sea:	98
	Attacked:	5
U863 (KL Dietrich von der Esch)	Type:	IXD2
	Left:	Kiel 03.07.1944
	Called at:	Horten and Bergen
	Left:	Bergen 26.07.1944
	Sunk:	29.09.1944
U180 (OL Rolf Riesen)	Type:	IXD2
	Left:	Bordeaux 24.08.1944
	Sunk:	26.08.1944
U219 (KK Walter Burghagen)	Type:	XB (Mine-layer used as transporter)
	Left:	Bordeaux 23.08.1944
	Arrived:	Batavia 11.12.1944
	Days at sea:	111
	Ships sunk:	?
U871 (KL Peter-Ottmar Grau)	Type:	IXD2
	Left:	Trondheim 31.08.1944
	Sunk:	26.09.1944
U864 (KK Rolf-Reimar Wolfram)	Type:	IXD2
	Left:	Bergen 07.02.1945
	Sunk:	09.02.1944
U234 (KL Johann-Heinrich Fehler)	Type:	XB (Mine-layer kitted out as transporter.)
	Left:	Kiel 24.03.1945 (Surrendered to the US at the end of the war)
U876 (KL Rolf Bahn)	Type:	IXD2 (Damaged before departure; cruise cancelled)

UIT23 (KK Heinrich Schäfer	Type:	ex-Italian *Reginaldo*
and Werner Striegler)		*Giuliani*
	Left:	?
	Arrived:	Singapore 17.06.1943
	Days at sea:	?
	Attacked:	3
UIT24 (OL Heinrich Pahls)	Type:	ex-Italian *Commandante Cappellini*
	Left:	?
	Arrived:	Singapore 09.07.1943
	Days at sea:	?
	Attacked:	5
UIT25 (OL Werner Striegler,	Type:	ex-Italian *Luigi Torelli*
KL Herbert Schrein, OL Alfred Meier)	Left:	?
	Arrived:	Singapore 26.08.1943
	Days at sea:	?
	Attacked:	3

Peter-Ottmar Grau (on the right, facing to the left) addresses the men at the end of the war around the time they scuttled their boats in Geltinger Bay close to the Danish frontier.

A German U-boat makes fast by the pier in Penang after a voyage from Europe.

14. Far East to Europe journeys from November 1943 to the end of the war

The following boats attempted return journeys to Europe:

U178 (KL Wilhelm Spahr)	Type:	IXD2
	Left:	Penang 27.11.1943
	Arrived:	Bordeaux 25.05.1944
	Days at sea:	180
	Attacked:	1
U181 (KS Kurt Freiwald)	Type:	IXD2
	Left:	Batavia 19.10.1944
	Arrived:	Batavia 01.01.1945 (Due to serious mechanical breakdown)
	Days at sea:	73
	Attacked:	1

Above and below: On arrival in Penang the Germans were surprised to see that the town consisted of two distinct opposites. On the one side there was ample evidence of incredible wealth, but many of the locals lived in the deepest poverty.

U188 (KL Siegfried Lüdden)	Type:	IXC/40
	Left:	Penang 08.01.1944
	Arrived:	Bordeaux 19.06.1944
	Days at sea:	163
	Attacked:	14
U1062 (OL Karl Albrecht)	Type:	VIIF (torpedo transporter)
	Left:	Penang 15.071944
	Sunk:	30.09.1944
U168 (KL Helmuth Pich)	Type:	IXC/40
	Left:	Batavia 05.10.1944
	Sunk:	06.10.1944
U196 (OL Werner Striegler)	Type:	IXD2
	Left:	Batavia 30.11.1944 (Lost shortly after leaving port)
U843 (KL Oskar Herwartz)	Type:	IXC/40
	Left:	Batavia 10.12.1944
	Arrived:	Bergen 04.04.1945
	Left:	Bergen 06.04.1945
	Sunk:	09.04.1945
	Days at sea:	117 + 2
	Attacked:	0
U861 (KK Jürgen Oesten)	Type:	IXD2
	Left:	Surabaya 15.01.1945
	Arrived:	Trondheim 19.04.1945
	Days at sea:	94
	Attacked:	0
U532 (FK Ottoheinrich Junker)	Type:	IXC/40
	Left:	Batavia 13.01.1945
	Arrived:	Liverpool 10.05.1945 (after the war ends)
	Days at sea:	118
	Attacked:	2
U510 (KL Alfred Eick)	Type:	IXC
	Left:	Batavia 11.01.1945
	Arrived:	St Nazaire 23.04.1945
	Days at sea:	96
	Attacked:	1
U183 (KL Fritz Schneewind)	Type:	IXC/40
	Left:	Batavia 21.04.1945
	Sunk:	23.04.1945

CHAPTER 3

Germany's Foreign Connections

This chapter is based on a confidential document written by Lt Cdr K. W. McMahan USNR and edited by Lt Cdr L. A. Griffiths RNVR as part of the Government Code and Cypher School (GC&CS) Naval History. This was distributed shortly after the war to people who knew about code-breaking activities. The text is valuable because it was not written for public consumption and therefore includes details that were not generally available at the time. Much of this information came from reading German U-boat signals and the exceedingly long radio exchanges between Berlin and Tokyo.

The biggest problem with German-Japanese co-operation was not so much the vast distance between the two countries but the lack of common background and culture. Although the first U-boat commanders making for the Far East left home with the impression that it would be possible to communicate through the worldwide international medium of English, this was not the case. *Vizeadmiral* Paul Wenneker, the German naval attaché in Tokyo, said that apart from a few close friends, there was never anyone with whom the staff could have a conversation in any European language, and he also complained that he very rarely had contact with anyone whose rank was higher than Captain. On top of this, the German Embassy never had an interpreter with a command of technical terms. Bearing in mind that much of the communications involved cutting-edge technology, this was indeed a serious handicap. The GC&CS Naval History states:

Fenced off from intimacy, the representatives of each nation were excluded from the deliberations and decisions of the other's high command. Throughout all the professions of support, which formed the official framework of their relations, it is difficult to find any continuous thread of mutual trust. If the Japanese were not suspicious of German intentions, they were apt to be offended by the German assumption of superiority in the knowledge and techniques of war.

The main underlying factor in all the co-operation between the two nations was keeping the supply and communication lines open. At the beginning of the war it was possible to send both people and goods along the Siberian railway, but this vital link broke when Russia joined the war only a few months before Japan. So transport became the greatest practical obstacle to bringing about the advantages of co-operation. The irony about this transport problem was that it fell to Germany, a recognised land power, to meet the demands, whereas Japan, with its claims of being a sea power, contributed very little other than supplying the fuel. From the very beginning, the shortage of Japanese shipping placed the main burden of providing vessels for running the blockade on Germany. When German merchant vessels were no longer in a position to tackle the Allied blockade, it was the German U-boat fleet that came to the rescue. The essential factor in the history of German-Japanese co-operation was the struggle to maintain the sea-lanes, and this was primarily a part of German naval history rather than that of Japan.

By being able to read a large proportion of the German radio codes, and due to the length of the voyages, Britain was in a good position to make adequate preparations to intercept these vital and most delicate links. Britain and America knew full well that the military needs of Germany and Japan dictated a policy of exchange. Both the Germans and Japanese appreciated the importance of this trade as well, although the Japanese side appeared to be far more reticent about making it work properly. This link was especially important because Japan and Germany complemented each other, with only very little duplication within both camps. Germany possessed advanced technical and scientific knowledge. It knew how to invent and then manufacture the complicated weapons, devices and equipment necessary for waging war. It did not, however, have access to important raw materials such as rubber and tin. Japan, on the other hand, controlled an empire of raw materials. These were not matched by technical ingenuity and industrial development, and therefore Japan needed assistance to make best use of these resources. There were also some materials, such as mercury, which were seriously lacking in the Far Eastern theatre, and such gaps could also be filled by sending supplies from Germany.

Before Japan's attack on the American naval base at Pearl Harbor, the Japanese authorities held back from open co-operation with Germany, although secretly they expressed a deep desire to help the German war effort. However, the disguise for any such assistance was immense and sometimes overpowering for the Germans. Then, immediately after Japan's entry into the war, the exchange of goods between the two countries proceeded at a rapid pace, with a considerable number of blockade runners making adventurous runs into France's Biscay ports. Many of the men sailed out again under the most dangerous circumstances, some ships managing more than one voyage.

The massive swastika on the side of the conning tower was ordered by the Japanese authorities to prevent their forces from attacking friendly submarines. (Probably U178.)

Decrypts circulating in Britain at this time give a slightly different picture. It would seem that the initial burst of co-operation fell flat rather quickly and it was not long before the airwaves contained complaints from Germans who were not allowed to be present when ships were being loaded in Singapore; others reported drawn-out delays with the delivery of promised goods and that substitutes were often produced instead of previously agreed products; fuel was in short supply and so forth. Each one was not terribly significant on its own, but when added together, this produced a noteworthy picture that all was not well with the Japanese-German co-operation in the Far East.

At the same time, Japan was making ever-increasing demands on Germany, asking for goods that were also in short supply in Europe. In addition, there were constant requests for ships. To analysts in Britain and the United States it looked very much as if the Japanese High Command was of the opinion that it could manage to win the war without Germany's help. All these undercurrents resulted in a slowdown of traffic at about the time that Germany was losing its grip in the Atlantic. The situation had deteriorated considerably by the time surface blockade running had to be given up due to increased enemy activity.

At the same time as German surface ships were wiped off the seas, or at least off the Atlantic, U-boats were also having an increasingly difficult period, and many history books would have us believe that this offensive collapsed beyond repair in May 1943. However, there was enough activity backstage to make the German High Command think that the U-boats would regain the offensive once the new weapons, already in production, appeared at the front. It was therefore not too difficult for the admirals to consider replacing the blockade-running merchant ships with submarines, although these would carry considerably less cargo.

At this critical stage it is most interesting to look at the state of technical development in Germany. Bletchley Park was producing such vast piles of readable signals that it was possible for British analysts to gain a good insight into what to expect from the new German weapons. The reason for this was that considerable traffic with so many secrets was flying back and forth between Germany and Japan, and this was a very fruitful period for the eavesdroppers. Germany was sending radar, radar search devices, standard torpedoes, mines, guns, radios and the like to Japan; many of these had their top secret specifications broadcast by radio. For some reason there were also a number of strange hang-ups with this exchange of information. For example, the Germans did not want the Japanese to know about the new acoustic torpedo, the T5 or *Zaunkönig*. In April 1944, when the first boats arrived in the Far East with these on board, they were ordered by radio to sink them in deep water before entering port. It would now be interesting to eavesdrop on the arguments within the German High Command, because shortly afterwards the U-boat Command sent another signal telling commanders to keep the acoustic torpedoes on board, but not to let the Japanese see them. It was German officers in Penang that objected most violently, telling the U-boat Command that torpedoes had to go into a common store run by the Japanese. So how could they be prevented from seeing the new torpedoes? In the end, after a lot of hassle, it was agreed that two of these new torpedoes should be given to Japan.

German help for the Japanese went much further than merely transferring equipment, weapons, and drawings. Japanese commercial and technical representatives, brought by German sea transport, were received in German industrial and naval establishments for purposes of training and inspection. In addition to this, German representatives were sent to Japan to assist there in setting up industrial establishments and technical processes. The Germans in Japan complained that they were hindered in their missions by lack of proper co-operation. On the other hand, Japanese representatives in Germany learned much of value, judging by the lengthy and detailed descriptions that were transmitted home. Some of this information must have been of great value to Britain in deciding how best to combat new German introductions. All this resulted in Japan making constant demands for space in U-boats sailing to the Indian Ocean in order to transport blueprints and purchases.

The two powers also exchanged political and military situation reports, and the Japanese maintained liaison officers in German naval intelligence centres. Now it is difficult to establish how useful this has been because in many cases Germany did not have a terribly accurate picture of the turn of events. In addition to this, the Germans tended to be far more optimistic with many of their new inventions that were due to come into service. The Japanese, in turn, gave the Germans an entirely false impression of Japanese naval achievements in the Pacific. All this added a considerable chaotic element to the information exchange and generally it is fair to say that regarding the exchange of intelligence, the Germans gave more than they received, both in intelligence about themselves and in intelligence about the enemy.

In general, German-Japanese naval co-operation falls into three periods. During the first twelve months after Japan's entry into the war, Germany was dominant and boldly assertive, taking the lead in negotiations and in action. The Japanese tended to make polite replies and then lapse into enigmatic silence, despite the efforts of Vice Admiral Nomura, the Japanese Three-Power Representative in Berlin, who gave freely of his own ideas concerning co-operation but was not well informed on Japanese worries in the Pacific or on the plans of the German Army. The actual achievements of the first period were confined largely to the exchange of raw materials and manufactures carried in German blockade runners.

The middle or transition period was one of adjustment to the prospects of war. Germany maintained its leadership in attempting to strengthen Japan's staying power with technical assistance and to bring Japan into a joint war against Allied merchant shipping. At the same time, the German Navy extended its area of submarine operations to the Indian Ocean. Maintenance of the essential link by sea between the two countries presented numerous problems, demanding new exertions and improvisation from the German Navy.

The third and final period, from the Allied invasion of France, D-Day, to the surrender of Germany, saw a shift of the initiative to Japan, as Japan sought to exploit the established German leadership in an effort to save itself from Allied naval power.

German-Japanese fighting co-operation

The failure to establish an open and equal exchange of intelligence between the German and Japanese Naval Commands about themselves as well as about their enemies reflected the basic failure to effect anything like fighting co-operation. Except on paper, such co-operation in the sense of joint naval operations, amounted to very little, yet without some statement concerning it, the illusory nature of German-Japanese co-operation cannot be fully appreciated. It would appear that Germany was urging Japan to enter the war as early as the beginning of 1941, but in general was kept in the dark as to Japan's decisions on such matters, and the attack on Pearl Harbor came as a great surprise to all, or at least to the vast majority of high-ranking Germans. It is unlikely that even Hitler was informed.

German plans to send U-boats around South Africa came initially from the Supreme Naval Command rather than the U-boat Command, and one of the main reasons for going into such long range operations was to draw Allied anti-submarine forces out of the trouble spots of the North Atlantic. Negotiations with Japan about sending U-boats into the Indian Ocean during 1942 suggested that Japan did not welcome German interference in that area. To understand this, it is necessary to remember that the first battle at El Alamein (North Africa) did not take place until July 1942, and the final defeat of Field Marshal Erwin Rommel there took place in October and November of that year. So, early in 1942, it looked to the Japanese that the German *Afrikakorps* might reach the Red Sea, allowing the German Navy to enter the Indian Ocean via the Suez Canal. On the other hand, if this German drive failed, then Japan could count on an increased presence of Allied forces in the Indian Ocean. Both these possibilities presented the Japanese High Command with a dilemma, which was later solved by events in the Pacific theatre. The result of the Pacific experiences was that after a while the setbacks there caused a change in attitude and made Japan happy to relinquish its Indian Ocean claims to the German Navy.

To put the thoughts of the above paragraph into perspective, one might look at various British naval staff histories. These were originally written during the war for limited circulation to higher officials, and the vast majority were modified between 1945 and 1955 with post-war additions. It states that in 1942, when reviewing the dismal picture of Allied performance, the Joint Staff Mission in Washington laid down three main defence tasks:

1. To keep Russia effectively in the war;
2. To prevent Germany and Japan from joining together in the Indian Ocean;
3. To check the Japanese advance on India and Australia.

So, although a meeting of German and Japanese forces in the Indian Ocean may look absurd these days, it would appear that this picture was obtained with considerable hindsight and at the time such a possibility was indeed a real threat.

Anticipating problems in the Indian Ocean with Japanese, Italian and German U-boats mingling in the same area, it was decided on 18 January 1942 to divide the area along the 70 degrees east line of longitude. This line runs through the sea to the west of India and puts the Maldives into the Japanese sphere. The bickering and discussion that went on about this would be enough to bore the majority of readers and the outcome is hardly significant for most historians, so these negotiations can be overlooked here. The Battle of Midway in June 1942, when the Japanese Navy suffered considerable losses, was far more to the point and put the question of co-operation in a different light. Following this, Japan desperately wanted the German aircraft carrier *Graf Zeppelin* finished so that it could operate in the Indian Ocean. Any person with an inkling of knowledge must surely ask how anyone could have expected it to get there. The *Bismarck* breakout had taken place a year earlier, in May 1941, and should have closed the minds to any breakout attempt by large surface units. The astonishing point about all the arguments reverberating between Berlin and Tokyo was that the concept of the Suez Canal coming under German jurisdiction played a significant role in general planning at this time. Perhaps this helps to emphasise the remoteness of the higher planners with their specialised staffs. They seem to have been a long way from reality. Even if this had happened, the obstacle of Gibraltar at the entrance to the Mediterranean would have limited German traffic to whatever could come out of Italian ports.

British analysts were certainly correct in their thinking that Germany had not the slightest inkling of what the Japanese were doing, and when the first boats of Group *Eisbär* appeared in the Indian Ocean, parts of the

The flag of Group *Eisbär* being hauled down for the last time shortly after the few remaining German boats had been scuttled in Geltinger Bay.

German Naval High Command were under the impression that they could well be meeting Japanese submarines. The interesting point is that the U-boat Command was hardly under any illusions of expecting help from Japan. At least, there is no mention of it in its official war diary.

Indian Ocean activities became a pantomime, and the organisation behind Axis submarine operations there cannot be described with a more appropriate word. For example, the Italian U-boat *Ammiraglio Cagni* sparked off some lively comments when negotiations were under way to refuel her from Japanese quarters. Apparently the Italians were informed that the Japanese Navy was in the process of sending a fleet of forty to fifty submarines into the waters around Madagascar. Bearing in mind that the German onslaught against the United States started with only five boats, this was indeed an incredible figure. The U-boat Command was so astonished that the officers immediately made contact with the Italian High Command. In reply to their request for further information, the German U-boat Chief, Admiral Karl Dönitz, was told to take the matter up directly with the Japanese. So the Italians were just as puzzled as the British intelligence analysts. It must have been an excitingly frustrating time for planners responsible for dispatching a significant thrust of U-boats to the Indian Ocean.

Following the Battle of Midway, the Japanese Navy became more and more involved in the Pacific, and less and less able to spare forces for the Indian Ocean. Nevertheless, an attempt seems to have been made to uphold a prior right in African waters. In July 1942, as the German Army approached Alexandria in Egypt, the German Navy was insistent that the decisive hour had come and that Japan must take up large-scale operations in the Indian Ocean to prevent the British from strengthening their stand at El Alamein with supplies from India via the Suez Canal. Japan agreed on the critical nature of the situation and gave the impression that naval assistance would be forthcoming. But officials in Berlin, including the Japanese representatives there, seem to have had no clear idea as to just what the Japanese Navy was going to do. Thus, when German U-boats sailed in August 1942 to operate off Cape Town, Admiral Fricke, then Chief of the Naval War Staff, was under the impression that Japanese submarines would appear off Durban and Port Elizabeth to complete the disruption of Allied shipping. Admiral Dönitz, on the other hand, made no mention in his log of any Japanese co-operation, nor did the U-boat operation order (*Eisbär*) refer to the possibility of encounters with Japanese submarines. The *Eisbär* operation was, however, not intended at first to penetrate deep into the Indian Ocean.

Today it is difficult to establish exactly how much Germany knew about British and American connections with Russia. There is enough evidence to suggest that co-operation between the three major states started long before Russia entered the war, and it could well be that the Persian Gulf connection had already come under close scrutiny by German intelligence by the time Germany invaded Russia. Britain was keen to develop and pay for the improvements to the railway line from Basra to the Caspian Sea and urged Russia as early as August 1941 not to enter Tehran in force for the time being. Britain was prepared to resume payments of oil royalties to the Shah of Persia, which had been suspended some time earlier, and also allow food from India into the country again if the government there could ensure a through route for war materials along the railway line. Some of this activity in Persia could not have gone unnoticed in Berlin because both the Arabian Sea and the approaches to the Persian Gulf became significant operations areas for long distance U-boats once these were in a position to make the long journey.

The later *Monsun* venture was a separate undertaking from what had gone on before because right from the early planning stages this involved contact with Japanese authorities. This planning was most important because not only did it involve German U-boats going into what had been regarded as Japanese waters but it also included a considerable transportation element, and that part of the equation was not an easy conundrum to deal with. Germany did employ cargo-carrying U-boats during the First World War, but in 1943 it had neither the necessary transporters nor the men with experience of getting them to sea.

Despite this sudden crossover of operations areas, there appears to have been no effort at running joint operations. The exchange of signals between Tokyo and Berlin suggested that there was only an iota of operational information exchange and Germany was very much groping in the dark. As a result, the German U-boat Command found a few unpleasant surprises along the way. For example, everything was running well when German officials discovered that the base offered by the Japanese could not provide diesel oil of the quality required by U-boats and some were already under way, making this a pressing problem. Japan had access to oil refineries, so producing such fuel should not have presented too great a problem. There were also difficulties with communications, as a result of which the Germans wanted to have their own radio transmitters, but Japan insisted on its own staff handling German signals. In the end what actually happened in the Indian Ocean must be looked upon more as a spontaneous miracle rather than the result of efficient joint planning.

The first U-boat to reach the Far East, U511, was warmly received at Penang in July 1943. Fritz Schneewind, the commander, had no alternative other than to become temporary chief of the first German submarine base in the Far East. The first regular commanding officer, Wilhelm Dommes, arrived as commander of U178 in August 1943. He had originally set out from Europe for an operation on the African side of the Indian Ocean and was almost on his way home when he received a signal asking whether he could reach Penang.

U178, under Wilhelm Dommes. Note the watertight seal in the front of the gun barrel.

So this new venture was a totally new challenge for him and, to make matters worse, by the time of his arrival he was both physically and mentally at rock bottom as a result of constant engagement over an incredibly long period.

The conditions that Dommes found in Penang were not ideal and rapidly got worse, despite a warm and friendly relationship with the local Japanese authorities. The first obvious step was to supply the base with provisions from Germany. These were going to take some time arriving and deliveries were not guaranteed. One of the biggest problems was the acute shortage of diesel oil already mentioned. Things got so bad that at one stage the 1,230 gross register tonnage (grt) German motor freighter *Quito*, belonging to North German Lloyd in Bremen, was sent around various ports in search of suitable fuel. Another distressing difficulty lay in Japan's inability to provide the necessary protection and escorts for U-boats near obvious hotspots where enemy submarines might be lurking.

In October 1944, it became obvious that Penang, the principal operating base, was no longer suitable because there was too much enemy submarine activity in its approaches. A concentration of British warships in Ceylon, the Burma Campaign and attacks on the Nicobar Islands quickly indicated that the base would have to be given up. The Japanese authorities provided alternative ports: Kobe in Japan and Singapore were used for main repairs, and Djakarta and Surabaya became cargo-handling ports, with the last named also providing reasonable repair facilities. Yet all bases suffered from a shortage of tools and there were many cases where local workers provided their own.

U178's second commander, Wilhelm Dommes, photographed at a reunion after the war.

Kurt Freiwald awarding the Iron Cross First Class to Radio Petty Officer Michalski. Freiwald was senior German officer in Singapore at the end of the war. He and his men were rounded up by the British authorities and made to march in temperatures of over 30 degrees Celsius to the point of exhaustion along a detoured route from their accommodation to the local prison. The British were good enough to send a lorry to pick up unconscious men unable to withstand the ordeal.

Above and below: U106, a standard long range boat of Type IXB, under Jürgen Oesten, alongside the blockade breaker *Anneliese Essberger*. Oesten was sent out with the objective of escorting the merchant ship back to France; at the same time the provisions supplied helped him to extend his operations area.

The Germans never allowed any of these helpers inside the U-boats, but were more than pleased with the results produced by this workforce in improvised machine shops. This is mentioned in more details in a later chapter.

The general situation in the Far East is summed up very well by the respected historian Capt. James Wise (USN) and Otto Giese (who ran the blockade aboard the *Anneliese Essberger* and then returned to the Far East as 2WO of U181 under KzS Kurt Freiwald) in an article entitled 'Hitler's Monsoon U-boats' (*Sea Classics*, June 1991). German U-boat activities in the Indian Ocean and in the waters around South Africa were a notable success, especially when one considers the loss in Allied tonnage and the fact that the war there did not start until after the offensive in the Atlantic had collapsed. An analysis of the effort indicates that 7 per cent of the total number of U-boats that made war patrols accounted for just over 7 per cent of total Allied shipping losses to U-boats. Thus while U-boat operations achieved significant successes, the transporting of war materials from the Far East to Germany fell far short of the planned expectations. Less than 1,000 tons of cargo reached Germany via returning U-boats. A single cargo ship could have carried eight times as much. Much of this cargo was carried by operational boats rather than the large transports engaged specifically for the purpose of carrying cargo. So the cargo-carrying aspect of Far East operations was an utter failure.

Wise and Giese lay the blame for the failure on a combination of facts. First, there was no senior naval officer or naval staff in the Far East and unlike other standard operating procedures in other areas, no post-deployment intelligence was evaluated so that it could be passed on to commanders. Thus many commanders operated on their own, with very little intelligence to help them. Secondly, communications remained poor and even mundane activities such as finding spaces in overcrowded shipyards could not be well organised. Thirdly, as has already been mentioned, there was only a little support to ensure safe passage through dangerous areas.

CHAPTER 4

Submarine Cargo Carriers

Although Germany took the lead in many of the joint operations with Japan, it was the Japanese submarine I-30 (KK Endo) that undertook the first voyage between the Far East and Europe, and this momentous event became the yardstick for preparing future ventures. I-30 arrived in Lorient in August 1942, later returning to Singapore to be sunk by a mine while preparing to enter harbour. (The first U-boat definitely destined for the Far East before it set out, U511 under KL Fritz Schneewind, did not leave until May 1943, so this was indeed a record-breaking voyage.)

The first plans to send German cargo-carrying U-boats to the Far East were made under the codename 'Mercator' and it seems as if this venture originated as a result of Ambassador Oshima suggesting the use of some of the older Mediterranean boats for long distance cargo-carrying missions. This term puzzled the British eavesdroppers until they realised he was referring to the larger Italian submarines in Bordeaux. They were given the cover name 'Akira' (or perhaps 'Aquila', depending on how one reads the Japanese phonetics) and varied in size from 950 to 1,300 tons. Using I-30's experience, they were thought to be capable of making two round-trips per year. As things turned out, the original Akira boats never made a journey at all. Two did not return from their mission before the conversion was due; the third never left Bordeaux.

The Japanese side was not a great deal luckier. Of four submarines that sailed for Europe only one, the 2,000/2,600 ton I-8 under KzS Uchino, made the round-trip without mishap. Two managed the round-trip but were sunk with some of the cargo still on board after docking briefly in Singapore, and one was sunk on the way to Europe. From such cargo figures as are available for these cruises, the total accomplishment appears to have been small, although some 90 out of a 100 passengers carried did reach their destination, and the materials carried to Japan, especially technical diagrams, were of primary importance to the country. (Today it is difficult to work out how British intelligence arrived at these passenger figures, but I-8 brought the best part of an entire U-boat crew to Europe and the remaining people were distributed among a number of other boats.)

From the German side, two boats were sent as gifts, U511 and U1224, but the latter was sunk on 13 May 1944 while en route to the Far East. This was an exceptionally heavy blow because there was a Japanese crew on board. These men, under the command of KL Georg Preuss, had come over in I-8, participated in the building process at Deutsche Werft in Hamburg, went through the German training programme and were then lost after about one month at sea.

In addition to those mentioned above, some forty other U-boats attempted a cruise to the Far East. Of these forty, two were forced to cancel their trips, one (U234) was interned in the United States after Germany's surrender and twenty-two were sunk on their way out, making it obvious that the seas had become dangerous even for submarines in remote areas. The remaining fifteen reached the Far East. Of these, four got back again, six were sunk while operating in Asiatic waters or returning, four were seized by the Japanese when Germany surrendered, and one surrendered to the Allies in Liverpool in compliance with the general surrender order of May 1945.

The total cargo successfully carried westbound for the period of nineteen months was approximately between 600 and 700 tons. The total eastbound cargo over a period of twenty-seven months, including operational supplies for the Penang U-boat base, probably came to something between 1,000 and 2,000 tons. These statistics convey to some extent the nature and fate of the venture as a whole. The operational side was highly successful, but the transport part of the operation ended in almost complete failure. Less than 1,000 tons was transported from the Far East to Europe. A merchant ship would have carried about eight times as much during one voyage and this figure was a long way below expectations. It was a hard effort with comparatively little gain.

Early transport cruises

It was in February 1943 that the first Indian Ocean cruise not primarily operational was undertaken by a German U-boat. This was when U180 under Werner Musenberg carried the Indian Subhas Chandra Bose and his adjutant to meet the Japanese I-29. This is dealt with in Chapter 8.

Back in European waters, U180 was making a concerted effort to avoid air attacks in the Biscay region when the first *Monsun* boats were being made ready. Among the curiosities of this *Monsun* undertaking is the fact that the *Monsun* order of 10 June 1943 did not include putting in at Penang as a primary consideration. The boats were to be refuelled at sea and then return to France after their operation. Penang was to be used only in case of emergency, if the refuelling at sea failed or if individuals needed repairs or a rest before returning. Note that this was unusual inasmuch that 'rests' were not usually incorporated in planning processes. The *Monsun* order may merely reflect the uncertainties that always attended German-Japanese co-operation. In any case, what eventually happened was part of the welter of improvisation that characterised the efforts to maintain a U-boat supply line to the Far East.

By the end of August 1943, there were only five *Monsun* boats left to continue the cruise to the Indian Ocean; five had been sunk by Allied action and one had been forced to put back because it had to give its valuable fuel to others due to the loss of the submarine tanker. Eventually the larger U-cruisers of Type IXD2 replaced the slightly smaller Type IXC boats. These had the advantage that they could make the trip without refuelling.

The two months that these crews of the first wave to Penang were to spend in the Far East, plus the two following two months, saw a significant turning point in the history of the U-boat transport venture. Transport was originally not the primary consideration of the *Monsun* group. As mentioned above, they were originally sent to the Indian Ocean to sink ships and then return to France, using Penang as a temporary port of call. While they were there the transport question became so important that it was allowed to encroach upon the operations. This was made clear to the commanders by radio in a signal saying that the transport of enriched ores to the homeland was absolutely essential to the war effort and every opportunity was to be taken to carry as much as possible. The U-boat Command even ordered the large deck guns to be removed and their ammunition stored on land so that there would be more space for carrying cargo.

The next wave of *Monsun* boats differed from the first by starting out with much of their armament already stripped before they left, so that they could carry as much cargo as possible. Yet although the emphasis had shifted from operations to transport, the boats were still free to attack shipping on the way, and this ended up as one of the most successful groups making for the Far East. Sinking twenty-one ships of about 119,000 tons in areas stretching from Ceylon to the Gulf of Aden and including the waters off Mauritius, this was indeed a most successful thrust.

Although the transport side of these operations is well known, very few details have emerged and thorough investigations by several researchers over a number of years have failed to turn up information regarding what was actually carried by each U-boat. It seemed as if this aspect of history would remain an enigma until a chance meeting many years ago made me look not in Germany but in Bletchley Park, where German U-boat signals were deciphered. There, among heaps of documents, the Government Code and Cypher School's Naval History of the War at Sea was found, and among these pages are copies of the decrypted cargo lists as they were intercepted through the radio. From these it has been possible to provide the following information:

Cargoes and Passengers carried by Long Distance Submarines between Europe and the Far East

- Keel cargo: The keel was a hollow steel girder with steel cross-sections to strengthen it. Most of it was welded, but one side of each section could be unscrewed to place old iron inside to act as ballast. Obviously these plates could be opened in dry dock and have anything heavy and non-corrosive placed inside. Steel bottles of mercury often replaced the original ballast.
- Deck casing: When fully surfaced, the top of the pressure hull was usually close to the surface of the water and all the long distance boats had a casing built on top to form the upper (outside) deck. The space between the two was just large enough for a man to crawl through on hands and knees. This space was used for accommodating anything that did not rattle, and since the area filled with water every time the boat dived, the cargo stored there also had to be resistant to seawater.

U850	(FK Klaus Ewerth) Type: IXD2 Left: Kiel 18.11.1943 Sunk: 20.12.1943	General cargo with 6 crates of Borkum and Naxos radar search receivers.
U172	(OL Hermann Hoffmann) Type: IXC Left: 22.11.1943 Sunk: 13.12.1943	Borkum radar search receiver.
U219	(KK Walter Burghagen) Type: XB (mine-layer used as transporter.) Left: Bordeaux 23.08.1944 Arrived: Batavia 11.12.1944	For Japanese Navy and Army: 991 bottles of mercury, 39 tons 868 bars of lead, 37 tons 8,505 bars of aluminium, 31 tons 62 boxes of raw optical glass, 42.84 tons Supplies for naval base 2 Junkers compressors Spare parts for surface ship *Bogota* 21 boxes of aircraft bombs for Arado seaplanes Medical supplies Navigational equipment Naval grid charts Radio sets and other communications equipment

U195	(OL Friedrich Steinfeld) Type: IXD1 (transporter) Left: Bordeaux 24.08.1944 Arrived: Batavia 28.12.1944	Spare parts including diesel parts Spare parts for surface ships *Havenstein, Havelland, Bogota* and *Quito* Radio gear Navigation equipment Medical supplies Ammunition For Japanese Navy and Army: 1,404 bottles of mercury, 54.4 tons 9,100 bars of aluminium, 31 tons 57 steel bars, 14.7 tons 112 boxes of glass, 78.5 tons 157 bars of lead, 64.37 tons
U1062	(OLzS Karl Albrecht) Type: VIIF (torpedo transporter) Left: Bergen 03.01.1944 Arrived: Penang 19.04.1944	22 torpedoes for Penang Radios Cypher material
U843	(KL Oskar Herwartz) Type: IXC/40 Left: Lorient 19.02.1944 Arrived: Batavia 11.06.1944	Supplies for Penang naval base, including 1 propeller
U851	(KK Hannes Weingaertner) Type: IXD2 Left: Kiel 26.02.1944 Sunk: Lost – unknown cause	1,878 bottles of mercury, about 75 tons 696 bars of lead, 9.5 tons Consumable stores for U-boats and U-boat shops, spare motor parts and compressor parts 500 batteries 2 x 37 mm AA guns with ammunition 170 kg lubricating oil Mail Cypher materials Radio equipment for German Embassy in Tokyo
U196	(OL Werner Striegler) Type: IXD2 Left: La Pallice 16.03.1944 Arrived: Penang 10.08.1944	2,197 bottles of mercury, 84.6 tons Consumable stores and spare parts for U-boats 1 port and 1 starboard propeller Radio equipment 14 U-boat torpedoes
U181	(KzS Kurt Freiwald) Type: IXD2 Left: Bordeaux 16.03.1944 Arrived: Penang 08.08.1944	Cypher material Supplies for Penang naval base

U537	(KL Peter Schrewe) Type: IXC/40 Left: Lorient 25.03.1944 Arrived: Batavia 02.08.44	Supplies for Penang naval base 1 radio direction finder 1 propeller 1 Fliege radar search receiver 3 other radar search receivers
U859	(KL Johann Jebsen) Type: IXD2 Left: Kiel 04.04.1944 Sunk: near Penang 23.09.1944	Cargo for Japanese Navy: 1,959 bottles of mercury, 77.34 tons 624 bars of lead, 25.58 tons Supplies for base 1 set of radar search receivers with spare parts 147 cases of communication equipment Consumable stores Spare parts for machinery for U-boats and workshops Navigation equipment 4 Fliege radar search receivers Ammunition 176 kg lubricating oil
U860	(FK Paul Büchel) Type: IXD2 Left: Kiel 11.04.1944 Sunk: 15.06.1944	For Japanese Navy: 2,610 bars of lead, 104.38 tons Supplies for base Replacement parts for U-boats and repair shops Radar search receivers 2 x 37 mm AA guns with ammunition Navigation instruments
U861	(KK Jürgen Oesten) Type: IXD2 Left: 20.04.1944 Arrived: Penang 23.09.1944	For Japanese Navy: lead, 109 tons Supplies for U-boat workshops Spare parts for Junkers compressors Bilge/ballast pumps Motors Navigation instruments 2 x 37 mm AA guns with spare parts and ammunition Aircraft ammunition
U198	(OL B. Heusinger von Waldegg) Type: IXD2 Left: Bordeaux 20.04.1944 Sunk: 10.08.1944	For Japanese Army and Navy: Supplies for base. Consumable stores for U-boats and repair shops Spare parts for torpedoes Electric and artillery spare parts Radio equipment Naval grid charts Lubricating oil Fliege radar search receivers and other radar detectors.

U490	(OL Wilhelm Gerlach) Type: XIV (tanker) Left: Kiel 04.05.1944 Sunk: 12.06.1944	fuel oil, 727.12 cubic metres lubricating oil, 19.52 cubic metres both for supplying to U-boats at sea.
U862	(KK Heinrich Timm) Type: IXD2 Left: Kiel 20.05.1944 Left: Narvik 03.06.1944 Arrived: Penang 09.09.1944	Supplies for Penang naval base Fliege radar search receivers Tunis radar search receivers
U863	(KL Dietrich von der Esch) Type: IXD2 Left: Kiel 03.07.1944 Left: Bergen 26.07.1944 Sunk: 29.09.1944	Supplies for Penang naval base Mail 2 boxes of Japanese naval attaché dispatches for Japanese Admiralty
U180	(OL Rolf Riesen) Type: IXD2 Left: Bordeaux 24.08.1944 Sunk: 26.08.1944	For Japanese Navy and Army: 6,669 bars of aluminium 1,843 bottles of mercury, 67.39 tons 100 crates of raw glass, 6,800 kg 12 Enigma machines with cypher data for 1945 Torpedoes Spare parts for Junkers compressors Auxiliary engine components Electric compressor Various tools Radios with spare parts Medical equipment
U871	(KL Peter-Ottmar Grau) Type: IXD2 Left: Trondheim 31.08.1944 Sunk: 26.09.1944	Supplies for Penang naval base Radar search receivers Main motor spare parts Mail, films, books and other welfare materials
U864	(KK Rolf-Reimar Wolfram) Type: IXD2 Left: Bergen 07.02.1945 Sunk: 09.02.1945	Drawings for the gears on the surface ship *Bogota* Nautical yearbooks for 1945 Set of parts for making rocket planes Contract for manufacturing rights of the Me 163 and Me 262 Parts for these aircraft Parts for Ju 1-6 Plans for Caproni submarine Set of *Zaunkönig* (acoustic torpedo) measuring devices Plans for Caproni Camprini aircraft Radar plans

		Plans for Satsuki type of U-boat 1,857 bottles of mercury Passengers: Messerschmitt engineers Schomers and Klingenberg Mitsubishi technical expert Yamato Junkers assembly engineer, name unknown
U234	(KL Johann-Heinrich Fehler) Type: XB (mine-layer) Left: Kiel 24.03.1945 Surrendered to the US at the end of the war	Lead, 67 tons Mercury, 24.11 tons Steel, 10.72 tons Optical glass, 66.46 tons Brass, ?? tons Instruments, munitions, medical supplies, drawings Production drawings for various aircraft Ammunition, 35.30 tons Ammunition, 1 ton Small arms and ammunitions for seaplanes Variety of equipment Mail, films and other welfare materials Radioactive materials – not included in the original list above Passengers: Japanese commanders Tomoaga and Shoshi Civilian engineers Bringewald and Ruf From the Luftwaffe: General Kessler, Colonel von Sandrath and OL Manzell From the Naval High Command: FK Falck Squadron Director Nirschlin Senior Construction Chief Schicke KL Bulle and OLzS Hellendorn
U178	(KL Wilhelm Spahr) Type: IXD2 Left: Penang 27.11.1943 Arrived: Bordeaux 25.05.1944	Rubber, 27.34 tons Tin, 110 tons Wolfram ore, 2 tons
U181	(KS Kurt Freiwald) Type: IXD2 Left: Batavia 19.10.1944 Arrived: Batavia 01.01.1945	In keel: Wolfram, 45.53 tons Tin, 46.92 tons Outside deck casing: Rubber, 63.32 tons Inside pressure hull: Molybdenum, 48.52 tons Wolfram, 13.15 tons Tin, 14.15 tons

		Opium, 3 tons Quinine, 2.7 tons Caffeine, 134 kg In diving tanks: Rubber, 79.86 tons
U188	(KL Siegfried Lüdden) Type: IXC/40 Left: Penang 08.01.1944 Arrived: Bordeaux 19.06.1944	Tin, 101 tons Rubber, 11.5 tons Tungsten, 16.3 tons Quinine, 500 kg Opium, 200 kg Wolfram Zinc ingots
U1062	(OL Karl Albrecht) Type: VIIF Left: Penang 15.07.1944 Sunk: 30.09.1944	General cargo, 60 tons Wolfram, 50 tons
U168	(KL Helmuth Pich) Type: IXC/40 Left: Batavia 05.10.1944 Sunk: 06.10.1944	Keel load of tin Tungsten, 29 tons in magazine Opium, quinine and vitamins
U196	(OL Werner Striegler) Type: IXD2 Left: Batavia 30.11.1944 Lost shortly after leaving port.	Metal ores (exact details not intercepted)
U843	(KL Oskar Herwartz) Type: IXC/40 Left: Batavia 10.12.1944 Arrived: Bergen 04.04.1945 Left: Bergen 06.04.1945 Sunk: 09.04.1945	Wolfram ore, 49.74 tons Molybdenum, 4.5 tons Opium, 1.3 tons Caffeine, 142 kg Tin, 57.21 tons Rubber, 30.81 tons Quinine, 300 kg
U861	(KK Jürgen Oesten) Type: IXD2 Left: Surabaya 15.01.1945 Arrived: Trondheim: 19.04.1945	Tin, 61.29 tons Wolfram, 59.82 tons Quinine, 3.25 tons Rock crystal, 120 kg Iodine, 577 kg Rubber, 48.44 tons Molybdenum, 900 kg
U532	(FK Ottoheinrich Junker) Type: IXC/40 Left: Batavia 13.01.1945	Quinine, 500 kg Opium, 200 kg Tin, 111 tons

	Arrived: Liverpool 10.05.1945 – after the end of the war	Rubber, 8.6 tons Wolfram, 11.8 tons Zinc ingots Vitamin concentrate
U510	(KL Alfred Eick) Type: IXC Left: Batavia 11.01.1945 Arrived: St Nazaire 23.04.1945	In keel: Wolfram, 45.4 tons Tin plates, 15.76 tons Rubber, 3.25 tons (probably in deck casing) In pressure hull: Molybdenum, 438 kg Wolfram ore, 64.65 tons Rubber, 5 tons Caffeine, 2 tons Rock crystal, 120 kg In deck casing: Rubber, 17 tons
U183	(KL Fritz Schneewind) Type: IXC/40 Left: Batavia 21.04.1945 Sunk: 23.04.1945	Rubber, 94.84 tons Tungsten, 21 tons Tin, 102 tons Opium, 250 kg Quinine, 500 kg Zinc ingots Wolfram ore Vitamin concentrate

CHAPTER 5

German Bases in Distant Waters

Neither the Kingdom of Prussia nor Imperial Germany had any great colonial aspirations, the first attempts to gain overseas territories not being made until 1884 (a little more than twelve years after the founding of the German nation). By that time, Britain had already established an empire stretching all the way around the globe, and other European countries such as France and the Netherlands also had colonies in far-off lands. The last German colony to be established, Kiautschou in China, was acquired through a treaty in 1897/98, and all these territories were officially lost again in 1918, at the end of the First World War, when they were confiscated by the victorious Allies. Despite this, small pockets of German interests remained around the globe and several shipping firms continued to establish offices with good facilities in distant lands. The offices of naval attachés in far-off capitals, including Tokyo, were re-established during the 1920s, so although there were no longer any German colonies, centres of German interest remained in foreign lands.

Being an industrial nation like Britain, Germany also depended on imports of raw materials, and merchant marine facilities were re-established rapidly after the end of the First World War. The government was well aware that individual shipping lines could not work efficiently without national help, so a concerted effort was made to set up the necessary infrastructure abroad for trade to flourish. This included founding what was later called the *Marinesonderdienst* (Special Naval Service) under KzS Werner Vermehren in Tokyo. Its initial objective was to set up the necessary infrastructure, such as good communications, and to acquire, store and distribute to ships essential raw materials that were not available in Europe.

Once the Second World War started, it became increasingly more difficult to run merchant shipping in and out of German ports. Indeed, although many books give the impression that the German Navy fired the first shots of the war when U30 (KL Fritz-Julius Lemp) sank the passenger ship *Athenia*, they fail to mention that by that time the Royal Navy had already made an impressive move against German shipping. The destroyer HMS *Somali* had already captured SS *Hannah Böge*. This problem of getting in and out of the German Bight was made considerably easier once the French Atlantic coast was occupied and blockade breakers could run mainly into Bordeaux.

The key figure behind this impressive organisation of fitting out blockade breakers was KzS Paul Wenneker, who had been the German naval attaché in Tokyo from 1933 until 1937. He then returned to Germany to become captain of the first pocket battleship, *Deutschland*. Returning to Tokyo in 1940, he was responsible for maintaining German interests in Japanese territories until the end of the war.

The Special Naval Service not only acquired raw materials but also made it possible to fit out, disguise and supply blockade breakers, and towards the beginning of the war it was instrumental in supplying a number of auxiliary cruisers (also known as raiders or ghost cruisers) in the Indian and Pacific oceans. So, although very little is known about this organisation, it did make a terrific contribution and laid the foundation stone for the later organisation that made U-boat voyages to the Far East possible.

The following details about the German ports in the Far East are based on notes made by Walter Schöppe from information supplied by KL Konrad Hoppe, who had travelled to the Far East as pilot officer aboard auxiliary cruiser *Michel* (KzS Hellmuth von Ruckteschell), having first served in the same capacity in auxiliary cruiser *Widder* under the same commander. Once in the Far East he became a watch officer aboard a U-boat and later commander for the German naval base at Surabaya. He had personal experience from working in all the German Far East bases.

The term 'Far East' throws one into immediate conflict with the Japanese, who called it the 'Southern Area'. It was made up of the old British and Dutch colonies of Monsoon Asia. Establishing facilities there was relatively easy because there were already a number of German civilians at a loose end in those ports. Some of them had helped merchant ships running the blockade back to Europe and they assisted with the acquisition of provisions for delivery to auxiliary cruisers. Many of these shipping businesses had been lying idle since trade was drastically reduced by the outbreak of war, and the men were more than happy to do deals with anyone willing to supplement what had consequently become rather lean times with little or no income. Indeed many of them, especially women of European origin, had been living under the most appalling conditions since hostilities had begun. Being without a regular income meant that many had to sell household items and jewellery to buy basic food.

The main difficulty with the establishment of bases in the Far East was coming to grips with Japanese mentality, something a few German officers

The Japanese rear admiral Ishioka, head of the Indian Ocean theatre, and his staff visit U178 on the U-boat's second trip to the Indian Ocean. KK Wilhelm Dommes is one step behind the rear admiral, to his left. The storage tubes sunk into the upper deck are clearly visible on the left.

never managed. There were times when dealings with the Japanese were indeed absurd. For example, at one stage the local commander demanded that the Germans should not listen to music composed or played by Jews. This was something the navy had not even thought about, and even the regulations in Germany were nowhere near as demanding as the political correctness required by the Japanese. Yet it was necessary to establish better than good connections with these authorities to secure approval rather than hindrance from those who commanded the occupation forces. Once this had been done, it was possible to bypass Japanese officialdom and deal directly with locals and, most important of all, to gain a foothold in the massive black market. Chinese entrepreneurs, more than willing to do business with the Germans, controlled many of these areas. They looked upon the Japanese as liberators from British oppression, but they also disliked the arrogant way in which the Japanese dealt with what they considered were inferior races. This co-operation with locals worked so well that it was not long before the Germans were able to secure better provisions than the Japanese, and the quality of work done by local tradesmen was often superior to that which Japan could provide through its wartime emergency programme.

The bases differed considerably and the way in which the Germans were able to conduct their business depended very much on who controlled the administration. Penang was easy inasmuch that it was entirely under naval management, and exceedingly good relations were established with the

Japanese rear admiral Ishioka. The Americans hanged him after the war because he was held responsible for crimes carried out secretly by his Chief of Staff. Apparently a number of women from a captured Dutch ship were raped before being killed.

Female company was indeed a major problem in those distant waters where young virulent men, cut off from sexual contact for months on end, arrived with a good amount of back pay. They had gone through a number of near-death experiences and were hell-bent on making use of the freedom in port by seeking out every opportunity to explore whatever amusements were on offer. This made it necessary to attach brothels directly to the naval barracks so that the German medical system could at least keep an eye on the girls in order to prevent rampant diseases being spread among the U-boat crews. Bearing in mind that the British colonial administrators had been living in grand opulence, there was no shortage of accommodation with marvellous facilities and this was often located in the best areas in or near the ports. Unfortunately, many of the U-boat crew members did not react too well to the well-to-do resorts in the cool hills because these were also somewhat isolated, the submariners preferring the hot hustle and bustle of the town to the emptiness of the jungle.

In addition to seeing to the medical needs of U-boat men and the local prostitutes, it fell to the German medical service to check on provisions being brought into the bases. This may have started out by dealing with fresh food bought locally, but it quickly developed into quite an undertaking whereby several factories had to be inspected and then have their packed products checked before they were issued. In addition to canning local produce, there was one factory that, after some adjustments, produced tinned bread, ideal for U-boats going on long journeys. Being invited to sample provisions destined for U-boats became one of the highlights for the Japanese, who hankered after being asked to attend these tasting sessions. The German medical service was developed so that it could deal with run-of-the-mill illnesses; for anything more serious the better Japanese facilities were made use of, including some excellent hospitals.

Men had to be given strict instructions about what they could and could not do when they went into the towns, where they found a multitude of local services to extract money from them. Some of the regulations were indeed harsh: men were forbidden from eating fruit unless it had been washed in guaranteed clean water; they could not eat ice cream because this could have been made from infected local produce; and so forth. It was even necessary to prohibit them from eating in the many attractive small bars and open stalls. There were a large number of highly attractive girls everywhere in town, pleased to make contact with the Germans. Many of those with European connections had been out of work for some time and were living literally on a starvation diet. Men were allowed to make contact with these and dance with them, but any form of physical contact was forbidden because the vast majority carried at least one infectious disease.

Konrad Hoppe said that he was most impressed with his own organisation because this worked so well that there were hardly any problems with sexually transmitted diseases finding their way to U-boats crews. At a reunion long after the war, one of the doctors told him the truth, which had been kept from the naval administration. Apparently the medical staff treated a good number of U-boat men suffering from the early stages of infection, but they never reported or recorded such cases because they knew it would result in the unfortunate sailors being court-martialled.

Hoppe gives a splendid account of his time in Djakarta during May 1944, when he accidentally ended up there, and the story of how he reached the place is even more fascinating than the facts he recorded. He was detailed to join U168 under KL Helmuth Pich in Penang because the first officer was admitted to hospital for an operation for acute appendicitis. This boat was not one of the exceptionally large U-cruisers but an ordinary Type IXC with the '40' modification. It left Penang on 28 January 1944, returning on 3 February because the first watch officer had been taken ill, and Hoppe was asked to fill the vacant position for an operation in the Indian Ocean. Shortly after this, both supply ships *Charlotte Schliemann* and *Brake* were sunk, leaving U168 to pick up survivors from the *Brake* and bring them back to Batavia, their nearest base. This was indeed a most momentous operation. There were almost 200 men on board, many of them injured, and some fell ill as a result of the insane conditions in the cramped submarine. The master of the *Brake*, for example, suffered a heart attack. The conditions were so cramped that there was standing room only and a rota had to be created so that everyone had an opportunity of at least sitting down for part of the time. In these dreadful conditions, the boat remained submerged for 24 hours to evade attacks by aircraft. Although it was possible to keep the air topped up with oxygen, the capacity of the system removing carbon dioxide from the air was not sufficient to deal with such volumes and the foul breathing conditions became quite horrendous. Yet the men of U168 managed to deal with the injuries and get their rescued comrades back to base. Once there, U168 was no longer fit for another prolonged voyage and since there was some spare shipyard capacity, it was decided to give the machinery a grand overhaul as well. During that period the first watch officer came over from Penang to retake his position, leaving Hoppe free to help out in the port. As things turned out, the next trip was the last for U168. It was just one day out from port when the Dutch submarine *Zwaadfisch* sank it. Twenty-three men were picked up.

Having arrived in Batavia aboard U168, Hoppe found that the German naval administration was running smoothly and there was nothing much for

Under KL Helmuth Pich, U168 attacked and sank six of these freight-carrying sailing ships in the Indian Ocean on 1 October 1943. The medical officer, Dr Balke, took this photograph. Wilhelm Dommes of U178 kept telling his men that these native craft, although small and insignificant-looking, made such a contribution to the enemy's war effort that destroying these small targets produced far more noteworthy results than sinking bigger ships in the North Atlantic.

him to do in the immediate future. So this became his first holiday for three years. Dutch people who held positions of authority before the arrival of the Japanese had been removed from office, but otherwise everything was very much as it had been before the war. In fact, it was difficult to see any trace of the war, although some items, especially cars, were in exceedingly short supply. The reason for the acute absence of cars is interesting. Apparently the locals dismantled them before Japanese forces arrived and then hid the various components in different locations. Hoppe found a good number of well-kept restaurants and even a cinema with a German lady as manager. The appearance of white faces among the colourful mixture of eastern races dominated by Chinese and Indians was welcomed by a large number of Dutch-speaking females who looked down upon the local population. As a result, there were no problems for the Germans in forming relationships with them. They were not only inviting but also terribly pretty, and this group included a good number of Germans who had married Dutch nationals before the war.

Only a very few of these females with European blood had volunteered to live in the safety of the camps set up by the Japanese, and those that did deeply regretted it. Many found their conditions deteriorating rapidly, especially towards the end of the war, and the treatment meted out by the Japanese became horrific. The women who remained living among the native population fared much better, although they did not have any income and it was almost impossible for them to buy anything with money. Whatever they wanted had to be traded on a barter system. Life was not easy for them, but it was better than suffering in an internment camp.

Despite the shortages created by the war, once again the Germans found themselves in a good position for dealing with the locals and managed to acquire a reasonable supply of what was needed, including tools and medical supplies. The Germans were not so aloof as the Japanese and allowed the local people to seek medical help from their naval centres. The local medical services were a little on the expensive side for many ordinary people, so the German influence was more than welcomed. The main problem with Batavia was that the Japanese Army was responsible for the administration and the rivalry between the various forces was carried over to the Germans, who had that unacceptable habit of sailing in ships. As a result, daily life was not terribly harmonious and silly little situations needed defusing frequently, so Hoppe was pleased when he was detailed to move away to help set up a new base in Surabaya.

Surabaya was the main base used by the Japanese Navy and for some reason they were hesitant in sharing the facilities with the Germans. Negotiations therefore took a while. The reason why the Germans were so keen to establish a base there was that it had already been a major Dutch port before war and contained an excellent official shipyard as well as a number of smaller private shipbuilding concerns. Hoppe wrote that when he arrived there in June 1944, together with officers from the supply ship *Brake* and an interpreter, he was immediately taken with the place. In those days it had only about 100,000 inhabitants, with the majority of locals living in small tinned-roofed buildings, and there were a number of other Europeans in addition to people who had settled there from the Netherlands. As a result, there was a splendid infrastructure to help newcomers settle into what looked like magical surroundings. The Japanese authorities supplied a massive hotel complex, large enough to accommodate at least two U-boats crews, and there were additional officers' quarters close to the river. Yet all this splendour was not available for immediate enjoyment because the German officers knew that the first U-boat was due to arrive in three weeks' time – not a long period for making a vast number of arrangements.

The first submarine to arrive was U537, also a Type IXC/40, under KL Peter Schrewe, which came into the port on 2 August 1944. Hoppe had known the commander since the early days when he was serving as a naval pilot on the Frisian island of Norderney. He was therefore specially motivated to do his best for an old friend. The only way everything could be got ready in time was thanks to the helpful Japanese authorities and to several Germans who contributed more than their best. Hoppe even found a German lady who was persuaded to act as chief cook. This was important because oriental food was not always terribly wholesome for European stomachs and considerable modifications were necessary to make local foods more enjoyable and easily digestible. The astonishing thing was that this woman, Frau Uhlhorn, did not have a great deal of culinary experience but started providing a daily hot cooked meal for about a hundred men, without either a gas or electric ovens. She employed some forty local cooks who prepared meals on small wood-burning stoves. Bearing in mind that rice formed the staple diet in the Far East, it was no mean achievement that she managed to provide fresh potatoes from a local farm, so that the men received the type of meal they were used to back home.

Even employing willing volunteers like Frau Uhlhorn presented some complications, and it took a while to get the message over that everyone in the German Navy should receive the same food. There was no differentiation between officers and men. Medical services remained very basic and Hoppe never managed to establish a German hospital. The best he ever found was a petty officer trained as a first aider. So it was necessary for the doctors on board the long distance U-boats to continue looking after their patients. There was no shortage of submarines calling, and most of the time it was usual for

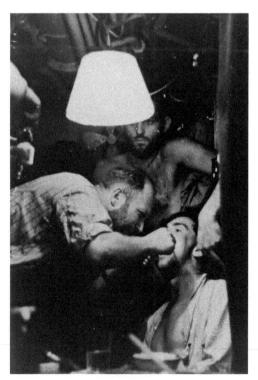

U178's medical officer Joachim Wüstenberg is dealing with the third watch officer's (LzS Kurt Schwazbach) infected tooth while *Maschinenmaat* Rudi Ohlweiser acts as a human vice to hold the patient.

there to be at least one submarine in port. Hoppe made the point that he had a gold crown fitted to one of his teeth by a local dentist. This lasted for twenty years after the war and was later recognised by German dentists as excellent workmanship.

As in many of the other bases, the Germans arriving there were provided with civilian clothing rather than military uniforms. One reason for this was that official clothing was not available, and the other was that the Japanese thought that ordinary clothes would be better from the security point of view. There was hardly any trouble with locals breaking the law, and many Germans found things becoming more awkward with non-naval Japanese authorities and for that reason they were required to wear special badges in some of the bases. Much of this clothing was of exceptional quality and considerably better than German war-issue materials. Yet, despite all the co-operation with the Japanese, there were still numerous little hitches. For example, the Germans were allowed to visit the approved brothels only when there were no Japanese there, so it was difficult to mix unofficially even if one wanted to exchange non-military information.

The social aspects remained unsatisfactory and Hoppe made every effort to change the way men could spend their free time. It was urgently necessary to provide more facilities for U-boat crews and to fit the buildings out so that they looked like a home rather than a military barracks running under strict hospital restrictions. For example, the Germans established what might be described as a European dance hall with live music and entertainment one would have found back home. The girls came from families with well-to-do connections to Europe and were paid for each dance with a ticket from a seaman. These tickets could then be exchanged for money at the end of the day. The Japanese came to like this idea so much that many officers became regular visitors. Of course, they were given free tickets by the Germans to help smooth things over in other areas. Since these dancing ladies did not live within the naval complex, the authorities lost control over them once they went home so it was therefore prohibited to have sexual contact with them.

One advantage in getting all this set up was that Surabaya was one of the few places with a German interpreter, Dr Schreiber. In most cases the Japanese supplied these and the Germans never knew whether their translations were accurate or modified to meet local political correctness. Schreiber came almost by accident and did a great deal to smooth out misunderstandings between the two cultures. Having worked as a German professor in a Japanese university meant that he had a good understanding of the local culture and his diplomatic skills created a most harmonious atmosphere. Even after the German defeat in May 1945, the relationships with the Japanese forces remained on a good footing, with a reasonable supply of necessities coming through, despite there no longer being a German state to pay for the services. Of course, the Germans were pleased to hand over any of their left-over resources to the Japanese rather than allowing them to be confiscated by the incoming Allied forces.

The problems really started once the news of the Japanese capitulation came through. Everything that was left was then distributed among the men, with the thought that whatever money remained would have to see them through possibly rather a long period. Things were certainly not easy, and at one stage it looked as if the Japanese authorities would evacuate all Germans to god-knows-where, and considerable pulling of strings was necessary to prevent a total breakdown in living conditions.

At first, British authorities took over control, then a provisional Dutch government was put in place, but this did not last long because the local Indonesians were on the verge of revolt. So there was a mishmash of events, with chaos ruling supreme.

CHAPTER 6

Life in Long Distance U-boats

When considering living conditions and food during the Second World War, it is particularly necessary to remember that life in those days was totally different to what it is now. People had different standards, lower expectations and an impressively strong urge to serve their country. Up to fifteen years before the war, London houses were still being built without central heating systems or indoor toilets, and in Germany the majority of older flats would not have had a bathroom. Not many, if any, U-boat men would have come from homes with a refrigerator or a washing machine, food came without a sell-by date, and only the very rich would have had cars. Having been brought up with such a comparatively simple way of life meant that the men did not regard the living conditions in submarines as spartan in the way that people would do today. What is more, people's working conditions in factories, both in Britain and in Germany, were often considerably worse than those imposed by the military, where men were generally well looked after.

The radio operator, author and historian Wolfgang Hirschfeld said that he chose to serve in larger U-boats because although they would remain at sea for longer than the smaller types, life in them was considerably more comfortable and one could work and live in a reasonable space without being squeezed into impossibly small confines. Commissioned officers and warrant officers were usually allocated their own bunk, while the rest had to put up with a hot bunking system whereby a man coming off duty would occupy a bed already slept in by his opposite number. Only a few of the lowest ranks and later additional gunners for the increased AA guns slept in hammocks. Despite this, some of the beds (even those for officers) were too short to stretch out in properly, so sleeping in those cramped conditions was not ideal or comfortable. Yet it was rated considerably better than being stuck in one of the small coastal or sea-going boats.

Matrosengefreiter Fritz Haak has just come off duty, after everybody else had already had their evening meal and every bunk is therefore occupied. He is sitting on a box, spreading his bread while the coffee pot and a cup are on the floor in front of him.

The men themselves often offered to make considerable sacrifices in order to remain at sea for long periods. For example, some gave up their bunk to store additional loaves of bread or other provisions. Some historians claim that callous leaders whipped the men into taking such action, but having talked to ex-U-boat men it is apparent that this originated in hateful propaganda departments rather than being based on facts. In reality very much the opposite happened. Dönitz ordered the U-boat Command to introduce stringent regulations to prevent men from overloading their living space and thereby unwittingly putting the boat and crew at risk.

It was not uncommon for the floor space of the accommodation areas to be piled so full of stores that there was hardly room to stand on what was carefully packed on the floor. Wooden boards were usually placed on top of tins to provide a reasonable floor surface so that men did not stumble over individual tins. (Tins in those days were made from considerably thicker material than they are now, and a hammer was required to flatten them.) Then, at the stage when the boat was filled to such an extent that there was no more room for any additional packages and the men had to stoop low to pass, another load of fresh food was likely to arrive. But with fifty or more men tucking into such goodies, they did not last terribly long.

The first major action once at sea was to trim or balance the boat so that it sat comfortably in the water when submerged. This could take up to half an hour or more and was done by controlling water inside a variety of tanks by working a complicated system of taps in the central control room. The controls of this so-called 'Christmas tree' or trimming panel were all slightly different, and the men allowed to work it had to be capable of identifying the controls in total darkness. Once the trim was established and there was sufficient depth under the keel, the next step was to try out a deep diving test to check that any repairs carried out in port would hold tight under extreme conditions of being depth charged.

Now the boat was in a position to proceed at cruising speed to its designated operations area, with four lookouts and the officer on duty on the top of the conning tower. While doing this, it was also necessary to practise the necessary manoeuvres required in an emergency and to continue with the usual maintenance jobs. Training, which gave newcomers the opportunity to learn new skills, also formed a part of the daily routine.

Hirschfeld explained in his diary that the majority of submariners quickly got used to the rough movements of submarines, but there were always a few, especially new recruits, who were violently seasick. Going out for some fresh air was out of the question, and life did become extremely harsh until men adjusted to the horrendous conditions. Even the best ventilation system failed to circulate the clear sea air to both ends of the boat, and many men, especially those accommodated in the extremities, had no alternative other than to get used to the stuffy conditions. After the war, several commanders remarked that they never really appreciated the conditions under which men lived at both ends of their U-boat, admitting that it was more than remarkable that there were hardly any disciplinary proceedings in those poorly ventilated and exceedingly cramped quarters. In addition to being unventilated, it needs to be remembered that the toilet did not have any windows or special air extraction system, so the powerful smells from fifty men were added to this foul air. The trick for dealing with seasickness was to provide buckets or large tins with a little used engine oil to float on top of whatever the men contributed. This was by no means ideal, but did contain some of the stench.

Bearing in mind that there were only two 'thrones' for fifty men, and one of these was often used as a larder at the beginning of the trip, men had to use buckets when the situation became too demanding. Now imagine these buckets in the living space and then a rough storm or a good dose of depth charges upsetting everything so that the mixture seeped down to imbed itself around the tins for the next meal. Not a pleasant thought, but men lived under such conditions without complaining. With no washing facilities at all, the interior of all U-boats quickly started to smell like a gymnasium changing room, with not-so-delicate odours from other quarters added to increase the ferocity of the experience.

The lavatory, or heads (plural, even if there was only one), was such a complicated piece of equipment that even the earlier pump-action types were

Above and below: U123, under KL Karl-Heinz Moehle, showing what a struggle it must have been for lookouts on top of the conning tower in even moderate seas.

The upper deck
lavatory or heads.

not the easiest to use, especially when conditions got rough. They were well below the surface of the surrounding sea even when the submarine was fully surfaced, meaning the flushing or pumping-out would, if men got it wrong, work in reverse and everything in the little room, including sausages hanging from the pipes, acquired notable freckles. At the beginning of the war it was only possible to pump out the contents when the boat was near the surface, special deep-water or high-pressure devices being added later to make the emptying of the bowl even more of a challenge. Dr Armin Wandel recorded several cases where men were so afraid to use this powerful little room that they chose to do their business on a bucket instead and even manufactured their own seats to fit on top.

A number of authors and historians have dismissed life in submarines as being similar to the conditions experienced by every other sailor at sea, some equating life in submarines to that in tanks. Whilst this may be true in some submarines on short missions, the existence inside any long range boat is considerably more severe than in any other fighting service. It seems that long before the war, Britain and the Netherlands, both with colonies in the Far East, started to look into the problems faced by submariners on long missions. Britain's Royal Navy sidestepped this rather important issue by sending out submarines with a fully equipped depot ship. That did not necessarily ease the problems for the individuals inside submarines, but it did break long voyages into a series of smaller steps, often with an abundance of ports of call on the way. The Royal Netherlands Navy was probably the first to seek solutions to help submariners travel both to and from the Far East and to cope with the hot tropical waters once they got there. Commander J. J. Wichers, for example, developed a reasonably efficient breathing pipe or snorkel long before the Second World War so that submarines could run their diesel engines without having to surface into the excruciatingly heat above the water. This was indeed a major problem, made worse by the appearance of metal ships whose armour did little to prevent the tropical heat from penetrating, ventilators having to be fitted to make life inside such vessels bearable. The metal parts of a submarine, even when almost all of the pressure hull remained below the waterline when fully surfaced, got so hot in the tropics that men would burn their feet if they walked on the outside steel without shoes. Indeed, it often got hot enough to fry an egg merely by cracking it on the deck.

In addition to the natural radiation from the sun, the running of diesel engines added considerable heat to the interior of a submarine in the tropics. However, this tended to be limited to the engine room, this heat not being distributed too far into other compartments. The reason for this was due to the vast volumes of air required to run the engines and the powerful ventilators sucking this hot air out of the interior. Of course, there is no way in which this system could prevent the radiated heat from the engines, and engineers had to put up with what would now be classed as unbearable conditions. Temperatures of 50 degrees Celsius and higher were not uncommon in submarine engine rooms, and in Germany engineers worked 6 hour shifts or watches for each spell of duty. Boats going to the tropics developed their own diving technique to overcome the incredible heat problem, especially the radiation from the diesel engines, by shutting them down half an hour or so before diving and then keeping the cooling systems running with ventilators on full blast.

Putting up with this immense heat was not the only hazard inside the engine room. The noise of the running diesel engines was so loud that there was no way in which one could have a conversation, and an engineer would not have known that the powerful alarm bells were ringing if the lights in the engine room had not started flashing at the same time. Although there are a considerable number of engines in museums, very few have the facility to run them as well. If they did, local authority health and safety regulations would probably prohibit visitors being present. The noise plus any auxiliary machinery, such as compressors, running at the same time can be described as deafening and unbearable. The U-boat diesel engine in Kiel Maschinenmuseum (Engine Museum) is a small one for a 250/300 tonner and the powerplants in the long range U-boats would have been considerably bigger. What is more, their diesel engine is displayed in a huge hall rather than inside a tight pressure hull. The din has got to be experienced – it cannot be described in words.

For the majority of the crew, private conversations were nearly impossible, even during such long-distance voyages. On the right is U178's medical officer, Dr Joachim Wüstenberg who died shortly after arriving in Singapore.

Modern air-conditioning systems keep humidity to below 30 per cent, and even humidity between 30 and 50 per cent is still regarded as bearable. Yet in the tropics, the humidity inside a Second World War submarine was rarely less than 70 per cent, and ranges between 70 and higher than 90 per cent were not uncommon. Marine engineers knew this long before Germany started building long range U-boats, but it was not regarded as critical until after the start of the war when the tropics became obvious areas of operation. The majority of long range boats had air-conditioning plants built into them, but none of these systems had been evaluated by the time the first boats embarked upon journeys into hot regions. The confined conditions meant that whatever air-conditioning system was going to be installed, it would have to work to the limits of its capabilities and nothing satisfactory was developed by Germany throughout the Second World War.

Humidity refers to the amount of water vapour in the air. This is completely invisible, thus the eye cannot determine the amount in the air. People often claim to see water vapour when it is hot enough to be classed as steam, but what they are seeing are tiny droplets of liquid water which have condensed again. So although people cannot see the humidity, they can definitely feel its irritating presence. As far as the submariners were concerned, the humidity was everywhere and there was no real practical solution to the problem. It got onto lockers where it was absorbed by dry clothing, so that after a while a powerful musty smell confronted one when opening the locker door and eventually the clothing developed a variety of colourful moulds, many of which could not be washed out again.

Much of the water vapour condensed on cool surfaces and was thus constantly dripping down walls or off pipes, This, together with waves and rain cascading through the hatch, found its way into the bilges at the bottom of the boat. These have wells or low points from where the water is pumped out again by bilge or ballast pumps. Of course, many of the bad smells inside a submarine are water-soluble and small amounts will dissolve in the water to turn it into an evil-smelling brew. Cooking, washing and drying clothes added to the general humidity inside the submarine, as did the breathing and sweating of men. All this, of course, also happens aboard surface ships, but there it is possible to isolate areas from each other and often there is no need to have a direct connection between living space and the bilges deep down in the bottom of the ship.

A considerable proportion of German food was preserved through natural drying and smoking. This could then be kept for long periods in a normal, dry atmosphere, but aboard U-boats it immediately started to absorb water and soften, sometimes to the point of going mushy and falling to pieces. It also acquired a good layer of mould mixed with oil vapour, which was also constantly present in submarines of the period. The growth of this mould was so rapid that squads of men had to go through the food every few days to wash it with salt water. While things like hams and large salami-type sausages could be hung up, other foods such as vegetables had to be laid in a heap and these were most susceptible to fermentation or, even worse, being converted into a foul-smelling mush. Anyone who has dealt with a pile of rotting potatoes or onions will know how offensive this can be.

The majority of long range U-boats had the kitchen or galley forward of the officers' accommodation and aft of the warrant officers' quarters in the forward half of the boat. This had a slight advantage over the smaller Type VII inasmuch that it was further away from source of hot oily fumes bursting out of the engine room. These oily noxious vapours condensed with great gusto on the first cool surfaces they met and therefore coated much in the galley with their characteristic flavour. Yet a vast array of moving parts throughout the entire hull had to be oiled on a regular basis, and nothing inside a U-boat was safe from oil odours. Some years before the First World War the Naval Office in Berlin appointed the famous Admiral Reinhard Scheer, who had a pocket battleship named after him, to inspect U-boats for the purpose of ascertaining whether the men should be allowed a confined-space addition to their pay. Turning up in Kiel, the first thing he was told was that he could not carry out his inspection in the way he was dressed or, if he did, he would never again wear his uniform on parade. Bowing to superior advice from a very much junior officer, he donned an old *Oberleutnant*'s jacket, already well stained with oil. The food he was given to taste was also well laced with the repugnant substance and this experience resulted in submariners being given higher

Above and below: U-boats usually carried two types of rain gear: raincoats with sou'westers, or heavier coats for better protection. Such rainwear was not issued personally to the men but to the boat and was shared by the lookouts. The problem with the 'Big Seal' was that one had to climb into it like a diver's dry suit and it could not be donned quickly when there was a sudden downpour or excessive spray.

By modern standards navigation was a highly skilled yet somewhat primitive undertaking during the Second World War and it was necessary to take accurate readings with sextants on the sun and stars to compute the boat's position.

pay than sailors on surface ships. During the Second World War, there were several commanders who would go to sea wearing the oldest of old clothes and sometimes even wore these for their debriefing immediately after the trip. Inside a submarine there was no escape from oil, dampness and nasty smells and that characteristic odour that hits one at the moment of entry still persists in some of the World War Two submarines now on display in museums.

The cooks in U-boats were of such comparatively low rank with so little responsibility that they were deemed incapable of packing stores on board a submarine. This tedious task was also a little below the supreme prestige of commissioned officers, so the task was handed over to the *Obersteuermann* or navigator, who was also the third watch officer. There was not a great deal of navigation to be done in port, so this person, usually with the rank of warrant officer, was ideal for the job. He did not select food but was responsible for stacking it in the right places. This was quite an exacting job because the provisions needed to be placed in the reverse order to that in which they were going to be consumed. To make matters a little more challenging, tins did not have paper or printed labels. Instead they had numbers impressed on them for identifying the contents. So the navigator made a detailed record of what was packed where. This was vital because some of the tins went deep down into the bilges where they were covered by a black liquid that had once been water before some powerful stench was added automatically. In most cases the food came from the flotilla looking after the boat, and the staff there would have calculated the quantities required. However, it was often possible to put in requests for special items, which were usually provided if they could be acquired.

Unfortunately for the crew, German designers did not include efficient food storage facilities in their U-boats. Several British seamen who ended up as prisoners of war remarked that it appeared strange that the Germans not only lacked special food storage areas but that no one seemed to have been trained in how such perishables could be prevented from deteriorating. Consequently a high proportion of the food went bad and had to be thrown away. Yet, despite this, U-boats were supplied with the best rations and often had foods that were unavailable elsewhere in Germany. At times the men had to do battle with the foods, especially with French cheeses. Spanish Civil War experiences had already taught U-boat men that cheeses must be supplied in wooden boxes rather than cardboard packages, but even with such strong packaging, some of the cheeses were exceedingly powerful at the best of times. The men might have enjoyed eating them, but living with them in close quarters was not the easiest of tasks, and noses had to develop an acute indifference to powerful smells.

Visitors to Second World War boats in museums will immediately be struck by the fact that there appears to be no large oven in the galley. The reason for this was twofold. First, such items were also missing from quite a few domestic kitchens throughout the land. Sunday roast lunches were hardly known in Germany at the time, the majority of housewives using their ovens only for baking cakes. In fact, a large proportion even forsook their oven for this task as well. Instead they mixed their cakes at home and then took the produce inside a baking tin to a local baker who would finish off the job for a small fee. Most of the food in homes throughout the land was cooked by frying, pot roasting or boiling, and it was common to have only one hot meal per day, with hot drinks or porridge at other times. So the absence of a large oven was not considered particularly inconvenient in those days. The second, and probably more important, reason for not having large ovens in U-boats was that they consumed too much power, which would have been detrimental if they had been used when the batteries were running low.

The big problem inside submarines was water, and this subject immediately throws up another anomaly in U-boat history. The galley had four taps labelled 'Washing Water', 'Filtered Drinking Water', 'Warm Seawater', and 'Drinking Water'. The strange thing was that drinking water was supplied through a hosepipe from a water tap in the harbour and washing water came via a fire hose outlet, but both were supplied by the same water main. So what was the difference? The answer lay in the storage tanks. Although not common, it did happen that dead cats, rats and other remains were sometimes found bloated inside the washing water tank. The insides of these were treated with a special paint to prevent the steel walls from rusting. Generally, drinking water was not rationed, although on some long journeys this became necessary because the water still, for converting seawater into pure water, was unable to produce enough. British submariners had considerably better drinking facilities than their German counterparts; the Americans went as far as providing cooled flavoured drinks, and many of their submarines also had an ice-making machine for the tropics. Washing water in U-boats was usually calculated on the basis of one small bathroom sinkful per man per week for washing himself and his underwear. Long distance boats heading into the tropics could not always carry so much water and therefore had to reduce the allocation. In some cases, men had to wash with salt water all the time.

Anyone looking around a U-boat near the galley will soon spot another tap labelled 'Milch' (milk), but this was not linked to cows. Instead it was connected to a tank containing a strong alkaline solution for quickly neutralising any area of the compartment below the floor which might have been contaminated by battery acid. Being slightly white in colour, the liquid was given this obvious name.

It is a wonder that the cooks ever managed to produce delicious meals in such cramped spaces with hardly any work surfaces and that more facilities were not provided for food preparation and for the men's ablutions. However, daily cooking was not much of a problem in a Type VII boat, where the galley was next to the engine room. This received a special supply of fresh air direct from the top of the conning tower and this system also sucked unwanted odours out of the galley, where a huge hood was fitted over the electric stove. Long range boats had a special air duct for the kitchen, but some of the steam and whatever was coming out of the pots also drifted along the corridor rather than being sucked out. The quality of the meals depended very much on the ability of the cook, who had his own bunk and did not stand watches like the other men. Instead he was expected to provide meals whenever they were required, without a great deal of regard to the general conditions of the natural elements. Despite this, action stations interrupted even the best plans and made the consumption of heavy meals impossible. The men then went without or kept up long periods of boredom with coffee and nibbles.

While chasing convoys in the North Atlantic, it was common for men not to be able to eat proper meals for days on end, grabbing whatever the cook passed round or left out for them. In long range boats the majority of commanders considered meal times sacrosanct and allowed only genuine emergencies to encroach upon them. During bad weather, when not chasing convoys, boats dropped down into the calm depths for a period of rest and recuperation at meal times. Some of the meals conjured up in that small galley were miraculous, although men did not necessarily enjoy them due to constipation caused by the lack of exercises. The better commanders knew that nothing could upset a harmonious life more than bad food and therefore ensured that meal times were something special. Of course, not all cooks produced enjoyable food and there were occasions where a commander ordered that the next man to complain about the food would do the cooking.

Another considerable problem was that things did not always work out as planned. The men of U30 (KL Fritz-Julius Lemp), for example, discovered that their bread had the wrong number impressed upon the tins. On opening them they found condensed milk instead, but the number for condensed milk also contained the same product, so they had nothing to chew on. Sometimes the food inside the tins was nowhere near edible and had to be ejected instead of being cooked. Of course, especially on long voyages when supply ships did not appear, the diet tended to become a little monotonous and at times even exceedingly scarce, with strict rationing.

Although the U-boat Office within the Supreme Naval Command responsible for designing and building submarines hardly considered the question of storing food, there were other departments giving attention to the type of food needed by submariners. It was not until the war was well under way that the U-boat Construction Office started including refrigerators and even deep freezes. The introduction of these did not go terribly smoothly and the first deep freezes installed in supply submarines presented the men with considerable problems. For example, the deep frozen food arrived by lorry on the quayside and had to remain there for a while before all of it could be taken below through the rather cumbersome hatches. While this was going on, the packages collected condensation on the outside and when all of these were

Men resting, with a sighting compass in the foreground.

placed in the freezer they stuck together into one huge hard lump that needed hammers and cold chisels to separate them. Today, even a schoolboy might imagine that such a loading process was fraught with dangers, but U-boat men then had no experience of such equipment and could not predict what was likely to happen.

There were no set menus for U-boats and very little in the way of specially prepared emergency-type rations such as those issued to the army. The exact composition of the stores varied considerably and depended upon local suppliers and on seasonal availability. Fresh fruit, for example, was more plentiful in summer and autumn and considerably more limited towards the end of the winter season. In view of this variation, it is difficult to provide an exact list of what U-boats might have taken to sea. Just to give some idea, the following is a list loaded by U160 (a Type IXC under KL Georg Lassen with fifty-two men on board) and recorded by Rudolf Schneider:

Supplies for U160: 52 men for 3 months

The numbers on the left indicate the quantities in kilograms, and a supply of fresh eggs, fruit and meat for immediate consumption would have arrived last of all for placing in easily accessible places. (T) indicates tinned, although many of the other items must have been tinned as well.

36	pork	60	celery roots
67	knuckles (*Eisbein*) (T)	48	frankfurters (T)
24	tongue sausage (T)	84	bacon
18	meatloaf or liver loaf (*Leberkäse*)	48	cooked sausage
		70	wheat flour
30	dried bread	70	sago
100	fruit	50	lentils with meat
50	biscuits	50	peas with meat
15	salad	12	ham (T)
15	cauliflower	30	oats
70	lard	20	pudding powder
10	vegetable oil	30	peas
65	cheese (T)	20	oxtail soup
50	plums	50	raspberry juice
50	peas	50	cherry juice
40	French beans for cutting	60	salt
30	spinach	0.2	caraway seeds
80	pickled cucumbers	25	salted herrings
35	tomato paste	60	prunes

50	fruit soups	20	mock turtle soup
35	manmade honey	110	jam
180	naval ration bread	50	orangeade
96	wholemeal bread	3	tea
50	linseed bread	50	coffee
72	pork (T)	200	sugar
18	frying sausages	12	sultanas
25	beef	1	pepper
18	sausage spread (*Teewurst*)	100	fresh fruit
12	meat aspic	25	roasted almonds
18	meat sausage	40	milk soup
42	corned beef	18	liver
30	ox tongues	36	bones with meat for making soup
70	crisp bread		
70	beer	42	pig tongues
180	dried carrots	200	chickens (T)
20	radishes	50	pumpernickel
50	margarine	415	lemons
50	fresh cheese	110	onions
100	pears	40	cucumbers
50	small plums	50	butter (fresh)
50	bilberries	25	meatloaf (T)
35	carrots (T)	100	apples
90	vegetables (fresh)	50	apricots
20	kale	25	beetroot
70	asparagus	40	French beans (snapping variety)
25	herbs for making soups		
0.1	bay leaves	60	mushrooms
25	dates	160	sauerkraut
90	dried ham	60	cucumbers (fresh)
54	liver pâté	90	sausages
60	sausages (T)	55	ham (smoked) (T)
80	macaroni	48	blood sausage
1	vinegar essence	48	meat sausage (T)
100	apple purée	90	rice
40	venison	40	pasta
72	veal	50	cabbage with meat
30	semolina	30	herring salad
25	chocolate	44	beef (T)
150	butter (T)	84	milk
10	glucose tablets	24	chocolate sweets
40	lentils	25	chocolates (filled)

30	peas (yellow)	12	soup salt
40	beans (white)	23	herrings (T)
40	honey (natural)	660	mixed flour bread
50	lemon juice	120	white bread
20	rum	73	wine (red)
12	cocoa	1750	potatoes
54	sardines		

While digging through the files in the U-boat Archive another researcher found the following details, copied them for me but unfortunately did not include the source. The provisions supplied to a Type IXC boat with a crew of fifty-five men for a twelve-week voyage are listed. Glancing at the list is likely to raise a number of questions, and some items in the following menu are not included in the list. Since the source is unknown, the reader must come up with his own explanations. The numbers on the left indicate kilograms.

36	pork	65	onions
18	frying sausages	50	butter (fresh)
18	liver	180	ration bread
25	knuckles (*Eisbein*)	96	wholemeal bread
45	beef	60	grey bread (*Feinbrot*)
18	veal	120	white bread
24	tongue sausage	175-0	potatoes
18	meat spread (*Teewurst*)	30	herring salad
18	liver sausage	40	game
12	Brunswick sausage	40	onions
12	aspic	1	various herbs and spices
12	hunter's sausage (*Jagdwurst*)	25	dates
18	liver loaf	33	red wine
18	meat sausage	72	pork (T)
36	marrow bones	144	beef (T)
270	eggs (10 crates)	42	ham (T)
416	lemons (13 crates)	48	frankfurters (large) (T)
300	fruit	90	salami
30	carrots	990	ham (smoked)
25	green beans	55	ham (T)
30	tomatoes	84	bacon
15	lettuce	54	liver sausage (T)
20	radishes	48	blood sausage (T)
40	cucumbers	48	hunter's sausage (T)
25	cauliflower	48	meat sausage (T)
15	greens	6	frankfurters (small) (T)

42   knuckles (*Eisbein*) (T)
42   corned beef
42   pig tongues (T)
24   pig heads (T)
30   beef tongues (T)
200 chickens (T)
50   white cabbage with meat (T)
50   lentils with meat (T)
50   peas with meat (T)
274 special bread (125 loaves)
660 bread (T)
30   hard bread
70   crisp bread
150 biscuits
50   pumpernickel
180 potatoes (dried)
5   onions (dried)
5   beans (dried)
20   lard
50   margarine
10   oil for cooking and salads
50   cheese (fresh)
25   cheese in tubes
65   cheese (T)
100 apples (stewed) (T)
100 pears (T)
100 cherries
50   plums
50   yellow plums
50   peaches
50   apricots
50   strawberries
50   blueberries
25   beetroot
50   peas
35   carrots
40   French beans
40   runner beans
90   mixed vegetables
60   mushrooms
120 kale
30   spinach

160 pickled cabbage (*Sauerkohl*)
120 asparagus (whole shoots)
80   asparagus (broken pieces)
60   cucumbers (fresh)
80   pickled cucumbers
25   mixed greens for making soup
35   tomato purée
60   celery (roots)
120 flour
80   macaroni
40   runner beans
90   rice
20   sago
30   semolina
30   oats (porridge oats)
150 butter (T)
20   pudding powder
30   peas (yellow)
30   peas (green)
40   beans (white)
40   lentils
110 jam
35   honey (artificial)
40   honey (natural)
50   raspberry juice
50   lemon juice
50   cherry juice
50   orange juice
50   coffee
20   coffee substitute
3   tea
20   rum
200 sugar
60   salt
1   pepper
5   vinegar essence
784 milk (28 crates)
75   chocolates (various)
10   glucose tablets
25   almonds (roasted)
75   gravy powder
20   oxtail soup

20	mock turtle soup	100	fresh fruit
12	flavouring essence for soups	43	herrings in tomato sauce (T)
10	meat stock	54	sardines in oil (300 T)
40	milk soup	25	herrings (salted) (T)
50	fruit soup	13	sultanas
60	prunes	12	cocoa powder

The following is the menu for the above list of provisions. Soups varied considerably: some were meat based, while others were sweet and made from fruit. When the U-boats were in warmer waters, the soups tended to be types that could be served cold. Breakfast usually consisted of coffee or cocoa with milk soups and crisp bread or rusks, jam and honey, and butter or eggs. The numbers indicate days at sea. L = Lunch, E = Evening meal.

1.
L: Soup, fried liver with mashed potatoes and fresh fruit.
E: Sausage, smoked meats, bread, butter and coffee.

2.
L: Soup, fried chicken, gravy, potatoes, red cabbage, fruit.
E: Meats, bread, butter and tea.

3.
L: Knuckle with sauerkraut, pea purée and potatoes, fresh fruit.
E: Liver sausage, cheese, bread, butter and coffee.

4.
L: Soup, chops, gravy, sprouts and potatoes, pudding with fruit juice.
E: Ham, sausage, bread, butter, cocoa.

5.
L: Stewed pickled beef, macaroni, potatoes, gravy, prunes.
E: Salami, liver loaf, bread, butter, cocoa.

6.
L: Soup, beefsteak with egg, cauliflower, potatoes and gravy, fresh fruit.
E: Camembert, fried herrings, bread, butter and coffee.

7.
L: Fried sausages, Bavarian cabbage, potatoes with gravy and fresh fruit.
E: Herring salad, cold sausage, bread, butter and tea.

8.
L: Potato soup with bacon, fresh fruit.
E: Swiss cheese (Emmental), salami, bread, butter, tea.

9.
L: Soup, veal, bean salad, potatoes with gravy, fresh fruit.
E: Meat spread, two boiled eggs, bread, butter, coffee.

10.
L: Soup, beef, potatoes, gravy.
E: Tongue sausage, Tilsit cheese, bread, butter and tea.
11.
L: Soup, rolled beef, cabbage, potatoes, gravy.
E: Ham sausage, sardines, bread, butter, cocoa.
12.
L: Lentil soup with frankfurters, strawberries with whipped cream.
E: Cold sausage, boiled egg, bread, butter, tea.
13.
L: Soup, goulash, potatoes, cucumber.
E: Edam cheese, meat sausage, bread, butter, coffee.
14.
L: Soup, spinach with eggs, potatoes, pudding.
E: Ham, radish, bread, butter and rose hip juice.
15.
L: Soup, veal burgers, potatoes, pudding with fruit juice.
E: Cheese, salami, cucumber, bread, butter, coffee.
16.
L: Rice pudding with sugar and cinnamon, stewed apples.
E: Fried eggs, fried potatoes, cucumber, lemon juice.
17.
L: Swedes with beef, pudding.
E: Pancakes with stewed apples, sausage, bread, butter, cocoa.
18.
L: Ox tongues, red cabbage, potatoes, gravy, pudding.
E: Ham, cheese, bread, butter, tea.
19.
L: Plums and dumplings, pudding.
E: Cold sausage, cucumber, boiled egg, bread, butter and apple juice.
20.
L: Soup, fried chicken, potatoes with gravy, sprouts, pudding.
E: Hoppel-poppel, pickled gherkins, tea.
21.
L: Soup, macaroni with ham and gravy, pudding and fruit juice.
E: Noodle soup with beef, boiled ham, bread, butter, apple juice.
22.
L: Soup, lapscous, pudding.
E: Cheese, fish, bread, butter and cocoa.
23.
L: Soup, duck, vegetables, potatoes and gravy.
E: Salami, boiled egg, cucumber, bread, butter, rose hip juice.

24.
L: Soup, asparagus with ham, potatoes, pudding with fruit juice.
E: Rice pudding with sugar and cinnamon, sardines, bread, butter and tea.

25.
L: Soup, beef goulash, mushrooms, macaroni, pears.
E: Corned beef, cheese, bread, butter, lemon juice.

26.
L: Soup, ox tongues, asparagus, potatoes with gravy, plums.
E: Cheese, boiled egg, bread, butter, coffee.

27.
L: Soup, veal, mixed vegetables, potatoes, cucumbers.
E: Potato pancakes, stewed apples, butter, tea.

28.
L: Potato salad with scrambled eggs, mixed pudding.
E: Ham with macaroni, tomato sauce, rose hip juice.

29.
L: Soup, turkey, potatoes with gravy, bean salad.
E: Scrambled eggs, bread, butter, cucumbers and tea.

30.
L: Soup, casserole, pudding.
E: Rice pudding, corned beef, bread, butter and coffee.

31.
L: Soup, eggs, spinach, potatoes, pudding.
E: Ham, sausage, bread, butter, tea.

32.
L: Soup, duck, potatoes, pudding.
E: Fish, ham, bread, butter, apple juice.

33.
L: Soup, ox tongue, asparagus, potatoes, stewed apples.
E: Rice pudding with a slice of corned beef, bread, butter, coffee.

34.
L: Noodle soup with beef, strawberries and whipped cream.
E: Cheese, sausage, bread, butter, tea.

35.
L: Soup, meat with onions, vegetables, potatoes, gravy, pudding, fruit juice.
E: Ham, boiled egg, bread, butter, cocoa.

36.
L: Plums with dumplings, gooseberry pudding.
E: Pancakes, ham, bread, butter, tea.

37.
L: Soup, beef goulash, vegetables, potatoes, dumplings, cucumber, pudding.
E: Salami, boiled eggs, bread, butter, tea.

38.
L: Soup, pea soup with meat, gravy, red cabbage, potatoes, pudding.
E: Cheese, sausage, bread, butter, coffee.
39.
L: Soup, pig tongues, mushrooms, potatoes, pudding.
E: Ham, sausage, bread, butter, coffee.
40.
L: Macaroni, bacon, tomato purée.
E: Cheese, corned beef, bread, butter, tea.
41.
L: Soup, lapscous, pudding.
E: Depending on what remains.
42.
L: Bean soup with beef and pork.
E: Depending on what remains.

Soup was provided each morning, alternating each day between meat brews and milk soup with bread. The menu was repeated for any more days at sea.

There are a number of obvious omissions in the above list, probably because fresh food does not seem to have been included. Looking at the huge number of potatoes, one must come to the conclusion that this is the total number of fresh and dried varieties. Generally fresh potatoes from a greengrocer could not be stored for more than three to six weeks; after that the men had to resort to using a dried powdered variety. This was not lacking in nutriments but was rather soft and could almost be drunk rather than chewed. Therefore the majority of men detested it. Bread also came quite high on the list of things that went bad quickly. First, it absorbed moisture, making it go soggy, and then layers of mould had to be scraped off before it could be eaten. Sadly, for some men there was no real substitute. Crisp bread was generally disliked because it was not filling enough and other hard tack substitutes were rather difficult to cope with as well. Even tinned bread was not ideal. It was hard and often had a rather sour taste that did not agree with everyone, leaving some with stomach pains. Tinned food was by far the most versatile, especially in the tropics where canned fruit, chocolate and sweets formed the main nourishment for the majority of men. Having lost the desire to eat due to the extreme temperatures, three or four men would share a large tin of juicy fruit.

A big problem as far as health was concerned was that the texture of the food worsened considerably as time went on; after a while most of it was so soft that there was nothing at all to chew on. This, together with the men not being able to brush their teeth properly, resulted in a variety of gum

Karl Hurkuck, a qualified confectioner, is baking a cake for the rear torpedo compartment where someone is due to have a birthday. Alcohol was not normally provided for the crew, but the birthday boy could call upon the commander to choose to drink either a cognac or a clear schnapps with him.

complaints. What is astonishing is that the flotilla medical staff that examined the men regularly, as well as before and after each long voyage, were specially trained to recognise symptoms of vitamin deficiencies, but hardly any were ever recorded. Yet men in long range U-boats fought raging battles with the pills they were given to get over potential problems. For example, the pills for helping to preserve the night vision of lookouts were so huge that it was possible to choke on them and some men dropped them into the bilges instead of eating them. On seeing this, other men immediately reported the matter to force sense into the culprits, telling them that everyone's life depended on them being able to see properly in the dark.

Not only did food differ starkly from one country to another until many years after the war, when international travel broadened national diets, in Germany there were also marked differences between the north and south. Bread, for example, formed a much more dominant part of the diet in the mountains of Bavaria than it did on the Low German plain. This meant that there were also differences in some U-boats, especially when a majority of members from the same area introduced strong local flavours into the menu. Thus, it is impossible to talk about a typical German diet, although some characteristics were common throughout the land. Cooked breakfasts, such as those served in Britain, hardly featured in Germany. One reason for this could well be that on average people started working much earlier, between 6 and 8 a.m., and often stopped for a second breakfast before lunch. The first breakfast was often dominated by something like porridge or milk soup made in such a vast variety of different ways that almost every housewife had her own recipe. This would have been followed by bread or by rolls with butter and jam, or perhaps some cheese and meats in a few cases, and usually accompanied by hot coffee. Tea was drunk predominantly along the North Sea coasts, often black with candy rather than sugar.

Again, the British cooked evening meal was hardly known in Germany, the majority having a hot meal during the middle of the day. This often consisted of just one main course with perhaps a little sweet to follow. The evening meal was again based on bread, but not the soft white types found in Britain. Since before the war, Germany had produced a vast variety of substantial breads and these were served with satisfying meats, cheeses or fish. Again, this would have been accompanied by a generous supply of coffee. All this was reflected in U-boat menus, which followed the national norms, with special meals being produced on Sundays and for other festive occasions such as birthdays.

CHAPTER 7

First Moves Far Afield: Freetown and Florida

The move into the waters off Freetown started more than year before the United States joined in the war and long before U-boats had any need to venture into tropical areas. U-boats had not spent a great deal of time in exceedingly cold seas either, so everything was new. There were only a few noteworthy surprises in those far-off waters because the U-boats making the long journeys found their destinations devoid of anti-submarine forces, and although they had to battle against the wits of stubborn old seadogs on the bridges of merchant ships, there was relatively little retaliation. It was therefore possible to chalk up comparatively high sinking figures, and the majority of boats came home with a good display of victory pennants fluttering from their extended periscopes. The few boats carrying mines found that they needed only a few to shut down the ports of major centres such as Lagos in Nigeria and Takoradi on the Gold Coast (Ghana) for a considerable period until minesweepers were brought in. It is also interesting to add that the first U-boats to come home without having sunk a great deal had been sent by the U-boat Command to the wrong areas.

The area off Freetown on the west coast of Africa saw the sinking of the first American ship of the war. The 4,999 grt SS *Robin Moor* was sunk on 21 May 1941. She crossed the path of U69 (KL Jost Metzler) shortly after the U-boat had been refuelled from the tanker *Egerland*. The absence of neutrality markings and flag made Metzler suspicious. Focusing on an unusual array of boxes being carried as deck cargo, he was under the impression that this was covering the guns of a special submarine trap. These were hardly used during the Second World War, but men of his age had grown up reading books about how Britain had lured unsuspecting U-boats close to well-armed disguised hunters during the First World War, and now he was not taking any chances. Approaching cautiously, he manoeuvred into such a position that the ship was kept constantly within the torpedo sights for firing the rear tube. (It was a Type VIIC.) At the same time, despite the first watch officer being on the

Right: A long range U-boat coming into port with its attack periscope holding up a row of victory pennants. The horseshoe-shaped object hanging on the conning tower wall is a lifebelt.

Below: U67, on the right, meeting a supply boat on the high seas. It looks as if there is a lookout manning the detachable loop on top of the periscope supports.

bridge to work the torpedo aimer, everybody else was ready for an emergency dive so that the boat could disappear in about 30 seconds.

Shortly after this incident Metzler wrote in his log:

The name *Robin Moor* was not recorded in any of our registers, making it look rather suspicious and I asked the master to come over to the U-boat with his papers [according to Prize Ordinance Regulations]. The ship stopped, boats were lowered and the first officer came alongside, but without any papers. He explained that the ship had only recently been bought and had been renamed from the old name of *Exmoor*. Now it was on its way from New York to South Africa. The first officer admitted that his cargo included partly assembled lorries and engines; all items listed as prohibited goods. I told him that I would have to sink his ship and ordered everybody off. At the same time I asked the master to come over with his papers. When the master came alongside, it was obvious from his papers that the cargo was definitely contraband going to a country engaged in warring activities against Germany. Therefore the ship would have to be sunk. We supplied the lifeboats with provisions, cognac and medical supplies and then shot a torpedo. Immediately after that we dived, not wanting to be caught on the surface by a gun possibly emerging from under those suspicious deck packages. Through the periscope it was possible to see the ship settling very slowly lower in the water and it was not too long before it became obvious that we needed to surface in order to finish her off with artillery. Thirty shells were fired over a considerable range of three kilometres before the ship finally dropped away from the surface. Since a large number of the crates from the deck were now floating in the water, I gave the order to sink them with gunfire from the smaller calibres. Tearing away parts of the packaging, it was now possible to see that they contained aluminium engine parts and our first watch officer, OLzS Hans-Jürgen Auffermann, who was in the Naval Air Arm until recently, confirmed that these were parts of aircraft engines. This was easy to believe because a vast number of aircraft wheels were floating among the boxes. SS *Robin Moor* finally dropped away from the surface at around 10.45 hours.

After that, U69 towed the lifeboats nearer to the African coast, but there is no mention of this in the log.

The next target, the 4,601 grt SS *Tewkesbury*, was spotted at 20.00 hours of that same day and also sunk by torpedo and gunfire, and following this U69 closed in on the coast to lay mines off Takoradi and Lagos. A few days later, on 31 May 1941, U69 torpedoed the 5,445 grt MV *Sangara* in the harbour at Accra, causing the ship to sink to the bottom in such shallow water that the superstructure remained above the surface. All this came without great retaliation from the opposition, although the German side was not too kind to its submariners. The ejection system for the torpedoes did not work terribly well, although no fault or damage was found anywhere, the port engine broke down for a short period, and the gyrocompass gave up the ghost.

The laying of mines, mentioned above, was not the easiest of undertakings. First, it was essential for the crew to be in the best possible conditions, since fast reactions could easily mean the difference between life and death. At the same time as getting the men ready and reminding them that they might need their escape apparatus, the interior of the boat was prepared for scuttling by unpacking and placing explosive charges in critical areas, specified by the chief engineer. Then came the inevitable discussions about who was going to be responsible for setting them off if the order to abandon ship had to be given.

These procedures were new to the majority of the men, including those who were responsible for making everything work smoothly, and it created a good deal of tension on top of the already strained atmosphere within the boat. Yet, despite the almost frightening preparations, the approach to Takoradi was more straightforward than when something similar had been tried during training. It was 21.00 hours on 26 May when U69 found itself on the previously ordered approach route close to the port. The lighting in the port and along the coast was somewhat subdued, but not fully blacked out, and parts of the small harbour were illuminated well enough to reveal the presence of six ships packed like sardines into the small space. There were lookout posts on the quays and even a slow-moving patrol boat. It was also obvious that none of these ships could be sunk or damaged by torpedoes because the idyllic little harbour was surrounded by a set of overlapping quays that offered excellent protection. Yet there was one ship lying at anchor just outside these walls of stone and it was very tempting to have a go at it, but although there was little movement among the lookout posts, Metzler did not risk it for fear of stirring up a hornets' nest. What was so astonishing was that he passed less than 200 metres from the ship lying at anchor but no one challenged the U-boat as it laid no more than half a dozen mines whilst a brilliant display of natural fluorescence lit up the activity.

Two days later the tension reappeared in what was becoming an increasingly hot situation. The temperature inside the U-boat in the shallow water had risen to 45 degrees Celsius, making life for the men almost unbearable. (In fact, this is so hot that modern regulations would not allow any employer to subject men to working in such conditions without special protection.) In addition to the heat, the weather conditions had deteriorated to such an extent that it was virtually impossible to see any features along the coast. Everything was shrouded in a mist, making it look like one of those badly exposed photos that were common before cameras with light meters were introduced.

Metzler did eventually find the entrance to the harbour at Lagos. This was rather tight and while trying out something quite unique, reversing in to lay the mines, he found that the boat was being driven against one of the harbour walls by the surf. Life aboard U69 under such conditions was not comfortable all, with breakers crashing over the deck. Being unable to control the boat, Metzler pulled out again, reversed and this time went in forwards, where he had more control over that infuriating surf. Although it worked, it did bring the boat close enough to the harbour wall to spot several machine gun batteries emerging out of the haze created by the waves. Yet these appeared to be unmanned, leaving the men in U69 in peace to boil while they discharged half a dozen mines. Luckily the opposition did not prevent a quick exit because some cross-currents were stopping the rudders from controlling the boat and it was a case of going where it wanted to rather than steering with the rudders. The men of U69 felt themselves lucky to have escaped from these detrimental natural obstacles.

America, especially the Caribbean and the Gulf of Mexico, presented U-boats with far more unexpected conundrums than the Freetown area on the other side of the Atlantic. One of the first objectives was to bombard oil installations on some of the main islands. This would have been an easy task in Europe because such complexes grew up by the water's edge as hideous eyesores, many of them squelching forth a variety of smoke and flames. In the Caribbean this was different. The people responsible for such industrial monstrosities there took so much care not to spoil the natural beauty that several U-boats failed to find the targets unless they went too close for comfort.

Although a few large U-boats of the First World War crossed the Atlantic, such long voyages through comparatively inhospitable waters far away from land were still very much an unknown venture during the Second World War. Paul Weidlich, the chief engineer of U518, was one of the few who have left excellent accounts in the German U-boat Museum. He contributed a copy of a confidential report he wrote for the U-boat Command towards the end of April 1943, immediately after having returned from a voyage to South America. This journey under KL Friedrich-Wilhelm Wissmann ended with a considerable row at the debriefing when it was discovered that eight out of fourteen torpedoes had been misses because they had been fired from too great a distance. So it was not an entirely joyous homecoming, but Weidlich could hardly be blamed for the shortcomings of his commander. Weidlich wrote:

The Men
Remaining submerged for more than fifty days put an enormous strain on all the men, particularly the technical division. The temperatures in the diesel and electro compartments were hardly bearable and often reached well over 50 degrees Celsius. This experience of sailing through tropical waters definitely proved that the additional room ventilators were nowhere near

adequate. Especially the technical staff suffered from boils, sores and other skin complaints. The majority of men had four to six large and many more small boils and this became so bad that there were always one or two men unfit for duty. Apart from this, the technical division did exceedingly well and things would have been better if there had been more salt-water soap.

The Engines
The exhaust temperatures of the diesel engines was a little higher than during the first mission to North American waters and the exhaust pipes often emitted glowing embers into the air. The engines were also liable to produce a faint smoke at times. The biggest difficulty lay in controlling the various vents and at one stage it was necessary to rig up some tackle in order to move them. The handles on the wheels broke off long before reaching the hot waters, suggesting that these systems could do with better oiling facilities. The valves also allowed water to seep in, but regrinding the seating prevented some of this.

The Torpedo Tubes
Having had some bad experiences with torpedo tube 3 during the first voyage, we were most surprised to find that this time tube 2 jammed open. Every effort to close it failed and in the end it was bashed shut with a sledgehammer from the outside. Working on the outside was not the easiest of tasks. There had been too much interference from aircraft to make this a practical proposition where we were. So the boat moved further out to sea into a less frequented area before literally banging it shut and then jamming it in such a way that it was unlikely to open, even if a depth charge detonated too close. This meant the tube remained out of action for the rest of the voyage.

Batteries
Despite the batteries having been serviced before leaving port, they still lost up to 2 mm of liquid per day and this increased once the boat reached tropical waters. The strong presence of aircraft made it necessary to remain submerged for exceptionally long periods of fourteen hours. This put an enormous strain on the batteries. With outside air temperatures of 29 degrees Celsius for something like fifty consecutive days meant the battery temperatures usually reached 43 degrees or more. Following an air attack a few of the batteries produced irregular results and one wonders whether these faults will recover with a long deep charge. Also annoying were the surfaces of the batteries. Some developed such obvious and wide cracks that it was necessary to use flames to melt the material so that it would reseal itself.

Much of the machinery built during the Second World War, whether small binoculars or large engines, was designed to be taken apart so that individual components could be replaced or the workings overhauled. The engines required frequent attention. The interesting point about Weidlich's report is that he provides some insight into the non-routine repairs carried out:

- The pipe for blowing the diving tanks showed serious signs of corrosion and collars had to be clamped on in places to prevent water from seeping in.
- During a routine diving test it was discovered that one of the main tanks had a porous section. The valve and the porous part were dismantled and repaired. The fault was caused by material failure.
- Some of the components of the valves for diving cells 1, 5 and 8 were not working properly. As a result, the main compressed air distributer was constantly filled with water. It was possible to clear this by opening and shutting the valve several times and it was necessary to work all the valves regularly to prevent them from sticking. It will be necessary to have all the seatings in the valves reground at the next overhaul in port.
- The refrigerator in the central control room failed due to an escape of the cooling gas. This gas was replaced, but no leaks were found and the fridge ran for some time until the gas had been used up. In the end we ran out of cooling gas and could no longer use the fridge, which was a serious blow in the hot tropical waters. It would be advantageous to take a second reserve bottle of gas on future missions.
- The fresh water generator broke down due to the water level indicator not working properly. This was repaired by soldering the flotation device but the system broke down again and this time we couldn't work out the reason.

And so the list continues.

Wolfgang Hirschfeld, radio operator of U109 (KL Heinrich or 'Ajax' Bleichrodt), has published one of the best accounts of what life was like inside U-boats, and the following is based on his books and subsequent interviews over a considerable period of time. He kept a secret logbook, so it is therefore easy to go back in time to read what was going on inside the U-boat between the entries of the official war diary. In March 1942, he made the point that the operations area on the western side of the Atlantic was no longer the most dangerous place to be. Both the Bay of Biscay and the bases themselves had become part of the front line of war. Hirschfeld was seriously perturbed by the goings-on in the French ports. Lorient, for example, had been hit by a number of major air raids. These hardly upset the U-boats inside their huge concrete shelters, and the men were also provided with well-built bunkers, so at night it was a simple case of merely running into the nearest shelter in one's pyjamas and with one's bedding to continue sleeping. Yet such protection was not provided for the locals, and many suffered enormously by having their houses, livelihoods and often their lives destroyed.

On 25 March 1942, U109 left Lorient together with U203 for Florida. Not much happened during the next few days, one boring routine being followed by another, to be interrupted only by practising everything Bleichrodt could think of. There were a few new faces on board; notably the first watch officer had arrived only a few days before departure. He was OLzS Werner Witte, who later commanded one of the first *Monsun* boats and was killed on 15 June 1943 when U509 was sunk in the Central Atlantic, north-west of Madeira. Life for radio operators had become somewhat easier since the U-boat Command had introduced the new coding machines at the beginning of February 1942. Now each sea area had its own frequency and coding system, meaning that it was no longer necessary to listen to every message that came flooding through the earphones. There was a slight disadvantage with this inasmuch that it was now no longer possible to hear what was going on elsewhere, but generally the radio operators were pleased to have less work, recording and decoding only messages pertinent to their area.

The first excitement came early in April when U109 was constantly followed by a shark. The men were not quite sure whether it was the same one or whether there were a number taking it in turns to follow the boat. Sharks did not have a good press, and the men were itching to have a go at it by feeding it with a hand grenade, but that would have made too much noise and permission was not forthcoming. The month brought with it what might be called 'April showers', only these had American dimensions and were so powerful that U109 hardly made any forward progress while the associated winds were blowing. All the engines could manage was to make a little headway, and Bleichrodt spent much time in the cellar avoiding the ferocious conditions on the surface. Whilst the situation was appreciated at first, it became so irksome after a few days that the crew started growing restless. All they could do was to lie in their bunks, using as little oxygen as possible and hoping that the storm would subside as quickly as it appeared. The U-boat Command no longer accepted handwritten logs, so every few days one of the radio operators had to type out a copy of the entries onto sheets of paper. This at least gave one person a little to be getting on with.

The usual discontent caused by men being squeezed together in a confined space was made worse when Bleichrodt received a negative reply to his question as to whether there was a possibility of being supplied with fuel before starting the return journey. The U-boat Command tersely commented that there were no chances at all, and he bitterly made a note in the log that U109 was waiting for better weather close to the American coat but also with

Testing the 105 mm quick firing gun on the bow of an ocean-going U-boat.

the prospect of coming home with a full load of torpedoes. There were no targets and not enough fuel to search for any. The astonishing thing with the persistent storms was that many of the crew had got so used to the punishing pitching and rolling that they were relatively happy to eat their meals without retreating into the calm depths. To stop their crockery from being strewn around the interior they chose to have their meals served in empty tin cans. Although the crockery was of superior, hotel quality, it could not be made to resist damage from hitting iron structures and much of it shattered as it literally went flying around the compartments, leaving the men to pick up and jettison the fragments.

Once the storm subsided, the men found themselves surrounded by flying fish gliding over the upper (outside) deck, and the few that hit the conning tower remained flapping on the woodwork. When the men had a bucketful, they were taken below and fried. Sadly for the men, the warm temperatures quickly gave way to considerably more hostile heat and the interior of the boat rose to a staggering 45 degrees Celsius in the hull, with 52 degrees being recorded inside the engine room when the diesel engines were running. To make matters worse, the inside of the hull had been dripping with condensation for days on end and all the men could do was to wear shorts while sitting on towels to absorb the perspiration dripping off them. Even the wooden cladding was not enough to prevent the dripping off the walls, with pools of water collecting everywhere. This, in turn, gave rise to numerous sores. The only consolation was that a few successes came the men's way and they did have a small refrigerator to make a little ice, but not enough for the entire crew at the same time. To make things a little more uncomfortable, the men found an abundance of natural fluorescence illuminating both the boat at night and torpedoes as they ran through the water towards their targets. Not ideal for surprise attacks.

In a way, everyone was pleased when the fuel ran out and Bleichrodt headed for home. The excursion to Florida was interesting, but not in the way that the men had imagined. For them it was nothing more than one torture after another, with nothing to make life even the slightest bit comfortable or profitable. Even the calm days were not to their liking. Then the waters were so clear and so shallow that a passing aircraft might spot the submerged boat stirring up the mud from the bed as it wrestled its way through the warm soup. On the way home, the men also spotted another fright-inducing American innovation: airships, called Blimps, in the sky. These were unarmed and the men would have loved to have a go at them, feeling confident that their best marksmen could bring them down, even with the large 105 mm quick firing gun, which had not been designed for hitting flying targets. Bleichrodt pointed out that although the Blimps might not have guns, they had a 'telephone' and could call up massive watchdogs with huge teeth lurking not too far away. He preferred to vanish into the depths before they spotted the U-boat.

U518's run to American waters and back

The following table, although not easy to digest at first sight, is interesting because it gives precise details of U518's voyage to the American side of the Atlantic. The chief engineer, Paul Weidlich, provided the information. In addition, he also supplied details of the quantity of pure water produced by the boat's still. This worked on the simple principle of boiling water and then cooling the steam to produce what was often referred to as distilled water. When running for 24 hours, the still produced 240 litres.

Days at sea	Distance travelled on surface (nm)	Distance travelled submerged (nm)	Time travelled on surface (hours-minutes)	Time travelled submerged (hours-minutes)	Fuel used (cubic metres)	Drinking water used (litres)
1	60	0	07-19	00-00	1.5	50
2	82	30	14-19	09-41	2.9	60
3	90	31	13-14	10-46	3.0	40
4	32	59	04-21	19-39	1.2	100
5	98	33	13-12	10-48	3.6	100
6	104	32	13-25	10-35	3.3	120
7	160	3	23-18	00-42	3.6	125
8	136	3	23-10	00-50	4.0	200
9	114	2.5	23-18	00-42	3.6	230
10	142	2	23-36	00-24	3.2	200
11	162	2.5	23-14	00-46	3.3	210
12	168	2	23-26	00-34	3.8	190
13	172	2.5	23-21	00-39	3.2	210
14	173	3	23-06	00-54	3.1	260
15	165	3.5	22-59	01-01	3.2	200
16	167	3	23-04	00-56	3.1	250
17	147	2	22-37	01-23	2.3	260
18	154	1.5	23-40	00-20	2.5	270
19	157	2	23-10	00-50	1.9	300
20	115	2	23-31	00-29	1.6	190
21	112	3	23-04	00-56	1.8	170
22	128	2	23-30	00-30	2.1	200
23	167	2	23-24	00-36	2.7	210
24	169	2.5	23-23	00-37	2.8	200

25	161	2.5	23-16	00-44	2.6	210
26	160	2	23-28	00-32	2.8	270
27	164	2	23-25	00-35	2.7	330
28	145	2	23-26	00-34	2.9	300
29	120	3	22-50	01-10	1.4	360
30	149	4	22-50	01-10	2.6	350
31	159	2	23-29	00-31	2.9	275
32	77	9	16-55	07-05	2.3	300
33	74	34	11-47	12-13	1.8	155
34	152	3	22-50	01-10	3.8	150
35	125	20	15-57	08-03	2.3	100
36	85	41	11-39	12-21	2.1	200
37	76	26	10-49	13-11	1.6	200
38	76	33	11-35	12-25	1.5	230
39	89	45	10-26	13-34	2.8	230
40	45	35	08-40	15-20	1.7	250
41	56	27	11-34	12-26	1.4	190
42	52	28	11-14	12-46	1.4	330
43	64	26	11-04	12-56	1.6	220
44	60	33	11-11	12-49	1.3	230
45	78	31	11-17	12-43	3.2	220
46	73	28	11-13	12-47	1.2	200
47	80	29	11-14	12-46	2.1	200
48	54	44	09-47	14-13	1.3	200
49	73	41	10-47	13-13	2.9	200
50	111	41	09-31	14-29	4.2	200
51	36	37	13-14	10-46	2.6	300
52	85	30	11-30	12-30	1.6	260
53	81	33	11-26	12-34	1.8	200
54	114	31	11-22	12-38	2.3	300
55	91	23	11-58	12-02	2.1	155

56	95	32	11-32	12-28	1.6	155
57	80	39	11-26	12-34	1.7	135
58	68	32	11-23	12-37	1.7	200
59	70	25	10-59	13-01	2.2	315
60	80	38	11-23	12-37	1.7	200
61	67	45	11-29	12-31	1.7	240
62	74	38	12-11	11-49	2.5	190
63	57	29	11-18	12-42	1.5	110
64	63	38	10-07	13-53	2.0	190
65	100	39	11-26	12-34	2.2	260
66	87	26	11-14	12-46	2.4	150
67	88	31	10-32	13-28	2.4	120
68	106	33	10-14	13-46	4.1	135
69	81	30	09-52	14-08	2.6	160
70	73	32	09-59	14-01	1.7	200
71	75	27	11-05	12-55	1.6	140
72	76	34	11-16	12-44	1.5	150
73	58	44	08-38	15-22	1.2	160
74	73	39	09-30	14-30	2.7	180
75	69	30	10-26	13-34	1.4	270
76	73	30	11-11	12-49	1.6	230
77	71	30	11-13	12-47	1.4	220
78	64	28	10-39	12-21	1.5	200
79	70	32	12-31	11-29	1.7	210
80	82	46	09-08	14-52	1.9	180
81	186	2	23-34	00-26	2.8	150
82	164	0	24-00	00-00	2.4	190
83	158	2	23-28	00-32	2.2	160
84	158	2.5	23-27	00-33	2.4	190
85	164	2.5	23-21	00-39	2.4	190
86	166	2	23-23	00-37	2.5	200

87	166	2	23-35	00-25	2.4	195
88	153	2.5	23-21	00-39	2.5	165
89	140	2	23-29	00-31	2.6	130
90	137	1.5	23-34	00-26	2.5	195
91	136	2	23-29	00-31	2.5	195
92	128	2	23-21	00-39	2.6	180
93	130	2.5	23-21	00-39	2.8	120
94	125	6.5	23-22	00-38	2.6	200
95	12	48	12-25	11-35	0.8	180
96	122	21	23-12	00-48	2.6	230
97	162	2	23-32	00-28	2.7	370
98	173	9.5	21-06	02-54	3.7	200
99	186	2.5	23-24	00-36	3.9	160
100	115	33.5	13-23	10-37	2.3	190
101	98	34	09-59	14-01	2.5	140
102	95	36.5	09-33	14-27	1.6	130
103	96	36	09-35	14-25	2.5	120
104	85	39	09-44	15-16	2.2	135
105	84	36	09-45	15-15	2.2	240
106	87	35	09-08	15-52	2.2	300
107	89	0	09-46	00-00	2.0	300

CHAPTER 8

U180 – The First U-boat with Motor Torpedo Boat Engines

This chapter is based on the official log, material compiled by Hermann Wien, Dieselobermaschinist of U180, from information provided by Werner Musenberg, its first commander, and in the GC&CS Naval History.

U180 and U195 were the only boats of Type IXD1 to be commissioned before production switched to the Type IXD2. Although similar, there were some marked differences between these types, and one does not have to delve too deeply before realising why only two IXD1s were built. First, the speed of more than 22 knots produced by six motor torpedo boat engines connected to two propellers (three per shaft) made these the fastest in the German fleet. They would have been ideal for water skiing if it had not been for the black exhaust they produced, so that from a distance they looked like one of those ugly coal-burning monsters from the First World War. This prominent discharge was obvious even at convoy chasing speeds, making it questionable whether they would ever have been capable of creeping up on a target for a surprise attack. Secondly, the noise of the engines was phenomenal, even for engineers used to working in noisy environments. Thirdly, fuel was guzzled up faster than one could calculate its consumption. So, although high speeds were possible, it was not always advisable to push the engines.

Having returned from his first voyage, Werner Musenberg, the commander of U180, was not amused and condemned the Type IXD1 as being nowhere near ready for operational use. The six engines occupied so much space that there was not enough room to service them properly. To get at all the vital parts it was necessary to cut the engine compartment open, extract the individual sections and then work on them. So complete servicing could only be done in port. Some bright spark came up with the idea of cooling the engines with fresh water but without providing enough stills to generate the vast quantities required. Consequently men were rationed to less than one small drinking glass of washing water per day for brushing teeth and had to clean themselves in salt water at all other times. This resulted in many developing a variety of skin complaints from mild rashes to serious boils oozing both blood and puss. Not ideal for short voyages and exceedingly difficult for long operations. U180 also ran into the situation where there was not enough fresh water for cooling all the engines and therefore had to shut down three for considerable periods to prevent serious overheating.

There were also a large number of pipes connecting the engines with the outside, and the junctions where these passed through the pressure hull leaked so badly that a ballast pump had to run constantly to remove it again. It was not unusual for an unbelievable four tons of water to leak in during a period of less than an hour, and at times a single pump was unable to cope with the quantities pouring in. Water then started slopping over the floor plates until another ballast pump could be switched on to help alleviate the problem.

Despite all the negative attributes discovered during trials, U180 did pass its final training tests and arrived in Kiel early in 1943 to be kitted out for its first operational voyage. Being such a huge monster and with it being common knowledge that other boats had gone as far as South Africa, it was not too difficult to guess that U180 would also be away for some time. *Dieselobermaschinist* Hermann Wien, a warrant officer with some experience, happened to have been the officer on duty the evening before the boat was due to leave and therefore witnessed a car pulling up alongside during the depths of night to deliver a number of packages and some suitcases. All very mysterious, especially as he had no idea that something out of the ordinary was afoot. The men bringing them ordered the few duty men on board not to mention this to anyone. The boat was lying by a specially dedicated pier belonging to the Fifth U-Flotilla, which specialised in kitting out boats going on their first operational patrol. Guards kept even men with naval dockyard passes from entering this sealed-off section. The reason was not so much to stop outsiders from entering the U-boats but to prevent pilfering of stores laid aside for loading. These usually arrived by lorry and it would take some time before all the packages could be taken on board. As a result, there were often huge piles of goodies lying around as a temptation for the light-fingered.

British decrypts would suggest that Musenberg was not much wiser than his diesel engineer and that plans for the future had not been discussed with him in great detail, for once at sea he sent a signal asking whether his mission was subject to operational limitations. The reply stated that he was free to attack shipping outside Lane A, the area set aside for German blockade runners.

Apart from the incident with the car, everything else went the same as it always did. The following morning, men wandered back from their land-based accommodation and paraded on deck, the commander spoke a few encouraging words and then gave orders for U180 to nose carefully out into

This and next page: Boats going on their first operational patrol were kitted out by the Fifth U-Flotilla in Kiel, which supplied everything from provisions and equipment to the latest intelligence. The loading process usually took several days and before leaving, the officers were usually asked to sign the flotilla's guest book. The following are pages from this guest book in which someone from the U-boat provided an illustration that was then signed by the officers.

the Kiel Fjord, before making for the open Baltic. It had passed the U-boat memorial at Möltenort and was running by the naval memorial at Laboe when the engines slowed down. This was unusual. Boats did not usually stop there. A small patrol boat came alongside and two men clambered on board. Dressed in civilian clothes, with black hats and sunglasses, they looked very like arch spies from some thriller shown in the local cinema. The crew were told that they were specialists for building bunkers, but no one believed this. Nobody could fathom why they should want to come on board in such an obviously dramatic fashion. Had they appeared in the harbour wearing naval uniforms no one would have batted an eyelid. Now their theatrical entry created all manner of speculative chatter, and the men on the bridge wondered what observers on land would have made of this incident. It was shortly after 8 a.m. and the majority of workers would have been active for an hour or so, so there were plenty of curious eyes on both sides of the narrow inlet.

It did not take long for the crew to work out that one of these men was Subhas Chandra Bose and the other his adjutant, Abid Hasan. Both had featured in several well-illustrated magazines and their dark skin and characteristic faces made it easy to recognise them. The two belonged to the All-India Congress, a group dedicated to fight, if necessary, in order to rid the Indian subcontinent of British domination. The magazines explained how Bose had escaped from British persecution in India to arrive in Germany shortly before Russia joined in the war. Apparently he had travelled along an arduous route via the Khyber Pass and then through Afghanistan and Russia to Berlin, where he was given permission to recruit Indians and other supporters. Hitler was interested in this assistance in order to weaken British influence in the Far East because unrest in that part of the world could have had a notable effect on the war in the West. All this happened shortly before Japan entered the war, when Germany was struggling on its own against the most widespread and powerful empire in the world. Unfortunately, the land route between India and Germany snapped shut when Russia entered the war and there was no safe way back. The only practical way of returning them to their supporters at home was by submarine via Japan. One of the reasons for going to this incredible effort of delivering the two men by submarine was for Bose to create the core of an army from Indian prisoners of war held by the Japanese. Unlike his contemporary Mahatma Gandhi, he was not opposed to using physical force to achieve his aims of liberating India from British rule.

On 9 February 1943, U180 left Kiel during the build-up to what was to become the largest convoy battle of all time, and this was the first long range U-boat cruise not dedicated primarily to operational activities. Bletchley Park had just got back into reading the U-boat radio code and opposition in the North Atlantic was so fierce that something as simple as moving forward became almost impossible. A vast number of aircraft prevented Musenberg from making progress during daylight, so he remained submerged for much of the time and surfaced only at night. To make matters worse, U180 also sailed into such wild weather that the Admiralty in London had ordered a special study to find out exactly what was going on in the North Atlantic. Expert meteorologists confirmed that the northern hemisphere was beset by an unusually large number of ferocious weather events, and men at sea were definitely not exaggerating when they described passing from one horrendous storm into another. It was an exceptionally unsettled period, out of character even for those treacherous winter months. Conditions were so severe that the karabiners for the steel cabled safety harnesses were bent and strict instructions had to be issued to lookouts never to allow the lines to slacken because a sharp jerk caused by a sudden hefty tug of a body being pulled away could snap them.

A year earlier, when similar conditions prevailed, U162 under KL Jürgen Wattenberg found that the battering from the waves had been so severe that the hydroplanes could no longer be turned to their extreme positions because the thick steel rod holding them had been bent. On this occasion the men also discovered that the outer doors of the upper bow torpedo tubes had been partly torn off and were hanging down in front of the lower tubes, putting all four out of action. This left Wattenberg with no alternative other than to request permission to return home. This signal had just been sent when there was such a great improvement in the weather that it was possible to flood the stern, raise the bow as high as possible and tackle the cause of the problem with hacksaws. It worked and U162 continued with its voyage to the Caribbean. Now, U180 was heading for similar conditions, making many men wonder if they would reach the other side of the extreme weather or if it would force them back. Cruising speed was severely reduced and U180 would either not reach its rendezvous in the Indian Ocean on time or would have to increase engine revolutions to consume more fuel. This immediately made it obvious that a refuelling would be necessary. The U-boat Command responded quickly and arranged for a U-tanker to supply 60 cubic metres of fuel, some lubricating oil and enough food for another two weeks. On 3 March 1943, U180 met with the supply boat U462 under OLzS Bruno Vowe almost midway between Spain's Cape Finisterre and America.

Life inside U180 must have been horrendous. Musenberg hardly had his sea legs. He had been the head of a personnel department from July 1937 until June 1941, when he started his U-boat training, and this was the first real sea-going experience for many of the crew as well. Bose and his adjutant were not the only ones suffering from violent seasickness. However, the North Atlantic torture had considerably abated by the time the boat reached U462 and soon after that the deluge coming down the conning tower was replaced by intense heat. Temperatures increased rapidly, turning the engine room into what can only be described as a moderate baking oven. It was not unusual to record 50 to 60 degrees Celsius there. The other great irritation was the deafening noise from the engines.

Bose spoke only a little German, in addition to coming over as being a little reserved, making it difficult to hold a conversation with him. Hasan was the complete opposite. He had such a considerable repertoire of jokes and anecdotes that the men enjoyed his company. He was 28 years of age and had been at Oxford University before going to Germany to study civil engineering. Although historians have sidelined Bose, there must have been much more to this colourful figure than has been made out; otherwise why would the British Government have offered £1,000 for his head? This was an enormous amount of money at the time (probably enough to buy four houses in London). He was eventually transferred to a Japanese submarine in the Indian Ocean but vanished shortly after that. It was assumed that he died in an air crash in a remote region, but there are enough alternative theories to make this political activist a fascinating subject for further study. Hasan survived the war, eventually spending some time working in the Indian Embassy in Peking.

Life was certainly not sweet and easy back home while U180 was making for the Indian Ocean, considerable persuasion being required to prevent the Japanese from backing out of the agreement to meet the U-boat at sea. Things were becoming rather critical for them. They had lost three Akira transport submarines and were not too happy at risking other submarines for what could turn out to be a foolhardy venture. Things became so critical that Musenberg was sent an officer-only message saying:

> Dispel by appropriate attitude and conduct of your whole crew the fears already entertained by the Japanese Command in regard to the Biscay cruise … Under no circumstances is the attention of the Japanese to be drawn to any special risks run in the Bay of Biscay.

Whether this helped or not is questionable because the two Japanese passengers taken on board when Bose and Hasan left experienced the full force of Allied attacks before U180 reached the comparative safety of the huge submarine bunkers in France.

The meeting with the Japanese submarine I-29 under Capt. Masao Teraoka on 25 April 1943 went as planned and without any great additional complications. So far there had been hardly any noteworthy incidents. A few ships were sighted in the distance, and U180 even got close enough to the Portuguese freighter *Alvaro Martins Homem* to identify it as neutral. The lookouts sighted an empty British life raft with half the provisions consumed, suggesting that its earlier occupants had either been taken off or come to a sticky end. Bearing in mind that U180 had now been at sea for eighty-three days, almost three full months, the men had done very well in avoiding unnecessary contact and bringing their passengers safely to their destination. The most miraculous occurrence was that Musenberg took on the British 8,132 grt tanker *Corbis* shortly after entering the Indian Ocean, sinking it on 18 April 1943. Tackling such a target with a huge boat whose engines were temperamental was not easy and demonstrated that he had considerable skill and tenacity.

Having exchanged recognition signals with the Japanese submarine, all Musenberg could do was to use the old International Signal Book to pass a message saying that they would remain close enough together until the weather improved for the planned transfer. The wind was blowing at force 3-4 from the south-south-east, with correspondingly choppy seas making any transfer of even experienced sailors too precarious. The weather and the sea had previously been dead calm with brilliant visibility for a long period, so Musenberg decided that it would be best to wait for better conditions. What followed was not terribly easy, although the Germans were impressed by the Japanese crew's co-operation and by their willingness to make everything run smoothly. The most difficult hurdle was general communication. No one on the German side spoke Japanese and in the end used a combination of German and English to make the necessary arrangements. This was done by sending a signalman and the first watch officer over to the other boat.

The next obstacle was entirely unforeseen. Lying side by side, but some distance apart for the transfer, the men discovered that the higher Japanese boat drifted off faster than U180, so some juggling was required to keep the two at the required positions. Ropes for hauling rubber dinghies back and forth did not fare much better. They kept breaking. Yet the enthusiasm from both sides eventually made it possible to bring over some 11 tons, consisting of 3 torpedoes, 146 crates and a mass of unwanted cockroaches, beetles and other crawling beasties. The Japanese had also come with a huge amount of provisions for the Germans, but none of those delicacies could be taken on board because there was neither room nor enough reserve buoyancy. As it was, U180 was now so full of hurriedly dumped boxes that the men had to crawl on all fours to get over them, and it would be some time before all these were stowed in more out-of-the-way locations. Things were coming over so quickly that packages had to be distributed evenly throughout the boat wherever there was room. The weight problem was far more worrying than the volume. U180 had left Germany 7 tons too heavy and, having loaded another 11 tons, much of the boat's reserve buoyancy had been used up. Musenberg had expected additional packages but not a vast heap of heavy gold ingots, each individually packed in a small wooden box. With a displacement of 2,500/3,650 tons against U180's 1,610/2,150, I-29 could carry considerably more cargo than the smaller U-boat.

The bunks vacated by Chandra Bose and Hasan did not remain cold for long. Two Japanese marine engineers, FK Tetsushiro Emi and KK Hideo Tomonaga, came on board U180 with the intention of going to Germany to study submarine construction. Tomonaga eventually attempted to return to Japan aboard U234 under KL Johann-Heinrich Fehler, whose surrender in the United States at the end of the war caused him to commit suicide.

Having met with I-29 in the Indian Ocean and handed over the two men, U180 had accomplished its main objective and turned back to Europe. Before doing so it was necessary to distribute the fifty bars of pure gold, each one weighing 40 kilograms, plus their wooden packing as ballast down in the lowest part of the hull. Their weight meant that they could seriously upset the trim or balance of the boat so drastically that there was no way that U180 could safely drop into an alarm dive. The chances were that the boat would go down for good without any hope of ever reaching the surface again. So dealing with the careful distribution of this weight was of the utmost importance. Even after everything had been carefully distributed, U180 was still left with a worryingly small amount of reserve buoyancy, but there was nothing that could be jettisoned. The men later found a pipe connection between the lubricating oil tank inside the pressure hull and another tank in the floodable area on the outside. Obviously, none of the planners thought that men might want to remove their valuable lubricating oil and this system was not connected to an electrical pump. So, the men improvised and moved several tons with a small emergency hand pump to lighten the load inside the pressure hull.

Originally the men just saw two strange Japanese characters come on board, but it was not long before these two became good friends and their thirst for knowledge was well rewarded. Being unafraid to get dirty, they ventured into the filthy extremities of the boat to see what was going on, and the Germans were thrilled when they told and retold the stories of their involvement in the attack on Pearl Harbor. However, the return journey did not go as smoothly as the early stages, and things became quite critical when the men discovered that their planned meeting with U463 would not take place because the tanker had been sunk. The rounding of the Cape of Good Hope and the journey further north became more and more difficult, with U180 being constantly forced under by large, fast aircraft. This happened so often that it became difficult to remain on the surface long enough to charge the batteries. Some of the aircraft came close enough to drop a few heavy explosions into the water. This was shortly after May 1943, and even if the men of U180 were unaware of the exact details of the carnage of Black May, they knew enough that they stood a greater chance of being sunk than reaching their new home port of Bordeaux in France. What is rather amazing, bearing in mind the heap of consolidated mechanical mishaps they were sailing with, is that U180 managed to sink another ship on the way. Even more astonishing was their last meal at sea. Once close to the French coast, the cook still managed to produce the most delicious celebratory meal, thanks to the boat having been fitted with a large deep freeze compartment in which a good supply of excellent meat still remained.

In Bordeaux, it seemed that everyone had turned out to greet U180; even the Gestapo were there to stop anyone getting near the boat. Of course, none of the guards knew why, and the U-boat men were sweating as well because they knew full well that one bar of gold was missing. Since no one had left the boat, and one bar weighed at least 40 kilograms, it was obvious that none of the sailors had appropriated it, but finding it was not easy either and in the end it was discovered because there was no other place that it could be. It lay submerged in the blackest mixture of whatever stank deep down in the bilges.

As far as further operations were concerned, U180 was dead. Even if someone had wanted to take the boat to sea, the engines would not have lasted very long and the chain of other serious faults made it necessary to give the hulk a complete refit. This took the best part of a year and it was on 24 August 1944, after D-Day, that the boat eventually left as a newly converted submarine tanker with snorkel under the command of OLzS Rolf Riesen. It did not get very far: it seems likely that it struck a mine only a couple of days after leaving harbour. There were no survivors from the crew of fifty-six.

CHAPTER 9

U195 – The Other Type with Motor Torpedo Boat Engines

The following account is based on material compiled by Franz Berger, U195's diesel mechanic, helped by Matthias Brünig (1WO) and Günther Neumann (radio operator).

U195 was one of two Type IXD1 U-boats built with six Daimler-Benz 20-cylinder diesel engines, which were replaced after the first operational cruise by two Germania 6-cylinder diesels. Most of the other features were similar to the Type IXD2. During the early stages of training, it was necessary for boats to run at several speeds along measured miles. These were marked by buoys in the water and by lining up two markers on the land so that accurate figures for engine revolutions and speed could be obtained. This most definitely confirmed that U195 and U180 of Type IXD1 were the fastest U-boats in the German fleet, with speeds in excess of 22 knots. Unfortunately, as mentioned previously, the engines also produced so much black smoke when running fast that it would have been difficult if not impossible to stalk unsuspecting targets.

It was eight o'clock on 20 March 1943 when U195 cast off from the passenger ship *St Louis* in Kiel's naval dockyard. This ocean-going giant, belonging to HAPAG of Hamburg, had been put out of business by the war and like many other huge liners now served as an accommodation ship. U195 stopped off briefly in southern Norway to top up fuel while the men inside stumbled over vast heaps of provisions. Constant pitching and rolling showed that some items had not been stacked properly, while other packages frequently got in the way, so a few adjustments were necessary before heading west into the 'Rose Garden' – a name derived from the thorns rather than the beauty of the flowers. On this occasion there was hardly any contact with enemy forces as U195 sailed into a full-scale hurricane with no holds barred. Everybody who did not have to be up remained in their bunks, large numbers were seasick, and the bow protruded out of the water so often that the speed indicator failed to register anything because there was no water washing past the outside sensor. Despite the chaos of cargo breaking loose and tumbling along the main passageway, water cascading down the conning tower and general bedlam, the second watch officer LzS Heinz Walter would not be put off from climbing up to the bridge to shoot the sun and stars whenever visibility allowed. From this the men knew that they were making only slight headway of about 20 nautical miles per day against the storm. Despite the carnage inside the boat, the storm did bring a few advantages inasmuch as there were no interruptions from enemy forces and U195 reached calmer waters without having experienced the ferocity of depth charges. Men who have undergone this ordeal have said that there is nothing more frightening, and it is impossible to describe the effect of a serious depth charge attack in words.

It was obvious that U195 would head south once clear of the United Kingdom, but nobody onboard knew exactly where they were going. The extra large pile of charts, including almost the entire globe except the South Pole and the west coast of North America, gave no indication of a possible destination. The journey times to operations areas had become so long that there was no point in giving commanders specific verbal instructions. Instead they were sent to sea and then had the latest intelligence and exact details of where to go broadcast from the land-based U-boat Command's Operations Room. Sadly for them, this was happening at a time when Bletchley Park was starting to read radio signals faster than the Germans and therefore had ample of warning not only of who was going where but also of when the boats were likely to arrive. Long distance aircraft from the RAF were already establishing themselves at vital points, and both the South Atlantic and the Indian Ocean provided ideal flying conditions for spotting submarines. The results were deadly, but not in Germany's favour.

The message 'MAKE FOR SOUTH ATLANTIC AND INDIAN OCEAN' came through U195's radio at the same time as the news that the commander had been promoted to the rank of *Korvettenkapitän*. Heinz Buchholz was, and still is, a bit of an enigma, but he was a likeable chap from the small town of Goldap in East Prussia, a good way east of the capital Königsberg (now Kaliningrad). This idyllic area consists of undulating hills rising out of either swamps or lakes. Buchholz was born in 1909, making him a good deal older than the majority of U-boat men, and had served as watch officer in three U-boats and commander of U24 and U15 before becoming an instructor at the Torpedo School in Flensburg. He was chief of the First U-Flotilla for a few months and was then given command of U195. The quality he brought with him for this posting was one of patience rather than going in for a quick kill. He died in February 1944 as commander of U177, a Type IXD2, whilst on his way to the Indian Ocean.

Calmer waters had been reached by U195 when the lookouts spotted a target illuminated by the day's last rays of sunshine. Unable to run the diesel engines at fast speed without that irritating black exhaust cloud, Buchholz waited until it was dark before approaching and when he got nearer he saw a fully illuminated passenger ship making for Portugal. Now, suddenly, the boot was on the other foot and he had to extract himself without being seen. Although the vessel was neutral, there was no guarantee that the position of the U-boat would not be advertised. Some days later, the men spotted another target, one that was obviously zigzagging and therefore had to belong to the enemy. The sinking of the 7,200 grt *James W Denver* on 12 April 1943 was followed by the 'Crossing the Line' ceremony on 25 April. It was a magnificently clear day with calm seas when the crew assembled on the upper deck to be cleansed of the dirt from the northern hemisphere. Following this, U195 ran into a ship approaching so fast that the majority of other U-boats would have had no hope of catching it, but Buchholz decided to try out the power of his motor torpedo boat engines and waited until after dark, when he hoped the black exhaust fumes would not be seen. This was not quite so straightforward because the sun was nowhere near setting, making it necessary to run alongside the target for several hours before starting an attack. The boat had to remain so far away that only the tips of the masts remained in view. What was even more unsettling was that the rear lookouts reported seeing a few sharks following, definitely a sign that they should not stop for the crew to have a swim. Submarines always presented a few surprises and U195 was no exception.

Having dealt with this target, the men spotted another one a few days later while cruising with only one engine. Buchholz jumped up to the top of the conning tower and immediately ordered the other five engines to be turned on. Diesel engines of the period were temperamental at the best of times and often required a considerable vocabulary of technical naval language before they did what was demanded of them. On this occasion they were cold enough to require some extra coaxing before they started running. Whatever the mechanics might have done, perhaps by being a little too generous on the gas lever, the engines erupted with their normal thunder and announced that they were on by sending a huge black cloud high into the sky. Whether this was spotted or not will probably never be known, because the target did not react until a torpedo hit it around midnight. This had not yet subsided when shells started flying over the conning tower. The target had some impressive artillery with the crew wide awake and their shooting so accurate that U195 immediately dropped into the cellar. Before leaving the surface the men noticed that the freighter was turning towards the U-boat, possibly with a view to ramming it. Later it was confirmed that this was the 6,797 grt *Cape Neddick*. It managed to escape and reach Walvis Bay for temporary repairs before making for Cape Town with its better dockyard facilities.

Above and below: The 'Crossing the Line' ceremony. Triton and his staff have come on board to cleanse the dirty northerners before entering southern waters.

It was necessary for U195 to withdraw as well. The engines also required a little attention. One had been out of action for a while and it looked as if the others would soon follow if they did not receive a decent talking to. Once in less frequented waters, the engineers discovered that the fault had not been built in by Daimler-Benz but was due to some leaking valves. Theoretically this should have presented the majority of men with some time off from normal duties, because the chief mechanic called on the commander personally to ask him not to consider any practice activities and definitely no emergency dive training while that one dead engine was lying as a heap of parts on the floor. It would have been too easy to send all the small bits rolling into the filthy bilges, and finding them again among tins of black bread would have taken a long time. The lookouts were not particularly happy while this was going on. Instead of the enjoyable warmth they had got used to, they were now surrounded by one shower after another and in between it looked a little like a cold sauna with a clammy mist penetrating even into the rain gear.

It has been said before that there were always surprises at sea and this was no exception. A few days later, the commander asked the duty officer if he could smell anything. Somewhere on land someone was having a barbecue, making it possible to smell food being cooked on a wood fire. The commander, who had 8 x 60 night glasses while the lookouts used 7 x 50 binoculars, immediately searched the horizon for land while the navigator confirmed that they were at least 15 miles from the coast. Weird things happen at sea. The chief engineer, KK (Ing.) Otto Elwert, made a contribution by saying that it was time to go back home if they wanted to reach France with what they had left in the fuel bunkers. This was just as well, because the calm air of the drifting smoke from the barbecue was quickly replaced by something far more ferocious, but the storm did not last too long.

As usual, a radio signal announcing that a boat was heading for home caused administrative cogs to grind into action. On this occasion U195 received a signal saying it was to meet up with U178 under KK Wilhelm Dommes with a view to taking a sick seaman back home. Around this time it also occurred to the men that one of the lookouts had been a fully qualified baker before volunteering to join the navy; therefore *Matrosenobergefreiter* (Leading Seaman) Kratz was excused duties whenever necessary to bake some highly delicious bread, much superior to the tinned black bread, and a replacement lookout was always found very quickly. The men were unanimous in saying that the bread and their Austrian cook, Leopold Widtmann from Vienna, were chiefly responsible for maintaining morale under these long monotonous periods at sea. Poldi, as he was called, was versatile enough to allow men with birthdays to choose the menu, and on most occasions everyone seemed to opt for his *Kaiserschmarrn*, a kind of special pancake, pulled apart during cooking and with dried fruit added, commonly served in the Alps.

U178 coming into port with victory pennants fluttering from the extended attack periscope.

It was the monotony of daily life, of being incarcerated in such a small confined space that was most difficult. For most of the time everything ran exactly as the day before and most of the men hardly ever saw the sky. However, something out of the ordinary did happen from time to time. One of those occasions was when a few test shots were fired with the 37 mm deck gun. Normally it pointed towards the conning tower, so it was advisable to turn it a little before using live ammunition. Moving it was pretty hard work, although everything worked well until it came to rotating the gun back into its parking position. Whatever the men did, nothing moved the barrel. It stood pointing out sideways until someone tied a rope to the end and pulled with the hydraulic capstan mounted on the bow. This was strong enough to haul the anchor as well and a little extra oil helped to do the trick. The gun was wriggled a bit until the oil penetrated to get it working again.

In many ways the men were passing through such idyllic situations that they almost forgot that there was a war on somewhere. The days were crystal clear, with the sun providing spectacular displays at dawn and dusk, and the sea was so devoid of any action that Buchholz often remained on the surface at these critical lighting times when aircraft could pounce out of the bright light. At night the boat created such fascinating fluorescence that small groups of men were allowed up to the top of the conning tower to watch the amazing spectacle. The calm surroundings presented a misleading picture; worrying news came through the radio. The boat had been at sea for a considerable

U154 with 37 mm quick firing gun
just aft of the conning tower.

period, having left in March 1943. It was now May, and boat after boat sent
serious reports of being under attack. At the same time a good number of
others failed to respond when the U-boat Command asked them to report
their positions. It was a grim period for the Germans. Black May was biting
hard and men as far away as the Indian Ocean were feeling the pain.

It was not too long before U195 also felt the presence of the air force in
southern waters. First, the boat met up with U193 under KK Hans Pauckstadt.
Being some three years younger than Buchholz, it was his duty to come on
board to discuss how the two boats were going to return home in the face of
such a strong threat from the air. He had a similar comfortable and easy-going
attitude to Buchholz, and both men agreed that everyone would continue to
eat the vitamin pills especially designed to help lookouts with their eyesight
and, at the same time, the first boat to detect the presence of radar with
its special detector was to hoist a green flag so that both boats could dive
simultaneously. This worked well, except that the air force was considerably
faster than the men had thought and one of the first emergency dives resulted
in the upper deck being shot to pieces. At the same time, *Matrosengefreiter*
(Able Seaman) List fell over board, just at that critical period when it was
no longer possible to halt the diving process. U195 was already running at
high speed and could not break off or turn to save the man. It was a painful

Matrosengefreiter Robert Ruste was always in a good mood, even when dealing with the filthiest of jobs. He came on board without having finished his basic U-boat training and as a result was punished occasionally when he did not follow the rules, but he never faltered and could always be relied upon to give his best.

case of going deep and on surfacing again it was of vital importance that one of the shot-through jumping wires on the stern be fastened in such a way that it could not wrap itself around the propellers before dealing with the man overboard routine. Heaving the heavy steel cable back on board was no easy matter. *Matrosengefreiter* Baensch was thrown overboard in the process, but the first watch officer, OLzS Matthias Brünig, reacted so quickly that he managed to pull him back on board without using a rope.

Arriving in the Gironde Estuary also presented considerable excitement. The water was not deep enough to dive, so a vast number of men were allowed on deck while a mine-detonating freighter sailed in front, accompanied by a minesweeper while a Ju 52 with a huge impressive ring for finding magnetic mines flew overhead. It was good that the escort was there, because the minesweeper hit a mine and there was only just enough time to beach it in shallow water. Dr Reuter, U195's medical officer, was immediately taken over by rubber dinghy to help with the wounded while U195 continued its journey upstream to Bordeaux. It was a strange anticlimax after such a long period at sea. The men talked a little about their aspirations for the future, enjoying a last meal together before dispersing to other duties. Many of them were deeply worried about what was happening at home. Much of this news had not penetrated through to the Indian Ocean, but now among friends they discovered that the Allied air forces had launched a massive bombing campaign, and those men with families in the areas affected by bombing raids were deeply worried. The only news from home was stale, and for the vast majority there was no way of getting current information by telephone. Now U195 was going to remain in dock for some time to have new engines fitted, so there were opportunities for the crew to go on well-earned leave.

CHAPTER 10

At the Receiving End – Torpedoes, Depth Charges and Mines

A diving submarine left the surface with a graceful curve, slid down at an angle and then levelled off again with another curve at the bottom, following a path similar in shape to a children's playground slide. If the boat accidentally went down at too steep an angle, then there was a great danger of it not being able to level off and the boat could plunge into the depths, never to return to the surface. Bearing in mind that a man walking from one end of a dived submarine to another could upset the trim or balance, then it is not too difficult to see that the correct settling of a submerged boat in the water was no easy matter.

This process of leaving the surface and levelling off in the depths required a downward distance of about 80 metres. This became a standard depth that all U-boats dived to and was identified as 'A' in Germany. Once at a depth of 80 metres it was necessary for the chief engineer to confirm that he had the boat under control, although often it was not necessary for him to do anything because it was obvious to all in the central control room. In an emergency he had another 120 metres of safe depth below him to wrestle with the controls in order to catch the boat and stop it plummeting deeper into the depths. Once the dived boat was under control, there were no problems in taking it deeper or performing any other manoeuvres. Going to periscope depth from the surface often required the same procedure. First a dive to 'A' and then, if the boat was under control, the chief engineer would use the hydroplanes for going back up top. Although the gauges recorded the water depths from the surface, for operational purposes U-boats usually recorded their depth from the levelling-off point of 80 metres. So 100 metres became A+20 and 60 metres A-20, and this original German system has been used in this book to capture the flavour of the times.

Periscope depth was not measured in metres but by a manometer in which a column of liquid moved along the side of a diagram showing the top of the conning tower with the extended periscope. The liquid in the tube indicated the outside water level. Submarines did not often rise out of the depths by blowing compressed air into their diving tanks, although this features in many books. The standard procedure was to use hydroplanes for taking the boat as high as possible. This was usually when the upper, outside, deck was close to the surface and the top of the conning tower was a few metres higher. At this stage the diesel engines were started and the exhaust fumes used to blow the water out of the diving tanks. This had the advantage of conserving compressed air and it reduced the risk of fire if shot at.

During August 1943, U170, a Type IXC/40, patrolled the Brazilian coast under the command of KL Günther Pfeffer and after that went on another mission to the area around Bermuda and the Bahamas before returning to Lorient in May 1944, just a few days before D-Day. There she was fitted with a snorkel and given a new commander, OLzS Hans-Gerold Hauber. On 1 August 1944, U170 left for the Freetown area of Africa. On the way back she was ordered to relieve a weather boat, but did not stay in this position for very long. Reporting a passing convoy, she was ordered to attack it.

At around midnight, at the beginning of 26 October 1944, U170 rose to the surface and continued running at snorkel depth until the second watch came on duty at 04.00 hours. There was a moderate north-westerly wind of force three with an almost calm sea and, being some distance west of northern Spain, conditions were comparatively comfortable with so little enemy interference that the boat surfaced shortly afterwards. Such moments of calm were always welcomed for getting rid of any unwanted rubbish and emptying the various buckets used when the men could not get into the heads. Shortly before 07.00 hours, U170 dived again. During the last 24 hours the boat had covered 28 nautical miles on the surface and 56 submerged, a considerable difference compared with earlier times. While travelling to Brazil just a little more than a year earlier, the boat managed somewhere in the region of at least 100 nautical miles on the surface each day.

Snorkeling was difficult at the best of times and exceedingly painful when the operators got it wrong or when the water washed over the head valve to shut off the air supply. Hirschfeld described his experiences of snorkeling. He, at least, experienced this first in Norway, in an area not frequented by enemy aircraft. U170 had its snorkel fitted in France and the crew had to try it out for the first time in the ferocity of the dangerous Bay of Biscay. He said that the experience of the air being sucked out by the diesel engines seemed to drive men insane and led some to try the most absurd tricks for finding air. Hirschfeld, for example, started opening drawers and lockers, hoping air might come out. When the punishment continued for a while, the ears became painful, some men found that the fillings in their teeth jumped out, and some had bleeding noses. In all, it was a most unpleasant experience and exceedingly painful when things did not go quite right.

The monotony of remaining submerged by day and extending the snorkel at night continued the next day and the day after that. The second watch had just taken up positions on 28 October when the diesel engines were shut down to sweep the surroundings with the sensitive sound detection gear. Although periscopes were manned during the snorkeling procedure, their field of vision was so limited that the duty officer could not see very far, so it was also necessary to shut off the engines in order to listen for any other noises in the vicinity. This sound detection gear could detect ships too far away for lookouts to see them from the top of the conning tower, so was very effective. Snorkeling stopped at 07.23 and shortly after that the sound detector picked up a heavy drone almost straight ahead; U170 crept quietly up to periscope depth but there was nothing to see. Propeller noises were slightly different, and it was difficult to establish the cause of the interference. The noise even moved around but without the men being able to draw any definite conclusions. The interruption lasted on and off until 13.22 hours when both the noise and the view through the periscope confirmed there was a zigzagging destroyer some 2 kilometres away. A torpedo was shot and U170 dropped exceedingly quietly down to A+50. This was necessary because the new acoustic torpedoes (T5 or *Zaunkönig*) could turn and home in on the boat that fired them. There was no guarantee that they would make for the intended target. Strangely, nothing could be heard other than water gushing past the sound detectors in the bow, and U170 moved up to periscope depth. A few minutes later no one needed a sensitive sound detector to hear a deafening explosion. This was followed by absolute silence. The annoying noise had gone without it having been identified. The U-boat went down to A⊠30 to wait for whatever was on the surface to fade away but in doing so picked up more curious noises. Once again nothing could be seen through the periscope. A little later a destroyer was spotted and shortly afterwards another one appeared. Then, suddenly, the commander spotted a big dream prize, an aircraft carrier of the HMS *Illustrious* type. Unfortunately for U170, it moved away, making it impossible to target, and the rest of the day passed in silence with the usual routine. At 21.00 hours, the snorkel was extended again, the boat was ventilated and the batteries charged. Slowly the crew dropped back into their boring but at least peaceful routine without abhorrent interruptions from weird noises punctuating the deep snoring of off-duty men.

The strange thing about this encounter was that whatever was near the receiving end of that torpedo explosion of a few days ago did not seem to have taken much notice of the U-boat. A few days later more noises were heard, this time accompanied by what the men called a circular saw. It is likely that no one in U170 at the time knew what it was and even if they did, it still came over as frightening. It was a special noise-making device or 'foxer' towed some distance behind vulnerable escorts in order to attract acoustic torpedoes. The U-boat remained in the depths, taking the occasional peep through the periscope, and by lunchtime of 31 October found that the weird combination of different buzzing sounds intermingled with propeller noises was a convoy of more than twenty ships. Taking the risk to push the periscope a little higher, it was still impossible to see the far end. There were too many ships to count in the brief time allowed for leaving the periscope sticking up into the air.

The difficulty was that merchant ships were surrounded by a large ring of escorts enclosing the convoy in a chain of Asdic impulses, and it was necessary to take on the nearest one in order to create a gap to break through. The procedure was the same as before: shoot an acoustic torpedo in the general direction of the noise and then dive to A+20. The boat had hardly levelled out when everyone heard that characteristic pinging of the Asdic detector nearby. The U-boat had been found. The problem with all sound detecting jobs was that the results depended very much on the skill of the operator, and even when both equipment and the human ear were working perfectly there would always be considerable interference cause by differences in salinity and in water temperatures. So the results were not always clear-cut and there was a little hope that the distance between the target and Asdic set was too long for echoes to return to the receiver. However, this did not appear to be the case on this occasion. A deafening explosion right on top of the boat announced dramatically that something had crept up quietly without having been noticed. The result was frightening. Everything shook. The lights went out. The manometers with their glass tubes burst and various machines gave up the ghost. Even more frightening was a distinct sound of water squirting into the dark interior. The deep diving gauge remained operational and indicated that the hull was sinking rapidly, leaving the men inside in a dire predicament. If they were to blow the tanks, the boat would rise like a cork and bounce about helplessly on the surface. Such a process could not be reversed once it had been started, so the blowing of tanks was a measure of last resort. Luckily the chief engineer kept his cool. He maintained his grip on the situation by blowing only one diving cell and using the ballast pump to remove the water from the interior. At this stage the men were hit by the unexpected. Something dropped onto the outside deck with a loud clang. The immediate reaction was that this had to be a depth charge set for greater depths and immediately put any thought of going any deeper out of the question.

Having halted the downward movement, it became obvious that the Asdic had caught the boat again and the escort on the surface was moving in for another set of big bangs. Once again a terrific explosion shattered the men, causing the boat to drop down into the depths. This time the huge ballast pump in the central control room failed to push the inrushing water out again and it was not until someone looked at the emergency depth gauge that they saw the boat had dropped down to 2A+45 or just a little over 200 metres. This was deep but not yet critical. Everybody knew that the boat would go a little deeper before being crushed by the surrounding water pressure. However, the central control room now resembled a metal merchant's scrap yard and a report from the forward torpedo room indicated that the depth gauges there were indicating 2A+70 or 230 metres. The boat was obviously still sinking slowly. The hydroplanes were adjusted electrically from the central control room and there was also a manual system worked by the same operator standing up and turning a huge wheel if the electrical power failed. If this was broken as well, then there was another set of controls with the necessary dials in the bow and stern compartments. These positions were manned during any submerged action. Now came the question of what to do next. Going much deeper was not advisable, so the men tried blowing some more tanks and using the electric motors to increase speed so that the hydroplanes would bite to help the boat rise. It worked. The gauges quivered violently as the needles turned to indicate U170 had gone up to A+40. This was quite miraculous because the boat had taken some 10 tons of water on board.

The curious point was that the enemy somehow lost interest, leaving U170 in peace to nurse its wounds. This left Hauber with enough time to make a list of the damage:

a. Upper (Outside) Deck
Ventilation duct buckled
Diesel air supply, both port and starboard leaking
Snorkel and exhaust pipes leaking
Various valves leaking
Exhaust pipe torn open
Air outlet for diving tank 7 torn
Snorkel has been moved slightly so that the upper fitting no longer meets the bracket at the top of the conning tower
Storage containers for rubber dinghies torn open
Two munitions containers dented
Linkage for the exhaust seals broken
Torpedo aiming device can't be rotated

b. Central Control Room
Half of the diving, regulation and water tanks torn open
Control valves for the high pressure air system broken or fallen off
A lot of screws and nuts have come loose or been torn out
Voice pipes to the top of the conning tower cannot be sealed properly
Magnetic compass not working
Sky periscope completely out of action
Attack periscope doesn't work very well
The connections to compressed air groups 2 and 5 leaking
Echo sounder broken

c. Diesel

Several welding seams for a variety of systems have been split

Port diesel clutch rattles

Emergency oil pump broken

Emergency cooling water pump broken

Further damage to pipes of the cooling water system and the engine oil system

d. Electric Motors

Ventilation duct for the battery torn open

Rudder position indicator broken

Engine telegraph broken

Revolution counter broken

Fresh water still broken

Various switches no longer working

U123, on the left, meets U138, a small Type IID under KL Wolfgang Lüth, in the Baltic during the summer of 1940. The sky or navigation periscope towards the left and the attack periscope, with the smaller head lens towards the right, are both partly raised. Ammunition for the 105 mm quick firing deck gun was stored below the radio compartment and had to be carried up a vertical ladder to the top of the conning tower, then down the ladder towards the rear (right) of the conning tower and along the slippery and narrow deck to the gun crew.

The stern of an ocean-going U-boat with 37 mm quick firing gun having suffered considerable damage as a result of having been fired without first removing the watertight seal at the end. Such incidents were usually accompanied by several serious injuries to the gun crew.

Now comes the interesting part of the whole experience. There was something decidedly strange about this chain of events: that second blast could not have come from the destroyer on the surface. The men argued that an escort would have dropped more than just a single depth charge. So where did that single explosion come from? It was just one single, well-placed explosion so close that the boat almost did not survive. At the time there was enough chaos, injuries and repairs that there was no time to reflect and no one said anything, but as time passed Hauber had that spine-chilling thought that this had been his own torpedo. He had fired a T5 anti-destroyer torpedo shortly before the detonation in difficult circumstances. First, he was set to fire from one of the bow tubes but the zigzagging induced him to abandon this plan and use one of the rear tubes instead. Thinking this through carefully, he wondered whether the settings for the bow tube had been transferred to the stern without making any allowances for the different angles. What neither he nor the U-boat Command knew until long after the war was that the German acoustic torpedoes had a major intrinsic fault. The vast majority did not hit the target. Instead they detonated some distance behind it, sometimes blowing the propellers off escorts but not sinking them. So Hauber's hypothesis could well have been correct. He wrote in his log that it was strange that there was only one detonation. Surely an escort on the surface would have dropped more than one depth charge? Later, back on the surface for a damage assessment, the men found some high-quality steel embedded in the upper deck. This must have come from something more expensive than a depth charge and could well have been from a torpedo. The men in both the bow and stern torpedo compartments heard noises shortly before the detonation, suggesting something with an engine was closing in at speed. Various machines running in the central control room prevented this almost silent sound from being heard. So it could well be that U170 was lucky in having survived an explosion from its own torpedo.

To add to the men's frustration, the U-boat Command asked for more weather reports and when these were transmitted there was no reply, suggesting they had not been heard. The French ports were already in a delicate situation by this time, bearing in mind it was now the beginning of November, almost six months after D-Day. Unable to go there, U170 continued northwards, to arrive in Flensburg on 4 December 1944.

On 27 June 1942, U171, a standard Type IXC under the command of KL Günther Pfeffer, left Kiel for the Gulf of Mexico. Coming out of the Baltic training grounds and making for the turbulent North Atlantic was not easy for the majority of the crew, but they rode the uneasy waters without trouble and refuelled from U460 (KL Friedrich Schäfer) to arrive at their destination without any great conflict other than the battle against the natural elements. The North Atlantic is cold and inhospitable at the best of times, even in summer, and the Gulf of Mexico was excruciatingly hot, making many of the young men on board wonder what they had let themselves in for. Just living in temperatures reaching the mid-forties Celsius was a real torture, with water constantly dripping off the walls so that all the men could do was to sit on towels. Theoretically they were allowed to undress completely only when washing, naval regulations stating quite firmly that swimming trunks or shorts and a shirt had to be worn at all other times. Many boats seem to have ignored this and allowed men to go about stripped to the waist, but commanders insisted that men on the top of the conning tower should be covered for most of the time to prevent sunburn and many boats even carried a good number of tropical helmets to protect those who had to be out and about under a hot sun.

The waters around America turned out to be more cruel than other distant regions inasmuch that there were too many surprises in the air to allow the men time off to swim or wash on deck. This was usually done either by just stopping the engines so that men could jump overboard or the bow diving tanks were partially flooded to the point where water washed over the front

A lookout with special sun sector sunglasses and cork tropical helmet.

part of the upper deck. Some boats went as far as building their own showers by connecting a fire hose to a pump and allowing the water to cascade down from the conning tower. Men of the First World War fared a little better because the first U-boat to cross the Atlantic, the unarmed freighter *Deutschland* under *Kapitän* Paul König had some of the cargo containers along both sides of the hull and it was easy to take the lids off a few, allow them to fill with water and use them as washtubs or tiny swimming pools. This made it unnecessary to stop or slow down. So, perhaps, one can say that the *Deutschland* was the first U-boat with a swimming pool on board. (König was a member of the merchant navy, not the *Kaiserliche Marine*, and therefore his rank did not have the military suffix '*zur See*'.)

The mouth of the mighty Mississippi delta was patrolled by U171 before she travelled on as far as Texas, sinking three ships in the process. This was not the type of bag required for even keeping pace with the numbers under construction, and looking back at these events with hindsight one wonders whether the great efforts and sacrifices made by the men were worth it. Before breaking through the more dangerous waters of the Bay of Biscay, U171 was refuelled from U461 (KK Wolf Stiebler), with orders to arrive in Lorient on 9 October 1942.

Fritz Müller, one of the 'lords' from the bow torpedo compartment, had just come off duty when the loud hooter was triggered to announce an attacking aircraft. The alarm bells were not rung because the water was too shallow for an emergency dive and everybody on board knew that this was going to be a case of fighting it out on the surface. Müller had hardly reached his position by the 20 mm anti-aircraft guns when the intruder was identified as a Junkers and the off-duty men trundled back slowly to their resting positions.

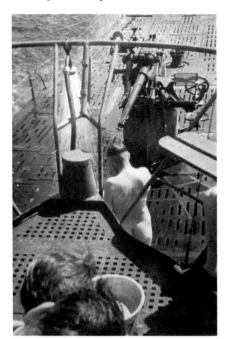

Right: A self-made shower. This merely pumped seawater onto the deck, but was very refreshing in the tropics.

Below: One of the storage containers by the side of the upper deck has been converted to serve as a bathtub.

The waves were unpleasant enough to make lying in a bunk uncomfortable so Müller found himself a hammock that allowed him to lie without being knocked against the sides. He had hardly settled down when the boat shook with terrifying noisy vibrations. The heavy iron steps up to the torpedo hatch fell off, missing him by only a few centimetres. Looking up in the darkness in the time between the lighting going out and emergency lighting coming on, he could see the hatch had been blown open by the explosion. Coming to his senses he noticed that the ladder had come close enough to tear his shirt but it had missed his body. His guardian angel was definitely working overtime.

Feeling around, Müller realised that all was not well with his back. There was some pain, but at that moment he was more concerned with the floor. It seemed to have jumped up and was not where it usually was. No one knew whether this had been a bomb, a torpedo hit or a mine. A torpedo hit seemed most likely because just a few hours earlier U171 had gone into an avoidance manoeuvre to get out of the way of a submarine lurking in the deeper water outside Lorient. Seeing the hatch open, Paul Ziska climbed through it onto the upper deck and Müller scrambled up after him to watch him make his way towards the conning tower. Müller had hardly stuck his head out when water washing over the deck flushed him back into the bow torpedo room. Hatches were designed to close on their own when this happened, so other than get a surprise, terribly wet and a few more bruises, all Müller had to do was to screw the locking mechanism shut to prevent the sea from flooding in. However, on this occasion this did not help. Water was flooding in from somewhere else and all the men could do was to take refuge on the upper bunks. Sitting on them, they soon found their feet dangling in the rising water. Everything seemed strange, almost as if it was a dream.

The hatch in the pressure-resisting bulkhead was open, so the men could see that there was no one along the corridor leading to the central room. The hatch at the far end, before the central control room, was closed, so it was impossible to know what was happening on the other side. There were no orders and the big question that needed answering was whether the boat had dived or whether it had sunk. The men wondered if there was still someone in control. These deliberations came to an abrupt halt when the boat crashed into the bed of the sea, confirming that it must have sunk rather than gone down in a controlled dive. While everyone made a thorough examination of their own body to see why they were hurting, one of the petty officers established that they were at a depth of about 60 metres.

Despite the chaos everyone remained calm, sitting on the upper bunks and coming to terms with the increasing pressure. They felt a little easier when the water stopped rising. At that point a teapot came floating past and each man splashed it a little so that it would continue on its journey to the forward end of the compartment. Reflex reactions in the men also ensured that the majority had put on their escape apparatus, the so-called Dräger lung, which should have contained enough oxygen for 15 minutes or so. One man did not have one and another found that his did not contain any oxygen. So, strange as it might sound, some of the men scrambled down to bring up a few spare lungs from below the bottom bunks. Everything went exactly as the men had practised during training, and they felt proud of their small achievement in proving that their escape apparatus was working properly.

Getting out was now becoming a bit of a problem. The men had screwed the hatch shut but they were unable to open it again – the water pressure on the outside was still too strong. Luckily there was a torpedo man onboard with enough experience to take the lead in what was to come. Müller reported that there was dead silence in the compartment; no one groaned, cried or moaned. During this deadly hush, in which everyone was left alone with their own thoughts and the knowledge that they would probably die during the next few minutes, the telephone rang. The torpedo tubes in which it was located were now well submerged, so it was necessary to dive down to find the handset. The message from the central control room was that there were only six men there and they would try to surface by blowing the tanks. This turned out to be just wishful thinking. Nothing much happened. As time passed, it became obvious that there was no way out. The U-boat was lying on the seabed without any hope of help for the stricken men. They shook hands, thinking this was the final farewell, when someone struck upon the idea of opening the torpedo tube flooding system so that more water would pour in to possibly equalise the pressure before everyone ran out of air.

The men did eventually manage to undo the locking mechanism of the hatch. It burst open with a loud bang and water poured down, forcing everyone from their sitting positions on the upper bunks. It was necessary to grab hold of something to prevent them from being washed away. No one wanted to end up at the far end by the torpedo tubes from where it would be more difficult to get out. Müller was conscious of hearing screams as the water gushed in. Opening his eyes again, he became aware of a painful if bearable burning, but it was necessary to find the hatch. It looked as if some men had the mouthpieces from their escape apparatus pulled out and were now drifting through the dim light. Müller could see a shadowy slow swimming motion ahead of him. It was a moment of weird fear. At one stage he had his nose clip torn off, but it was attached with a piece of string and he found it again and replaced it. As he did so, he felt a burning sensation in his lungs and added some more oxygen from the cylinder inside his air bag.

Müller did eventually get out and found himself on the surface, having hit his head against the net deflector wire running from the bow to the top of the conning tower. While still fighting for air and unsure where he was in relation to the surface, he found his breathing getting considerably more difficult. Making use of what he had learnt on his U-boat induction course, he was eventually able to control his breathing reasonably well, except that he also gulped down a mouthful of water. The first reaction was to spit or to blow it out, but in a flash he remembered that this would result in a corrosive potash solution forming inside the tin used to remove carbon dioxide. This tin was located inside the air bag of the escape apparatus and getting this liquid into the body would be deadly. So instead of spitting it out, he swallowed it and continued breathing with some difficulty. Once on the surface he found a colleague who had experienced the same thing but had spat the water into the escape apparatus bag. He died in some discomfort some half an hour later. Seeing the sky, Müller realised he had survived the sinking, but in his joy forgot to close the tap in the mouthpiece so that the air in the apparatus escaped and he had to inflate it again before using it as life jacket.

A large freighter used as mine detonator and a minesweeper had already been alongside for some time, picking up survivors as Müller appeared on the surface and it was not too long before they also fished him out of the water. To his surprise he still had enough strength to climb up the ladder on the side. Hot drinks, blankets and dry clothes appeared and Müller knew he was among friends who would look after him. Later they told him how they had heard the news of the sinking from the aircraft and had made for the spot as fast as they could. Apparently U171 had run onto a mine and the diesel engines were still running when the hull cascaded down into the depths. So it seemed likely that the engines sucked the air out of the rear compartment, killing everyone inside. The men received new clothes as soon as they landed, and many were surprised that Dönitz himself, the navy's Supreme Commander-in-Chief, should find time to listen to every man telling of his experience during this incredible escape. Müller went home for two weeks' leave and then reported to join a new boat, U170, in Bremerhaven.

CHAPTER 11

U178 – The First Thrust to South Africa

U-boat men coming to Bremen to learn about the technicalities of their new boats at the shipyard were initially kept at the navy's expense in hotels, military accommodation or in Deschimag AG Weser's own hostel. Hostel was really the wrong term; in fact, it was more comfortable than the majority of hotels and one was looked after very well indeed. Bremen was very much like any other large city. It was anonymous but compact and therefore easy to get around – and it still boasts one of the biggest wine cellars in the country (an ideal place for U-boat research). Having been a major seaport meant that up to the beginning of the war it had also had a notable entertainment quarter, but this had declined by the time the first very long range U-boats were laid down. Yet, apart from the irritating blackout, one hardly noticed that there was a war on. Air raids were more irksome nuisances than serious threats. Things were slightly different down by the river in Germany's biggest shipyard. Although a long way inland, the tidal Weser brought the smell of the sea and damp winds from the German Bight, making the waterfront decidedly uncomfortable. The locals went down to the riverbank on hot summer days to cool off from the oppressive heat, but in winter they avoided this windswept area.

Obermaschinisten (chief mechanics) Johann Becker (diesel engines) and Rudolf Haerle (electro-motors) were the first members of U178's crew to be appointed, as early as April 1941. The boat had been laid down on Christmas Eve 1940 but was not launched until 28 October 1941. The reason for sending these two experienced men so early was so they could modify the Operation and Safety Regulations of the Type IXC to suit this new, enlarged boat. This was quite some undertaking because not only did the machinery occupy half the boat, the engines would need to run at the most economical speeds for long periods without any back-up from shipyard maintenance personnel. It was very much a case of building the boat in such a way that as many repairs as possible could be carried out by the crew on the high seas. It was therefore

Left: Two men from U178.

Below: Men from U178 wearing U-boat overalls.

essential that experienced submarine engineers were at hand to ensure that one stage of construction was not built on top of an earlier installation in such a way that it obstructed access.

The chief engineer, Dipl.-Ing. KL (Ing.) Johannes Gottwald, did not arrive until July 1941 to lead the rest of the technical division in the boat's construction. Non-commissioned officers and other members of his team, including the torpedo mechanics and radio operators, followed in August 1941. The building yard of Deschimag AG Weser was already running beyond pre-war capacity and the normal accommodation facilities near the harbour were no longer able to put up so many men. Thus a good number were shunted into the Lloyds Hostel (Lloydsheim) where the lower ranks lived with ten men in one room and four non-commissioned officers shared a room. This hostel, built during the middle of the nineteenth century, was located in Bremen-Findorff's Admiralstrasse and had originally served as temporary accommodation for emigrants waiting to leave the country. It was subsequently converted into a youth hostel before being requisitioned by the military. Its location was several miles from the shipyard, far too long to walk, so a special tram was laid on to take the men to work and to bring them home again in the evening. Breakfast was provided in the hostel, and for lunch the men had to make their own way to what was once a dance hall that had been converted into a military canteen. This was located in Lindenstrasse, close to the shipyard.

The Type IXD2 boats were fitted with a new innovation in the form of battery acid cut-off and isolation units, and since none of the men had seen these before they asked for a lesson to explain how the system worked. Batteries had already been installed by this time, so Haerle requested special permission for the men to see this in action inside the narrow confines of the battery compartment. This was by no means straightforward because the gases given off by the batteries, already in use, were highly explosive and it was essential that the shipyard workers knew what was going on. In fact the regulations regarding entry to this space were so strict that special permission had to be asked from the chief engineer before any member of the crew could open the hatches leading down to the battery compartments. The space there was so limited that two sledges on rails had to be rolled along above the batteries with a man lying on top. He was supplied with a miner's type of headlamp so that both his hands were free for the necessary maintenance work.

The plan for the lesson was for Haerle and *Maschinenmaat* (petty officer mechanic) Hans Bandy to demonstrate to men looking in through the open hatch of the warrant officers' quarters. For some reason, the shipyard staff had switched off the battery ventilators too early that day and a spark, created when Haerle's headlamp was switched on, caused an enormous explosion of the remaining gases in the compartment. Both of the men in the battery

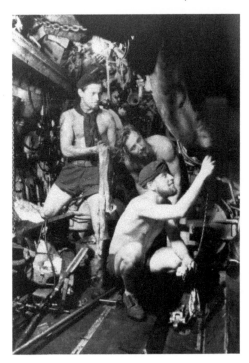

U178: a torpedo has been brought down from an external storage tube and is now undergoing a thorough overhaul to check that it is in perfect condition. The men are (from left to right): *Matrosengefreiter* Robert Rustemeyer, *Torpedomechaniker-obergefreiter* Heinrich Koch and *Torpedomechanikersmaat* Heinz Matthies.

compartment were seriously burned but were able to leave hospital after treatment. Unfortunately, some of the other men by the hatch were not so lucky and suffered considerably worse injuries. Gerhard Engelmann was so badly wounded that he was not only removed from U178's crew but was also declared unfit for further submarine service.

The crew of U178 was complete by the time the boat was commissioned on 14 February 1941. Among the men were two *Oberfähnriche* (sub-lieutenants) Dieter Bornkessel and Klaus Dönitz, the son of the U-boat chief. Klaus Dönitz had already been injured by this time and suffered from epileptic attacks. On one occasion it was only the quick thinking of the men around him that prevented him from tumbling into the water. As a result, FK Hans Ibbeken, who was on first name terms with the U-boat chief Karl Dönitz, wrote a letter requesting that his son be removed from U178. The Commander-in-Chief was a tough nut, and there was no way that any of his friends or relatives would receive favours from him. He later sent his son back into action aboard a motor torpedo boat, on which he was finally killed in May 1944. In between his appointment to U178 and the motor torpedo boat Klaus Dönitz had served as secretary aboard the accommodation ship *St Louis* in Kiel harbour. Bornkessel remained with U178 for only three months as third watch officer and was moved to another post in June 1942. By the end of the war he had commanded U2332 and U2370, both small electro-boats of Type XXIII.

U178, under KzS Hans Ibbeken, with its white swan emblem on the conning tower, running into the Bordeaux at the end of its first operational war cruise.

Although U177 was the first of its type to be launched, U178 became the first very long distance submarine to be commissioned on 14 February 1942 by Ibbeken. He was a complicated mixture of age, experience and personality – not the easiest of people to trust with secrets in thorny private situations. Born in September 1899, he was one of the oldest commanders, and his high rank also suggested that he was a little beyond the task in hand. The men did not take an instant liking to him. He had been commander of Flotilla Saltzwedel in Wilhelmshaven and at the same time flag officer for U-boats West, so some of the men wondered why he had stepped down to be in charge of a brand-new U-boat. Whatever their thoughts, none of these personal feelings interfered with the stringent training of the following weeks. The Baltic was cold, partly still frozen solid, but nothing much of importance happened. It was hard work, with little time to reflect on personal thoughts, but at least this training proved that the 'old man' seemed more than capable of doing the job he had been appointed to. He was a strict disciplinarian but fair, welding the diverse bunch of men into an efficient team.

If there were any personal problems requiring input from higher authority then the men tended to turn to Wilhelm Spahr, the first watch officer. A passionate sailor with salt water running through his veins, he had joined the navy long before 1939, and by the start of the war had risen through the ranks

Shore-based staff were usually allowed time off work to greet incoming and outgoing U-boats. Often there were enough females willing to kiss the still stinking commander, but many of the men resented this attention, some of them asking, 'Who will come and kiss us?' On the left is Hans Ibbeken, after U178's first operational cruise to the Indian Ocean.

to become the navigator cum quartermaster in U47 under Günther Prien. He was the chap who steered the boat into the Royal Navy's anchorage at Scapa Flow to sink the battleship HMS *Royal Oak* in October 1939. He had received a commission by the time he joined U178; holding the rank of *Oberleutnant zur See*, he was probably one of the most experienced officers in the entire U-boat arm. Unfortunately for the High Command, he lacked the natural killer instinct and was likely to allow humanitarian issues to influence his decision-making. This made him the life and soul of the boat, with many of the men following him blindly because they knew they were in capable hands.

The men of U178 saw little of the coming spring but did feel the warmth of summer while training, and it was late August 1942 when the boat tied up at a pier in Kiel especially set aside by the Fifth U-Flotilla for provisioning U-boats going on their first war patrol. By that time Ibbeken had been promoted to *Kapitän zur See*. On 8 September, the boat headed out to sea. It was topped up with fuel in Kristiansand, Norway, before heading west to skirt around the north of Scotland. RAF Coastal Command made its first impression on the men by giving U178 such a hammering that it continued with a definite list, but the cause, a leaking tank, was rectified before not too long and the boat continued southwards into calmer waters where there were also fewer aircraft. This incident gave the men considerable confidence because at first they had been under the impression that they would have to return to port for repairs. Everybody was exceptionally pleased when they found that they

Above: U178's first watch officer, Wilhelm Spahr, who was the life and soul of the boat and very much liked by the crew, photographed after the war.

Right: U178 with the commander, KzS Hans Ibbeken, on top of the conning tower.

could correct a serious list themselves without any input from a shipyard. They also considered themselves lucky, as another boat, U262 under KL Hans Lange, with which they had left Norway, was sunk with all hands around the time that U178 was damaged.

Nothing much happened until the men's thirty-third day at sea when the second watch was looking forward to coming off duty after a four-hour spell on the top of the conning tower. Just at that critical moment something untoward was spotted and U178 dropped into the depths while everyone rushed to action stations. It did not take long before the commander at the periscope realised that he had a giant of unexpected proportions bearing down on him. This was the sort of situation every submariner dreamed about, and many who experienced such an event found the target was just a little too fast and at too difficult an angle to tackle. So all they could do was to watch while the monster passed beyond torpedo range. This two-funnelled passenger ship was zigzagging as well, and Ibbeken was in the process of giving up when it turned directly towards him. This was a brilliant opportunity. The first torpedo was fired at 08.19 hours. Unfortunately for the Germans, the then unidentified target, the 20,119 grt *Duchess of Atholl*, had been built during the mid-1920s, when the disaster of the *Titanic* and watertight compartments was still reverberating among all marine engineers, so every torpedo tube had to be emptied before the ship went down. On the one hand, the men were delighted because it made more space in the cramped interior, but on the other it was rather a high sacrifice of valuable hitting power for just one ship.

This dramatic action took place on 10 October 1942, close to Ascension Island, some 7 degrees south of the Equator. Sadly for U178, the presence of U-boats off the Cape Town area of South Africa had already been well advertised two days earlier when U179 (KK Ernst Sobe) sank the 6,558 grt SS *City of Athens*. On this occasion the Royal Navy destroyer HMS *Active*, under Lt Cdr M. W. Tomkinson, intercepted the distress call and coincidentally ran over the top of the submerged U-boat while on the way to help survivors. The chase was simple, despite the considerable wriggling of the giant in the depths. Having been forced to the surface by some well-placed depth charges, the U-boat dived again and just at that critical moment the destroyer raised enough steam to ram the hapless opponent. Sixty-one men in U179 perished in an instant, but this gave HMS *Active* plenty of time to pick a slow path through the wreckage, collecting survivors from the *City of Athens*. It was a horrendous scene: searchlights illuminated a mass of packages, deckchairs and fragments from the ship floating on the sea like a massive carpet. On 18 September 1942, U179 had used its radio transmitter for the last time, the sinking taking place on 8 October, so the men in U178 were blissfully unaware that their companion had been lost and that the defences around South Africa were now on full alert for further intruders.

The interesting point about this encounter was that the secret Submarine Tracking Room under Rodger Winn at the Admiralty in London had forecast the presence of U-boats off Cape Town as early as the beginning of September. At that time there were still enough sceptics to think that any noteworthy encounter in those far-off waters was more likely to come from Japanese submarines than from boats that had left Europe. The men of HMS *Active* had got close enough to their target to confirm that it had not come from the Far East; instead it had the silhouette typical of the more dreaded U-boat from Germany.

So U178 found itself just over the Equator when the interior was rearranged to load torpedoes into the six empty tubes and thus make the crowded rooms in the bow and stern a little bit more comfortable. Unfortunately, things were not going too well for the men. Disagreements created by sixty men cooped up inside such a small space were common to all submarines and everyone found their own way of preserving their sanity. Now the daily grind of extreme boredom helped to upset the harmony of operations. Ibbeken had already been renamed 'Ibbo' with such poisonous pronunciation that even the officers were objecting to his presence. They could not understand why he had found it necessary to transmit three messages back to base on three consecutive days. This not only provided the enemy with an ideal means of working out the U-boat's position but also made it possible for them to calculate the course and cruising speed. The action was labelled as irresponsible and outrageous, with prophesies that they would end their days in a similar manner to the pocket battleship *Admiral Graf Spee* which had been hunted down by a number of cruisers as a result of the opposition being able to predict its destination.

Ibbeken was not the only problem. Around this time, the men also had their worst fears confirmed. A detailed inventory of the provisions consumed showed that the Fifth U-Flotilla in Kiel had seriously miscalculated and there was nowhere near enough food for the planned voyage. Each boat not only kept a record of the food loaded but also added details of where each item was stored. So each day it was possible to cross off what had been consumed and the cook could work out exactly what he had left. Ibbo had not been responsible for this, but many men attached a high proportion of the blame to him.

The basic problem was that the bread had been delivered in tins weighing 425 grams but the quantities were calculated on tins containing 700 grams, so the men were short by some 40 per cent. As a result, bread was immediately rationed to 210 grams per head per day, and biscuits, rusks and crisp bread were rationed as well, something the men were not used to at all – usually they could eat as much as they liked. Things got even worse when a thorough calculation of the remaining fresh water revealed that the men had used far greater quantities than originally planned and the water distillation plant in the central control room was not producing the quantities expected. There was therefore no alternative other than to ration drinking water to half a litre per man per day.

The shortage of food, something many U-boat men rarely experienced, was bearable inasmuch as the lack of exercise meant there was also a general lack of appetite, but negotiating the exceedingly hot tropics without adequate drinks made the men extremely miserable. The annoying thing was that there was an excessive amount of water dripping off the cool walls and everyone was constantly bathed in sweat, but none of this was of much use for drinking. The condensation off the walls tasted like oil or rust and was rejected by even the most thirst-ridden member of the crew. The torpedo mechanics had opportunities of draining off a little distilled water destined for the batteries, but this tasted so foul that honey or a little seawater had to be added to make it palatable and there was no way that anyone could do this secretly inside a submarine like U178. The bread situation improved slightly towards the end of October 1942, when U159 under KL Helmut Witte delivered another 112 tins. He also handed over a leading seaman who was too ill for the first-aider to treat, as U178 had a doctor on board who could cope with more complicated medical problems.

Fortunately for the men, the wind turned to blow from the south and brought with it grey clouds, mountainous seas, cold temperatures and a few accompanying albatrosses. No one would ever have guessed that they were

Dr Joachim Wüstenberg, medical officer of U178.

The stern of U862, a very long range Type IXD2, under Heinrich Timm.

running along the coast of what is now Namibia, which had been German South-West Africa until the end of the First World War. The storm certainly blew away all indications that the great Kalahari Desert was only a few miles to the east. No one, other than the duty watch, volunteered to go up to the top of the conning tower and smokers preferred to assemble in the commander's conning tower control room. Some enterprising chap even installed a home-made electric cigarette lighter. At this stage the radio room relayed a number of entertaining concerts from Cape Town through the boat's loudspeaker system. The music was different enough to provide welcome relief from the enforced monotony. Although there was an excellent collection of 78 rpm records on board U178, the commander having asked a music professor in Danzig to make the selection specially for this long journey, it was always good to hear something new. This was considerably better than the situation on U862, where the commander KK Heinrich Timm, a classical music enthusiast, had the selection weighted in favour of symphonies, sonatas and piano concertos. One of his crew remarked that the unbearable tropical heat was considerably less annoying than having to listen to this background drone coming through the loudspeakers.

U178's *Obersteuermann* Johannes Kunz warning his duty watch to keep their eyes open. He was the sort of bloke with a fierce bark, but was popular among the crew because everyone knew that his encouraging words were necessary if the boat was to survive.

The force 7 storm subsided as rapidly as it had appeared, with a resultant increase in temperature, and everyone inside the cramped U-boat was again thoroughly aware that they were in a hot region. It was not long before the navigator announced that they had broken a record and had now gone further south than any other U-boat. Only a few surface raiders, including the auxiliary cruiser *Atlantis* under KzS Bernhard Rogge and the *Pinguin* under KzS Ernst-Felix Krüder, had been so far south, and the legacy these ships had left behind soon came to haunt U178. Five drifting mines, probably laid by the *Atlantis*, were spotted as the U-boat rounded the Cape of Good Hope.

It was 6 a.m. on 27 October 1942 when the next significant action announced itself with a sudden flood of orders pouring from the top of the conning tower faster than the duty watch during an emergency: 'Turn on both main diesel engines. Commander to the bridge. Action stations.' (The boat had been cruising on diesel-electric drive, using the smaller powerplants to generate the necessary electricity, and starting the main engines when cold usually took several minutes when they were co-operative and a little longer when bloody-minded.)

Following this nothing much else happened, other than the nauseating chocking of the main diesels rattling into action. Twenty minutes later they were shut off again so that the boat could dive for the attack. This meant going down to about 80 metres or so, catching the best balance or trim and then using the hydroplanes to climb back up to periscope depth. The commander remained in the control room inside the conning tower while this was going on, and the Type IX boats were large enough to accommodate the action helmsman as well in that small compartment. Usually a petty officer would also be standing by to work the torpedo calculator or 'fruit machine' as it was called in the Royal Navy. Sitting on a saddle, the commander could rotate the periscope by pressing a button with either his left or right foot. The helmsman, holding onto two handles, could press one of two buttons under his wrists for turning the rudders either left or right. Obviously, he had a set of dials to indicate the exact position. The prospects this morning did not feel terribly positive and 'Petty officer standing by' definitely did not reflect the true goings-on on this occasion. The poor man was holding on for all he was worth, hoping the rolling and pitching would not throw him off balance. He was surrounded by a mass of pipes and other projections that would cause painful injuries if bumped into, and leaning against things was not that comfortable either. Everything was dripping wet due to water having cascaded through the hatch above, and it was too warm for wearing coats. In addition to being knocked about by the waves, the boat was heaving up and down, leaving the men with the feeling that one gets in one's stomach in a fast-moving lift. The majority of submarines had a few chaps who were unable to adjust to this stress on the body and often felt seasick while on the surface. The punishment was far worse than any modern fairground ride and lasted much longer.

Ibbeken was already in a bad mood, cursing the chief engineer down below in the central control room for not keeping the boat at periscope depth. Perhaps he should have aborted the attack, but his ill temper persisted for more than 30 minutes before two torpedoes were fired. Neither of them hit anything and the tenseness of the hunt continued until shortly after 10 a.m., when he ordered the two empty tubes to be reloaded. This was still going on when another ship was heard to approach. This time Ibbeken did not respond, saying there was no point in pursuing the target due to the heavy swell. The weather gods were obviously against U178 and the ship was well out of sight by the time Ibbeken had another look. Following this, the sea quickly calmed down to a mirror smooth surface, which lasted until mid-morning of the following day when the wind started increasing, with noticeable waves spluttering over the upper (outside) deck again. The ferocity of this weather attack increased until the waves were some 7-8 metres high (23-26 feet).

At that critical stage, when everyone was thoroughly fed up, another ship appeared. Ibbeken tried a different tack this time. Seeing that the vessel was running roughly the same course as the U-boat, he turned onto an identical heading to run well ahead of it while remaining just out of its sight. His idea was to keep this up until the weather improved or darkness could cover a surface attack. Again, things did not quite work out. After 3 hours or so, U178 ran into a tropical storm with the sort of bible-black colour that should be avoided at all costs. However, on this occasion it was important to remain close to the target chugging on behind. Not only was visibility cut to almost nil but the power of the downpour was so strong that the men thought warm hailstones were hitting them. What was coming down was water, with a power the men had never felt before. Luckily it did not last long and the sky quickly lightened again, but the ship had gone without leaving any indication of the direction it might be heading in. This produced a strong division among the men. Some wanted to look for it, but those with more experience knew that this would be a waste of time and fuel. In any case, conditions were far from perfect, and the beautiful tranquillity of the southern oceans typically portrayed in films seemed nothing more than fantasy.

Other than being reasonably warm, the westerly force 6 wind was now hitting the lookouts sideways on as they headed in a northerly direction through the Indian Ocean, over waves with a sea state of 8-9. The area was empty of shipping as well, as if U178 had strayed away from the main traffic lanes, and first watch officer Spahr suggested that it might be better to close in on the coast. On this occasion the proposal did not produce a negative comment from the commander, who obliged by heading in the right direction. Spahr and many of the men were for going in close to the port of Durban to aim at any worthwhile target there. However, Ibbeken was not in agreement. Part of his orders were to remain in the Indian Ocean for a long as possible and he was told that it would be better to sink a single ship occasionally in order to tie up the opposition's hunting forces and hopefully induce both Britain and the United States to divert hunters from the North Atlantic into those far-off waters.

The big problem as far as the men in U178, the U-boat Command and the Naval High Command in Berlin were concerned was that no one had the faintest idea about what was going on in the shipping lanes around South Africa. The first raiders to sail that far during the spring of 1940 had a reasonable team on board for listening to foreign broadcasts and evaluating the sparse news that reached them, but even the huge U-cruisers, like U178, had insufficient space for such far-reaching trappings. So they were literally groping in the dark and things had changed considerably since those early surface raider days. Pocket battleship *Admiral Scheer* did penetrate into the Indian Ocean under KzS Theodor Kranke during the first few months of 1941, but that was also more than a year before U178's venture. So it was very much a case of being the first U-boat to stumble blindly into unexplored regions, hoping for good fortune without much support from any intelligence back-up.

It was first light on 31 October 1942 when the African coast came into sight, but there was hardly time for everyone to climb up to the top of the conning tower to enjoy the view before an aircraft appeared out of the sun, as if coming in to attack. Strangely enough it probably was not expecting to meet a U-boat. It did not react at all, and it looked very much as if U178 had not been spotted. A short time later, when the boat resurfaced, only a couple of smoke clouds from what looked like patrol vessels burning poor quality coal were spotted. Thus, rather than enjoying the sun and studying the coast, the men spent much of the time submerged, avoiding being surprised by whatever was likely to come out of Africa. Closing in on Cape Lucia, U178 surveyed the passing traffic from down in the cellar with its highly sensitive and directional sound detectors.

This was not a bad move and produced some results, but it also sparked off another set of arguments. First, Ibbeken wanted to surface immediately after sinking the British 8,233 grt freighter *Mendoza* to discover its name, route and cargo, but an aircraft had been seen flying over it and the men in the central control room objected to such an extent that the order to surface was cancelled. This decision had only just been reached when several distant detonations indicated that countermeasures were already at sea. These were heavy enough to break a number of the glass gauges in the central control room, confirming that the decision to remain submerged had been correct.

A couple of hours later, when U178 did eventually reach the surface to ventilate the boat, the men were hit by another calamity. It proved impossible to engage one of the clutches connecting the engines to the propeller and neither muscle strength nor compressed air moved the machinery. Once again another noisy and unnecessary argument erupted, with both deck and machine watches hurling abuse at each other. It seems that the commander also lost his nerve and screamed the most offensive and foul language at the chief engineer, KL (Ing.) Johannes Gottwald. Gottwald was not only an expert in his field but was blessed with such an unnatural calm that he always seemed to maintain the same peaceful attitude, even when surrounded by the most chaotic situation. Ibbeken, realising that he had gone too far, apologised later that evening.

Eventually, when U178 reached the surface at 19.00 hours, the lookouts found a very pleasant temperature of 22 degrees Celsius and such a benign sea that the engineering division could continue tackling that problematic clutch, which was still objecting to being moved. It was now the evening of Sunday 1 November 1942, the men's fifty-fifth day at sea. Food was rationed, there was hardly any drinking water and one of the propellers could not be connected to its engine, so the general atmosphere was not the brightest, and men were looking for a scapegoat by trying to connect the chain of bad luck to some superstitious event. The idea was to find another irrational action that would perhaps put an end to the bad luck.

Almost all of the following day was spent down in the depths, wrestling with the clutch and using the appropriate sailor's vocabulary to induce movement and to find some means of bringing better fortunes. It was five o'clock in the afternoon when U178 returned to the surface. The evening meal was being served, or perhaps 'distributed throughout the boat' might be a better way of describing the procedure, when the call came, 'Ship in sight.' The duty officer, Friedrich Petran, had been jinxed for some time. Something out of the ordinary often happened when he was on duty and on this occasion Spahr did not wait for the commander to react. Instead he jumped up instantly and, without getting dressed, climbed to the top of the conning tower. Immediately he recognised that it was not a ship but two destroyers close together. Taking command, Spahr turned U178 to present the smallest possible silhouette to the approaching destruction. Diving was out of the question because they were only about 500 metres away and any disturbance on the surface might easily be spotted. It was a nail-biting situation. Extreme silence and utmost care were called for. One false move and U178 would be no more.

U-boats did not have weapons capable of tackling destroyers; all they could do was to run away. On this occasion the approaching hostile depth charges were so close and the submerged boat so slow that more than luck would be required to survive. However, U178 was not spotted and the two warships vanished almost as quickly as they had appeared. Running away on the surface at fast speed was not much of an option either. That clutch was still not showing any signs of wanting to move, which meant that the maximum speed would not be much more than about 10 knots. The engineers had not yet exhausted their vocabulary of swear words and were still cursing the machinery, but it was not until the following day, 3 November, that Gottwald announced that everything seemed to be back to normal. He then asked for permission to try a few declutching tests. Everything worked again, much to the relief of the entire crew, some of whom had already been talking about the possibility of being marooned on the African coast.

The first watch change, at 04.00 hours on 4 November, saw U178 lying at periscope depth off Lourenço Marques (now Maputo). The periscopes gave a reasonable view of the coast and although the men would have preferred to see it from the surface, they feared those interfering aircraft, which had been seen on too many occasions. The men's patience on that hot sunny day was not rewarded until shortly before midnight when a ship without neutrality markings came into sight. It went down exceedingly quickly. This time torpedo aiming and machinery functioned without a hitch. Once again there erupted a bitter battle of words, with Ibbeken wanting to surface but Spahr warning against such a move. They were too close to the coast and retribution might be quick in coming. The warning was not heeded. Ibbeken desperately wanted to know the name and details of the ship and therefore surfaced to find one of its lifeboats. This move immediately showed that the peaceful coast was not as serene as it appeared: the lookouts had hardly settled on the top of the conning tower when the terrifying whistle of shells flying overhead made them duck. It was too dark to make out who was doing the shooting, other than that the shells seemed to be coming from Portuguese waters. Without having discovered any information about its quarry U178 dived again. Post-war documents indicate that the vessel that had been sunk was the Norwegian 2,561 grt freighter *Hai Hing*.

It was shortly after lunch on the following day that everyone in U178 was called back to action stations. It was a quick hunt lasting for about 15 minutes and resulted in the British 5,244 grt freighter *Trekieve* being hit. Ibbeken gave the order to surface just two minutes later, again much to the consternation of the crew, who still had those vivid memories of aircraft flying overhead. Yet the commander was not to be put off. He wanted to know the name of the ship, its cargo and where it was making for. This time the rumblings down below were not so quiet and no one was left in any doubt that the men considered this to have been a careless and outrageous decision with a total lack of conscience. It was now common knowledge that many of them felt that either the commander was replaced or the men would leave at the next opportunity. Spahr did a lot to calm the situation and at least managed to get Ibbeken to agree to dive at sun up and sun down. Remaining on the surface when the sun was so low in the sky presented an ideal opportunity to attack the boat by approaching it with the bright light in the rear, so that it was almost impossible for lookouts to spot the approaching attacker.

The temperatures inside the submarine had been uncomfortably hot during the last few days, but now they were heading towards Madagascar it started to become steadily colder and the night of 9 November was rather stormy. At first light the following day the horizon was barely visible and the conning tower control room resembled a turbulent bathroom, with water constantly rushing down through the closed but unsecured hatch. The hatch leading from this compartment to the central control room immediately below was kept closed and the water was allowed to drain into the bilges through pipes, from where ballast pumps sucked it out again. All this combined with only a few ships having been sunk put Ibbeken into a bad mood, and the acute absence of shipping induced him to explore the East London–Durban routes. The storm was subsiding a little when the chief engineer discovered that they had used considerably more fuel than anticipated and could remain in their operations area for only another ten days. There followed a period of bright sunshine accompanied by calm seas, but Ibbeken again refused to dive at sun up and sun down, creating considerable unrest among the crew. The ill feelings and arguments were now penetrating into every aspect of daily life and it seemed as if the men were arguing about the most ridiculous trivialities; things that would not usually have attracted comment were now creating friction between the engineer and deck divisions, with one trying to score points off the other.

It was 05.30 hours on 13 November when the next ship came into sight, and this one was obliging enough to run straight towards U178. So it was a case of just diving and waiting with an electric torpedo, the type that does not leave a wake or bubbles as it speeds through the water. Less than hour later, the British 3,764 grt *Louise Moller* was no more. This put Spahr into a deep depression and into another conflict with the commander. He saw what he thought was the master of the ship waving to them while clinging to a small piece of floating wreckage, but Ibbeken refused to help, saying that the men should think about women and children burning back home instead. Yet, despite the goings-on in Germany, many men thought that leaving the chap there was barbaric. Sometime afterwards they passed a number of lifeboats and managed to convey a message to the survivors to look for the unfortunate soul on the wreckage.

The ill feelings, now growing more rapidly than the mould on the food, spread throughout the boat while the monotony of daily life continued unabated. There was some action, U178 attacked, heard what the men thought were depth charges aimed at another boat, probably U181, but generally there was nothing much to write home about. Ibbeken had taken to his bunk for much of the day and then at night he complained about not being able to sleep. He also took to smoking on top of the conning tower, something that was usually strictly prohibited during the hours of darkness. At night, smokers had to remain within the conning tower control room so as not to show any light to watching eyes. To make matters worse, he was striking matches to light his cigarettes.

In the meantime, U178 got to know about the Allied landings in North Africa. However, the men were not terribly concerned, saying that it would not be long before Rommel pushed them back into the sea. On their seventy-eighth day at sea the radio news was more depressing. Hoping they might start their homeward run any moment, the men were disappointed by a signal from Germany suggesting that they might have to remain in the Indian Ocean longer than anticipated. There was no chance of returning home once they had expended all their torpedoes. It was unclear exactly what was going on and what had given rise to such orders, but the men were used to obeying orders and did not question the matter any further.

It was Sunday 29 November 1942, the first Sunday of Advent, when Commander-in-Chief Karl Dönitz issued the order to commence the return journey, which added a pleasant touch to the festivities. The men made their

U181, under Kurt Freiwald, transferring a torpedo from the upper (outside) deck to the bow compartment. Oddly, the torpedo is obviously the wrong way round to fit into the torpedo compartment. It looks as if the gear for raising one of the outside storage containers is in place in the left foreground, so it seems unlikely that the torpedo has been passed over from a supply ship.

own Advent wreaths by twisting parts cut from potato sacks. This created a pleasant atmosphere throughout the boat, with the smell of real coffee made from freshly ground beans percolating through the stuffy interior. Considerable ingenuity went into the production of these wreaths. Green paint added the right colour and white cotton wool gave a hint of snow, although the temperatures were still exceedingly hot. There were even candles with flames, but all carved from wood and painted. Of course, the men were not allowed to light candles inside the boat because the ventilation system was too poor to extract both the hydrogen and oxygen given off by the batteries and an open flame could not only create a fire but also trigger off a vicious explosion if the proportions of the two gasses were right. The engine room occupied all the space within the pressure hull and therefore there were no batteries underneath it. In fact, the engineers often played with fire by opening the cylinder vents to examine the flames shooting out. The reason for this was to check that every cylinder was firing properly because it was better than waiting for the temperature gauges to rise, indicating a problem within a cylinder. The engine compartments, of course, had their own direct ventilation system made up of huge ducts running down from the top of the conning tower. These opened inside the conning tower wall and can often be seen in photographs as a grating covering the huge entry ports.

The main subject of conversation, the shortage of fuel, prompted one of the 'heroes' to come up with the bright idea of emulating those U-boats of the First World War that went as far as setting sails. Each mattress was encased in a protective canvass sleeve that had by then been in constant use for rather a long time by men who could not wash properly. So it was thought that an airing might do them some good and *Stabshauptgefreiter* (Senior Leading Seaman) Erich Künzel and *Matrosengefreiter* (Able Seaman) Karl Hurkuck collected enough to stitch together a reasonable sail, the idea being that it would be hung from an extended periscope. This incident was not recorded in the boat's log and one wonders why none of the officers objected to the scheme from the very beginning. Spahr foresaw all sorts of problems long before they made the slightest appearance. Having raised the sail, the men found it helped them to make just over one knot, but the monstrosity was so huge that they could not have created a better advert of their presence. In the end the invention was dismantled, but not before the sailing lobby could claim some success, although the men did agree that it would never get them get home.

A terrific argument erupted within the boat while this was going on. It started with the chief engineer finding two sunglasses left lying around by the lookouts. The men had now been at sea for eighty-seven days or almost three months, and small things like that could easily upset the delicate balance between the seamen and engineer division. The problem was sorted eventually, but not before the air had been filled with an abundance of hasty accusations accompanied by ill feelings. Some of the men were not so bothered about this silly argument and many of the officers objected far more to the way Ibbo was behaving. He had developed some allergies and kept scratching himself for much of the time. The men did not like having to witness this performance at meal times, but there was little they could do and there was no one to complain to.

Permission might have been given for U178 to return home, but every tube still had a torpedo in it and it was not too long before another ship came into sight. It was late in the afternoon when the U-boat surfaced for an attack. On top of the conning tower with a stopwatch in his hand, Spahr was timing the electric torpedo when the man operating the sound detector reported that the noise from its propeller had started increasing in volume. Spahr reacted instantly with an alarm (an emergency dive). The boat crashed into the depths and the chief engineer automatically ordered the rudders to be set so as to expose the smallest target to the approaching destruction. The air was tense. All this happened within 30 seconds of firing the torpedo, so one did not

U515, a standard long range boat of Type IXC under Werner Henke, with navigator and Quartermaster Wilden wearing a tropical helmet. Behind him is Able Seaman Dewaldt and in front Chief Petty Officer Lamprecht. The men are wearing special sunglasses for lookouts facing into the sun. These fitted snugly to the face and binoculars butted against them so that the light intensity would not change when looking through the binoculars. The navigator, a warrant officer, usually doubled up as third watch officer in the majority of U-boats.

need a great deal of sense to conclude that its return journey would not take much longer. Spahr was right. The men did not need the sound detector any longer to hear it pass right over the top of the conning tower. Instead of being pleased, Ibbeken blasted Spahr, asking him fiercely, 'Who do you think is the commander here? Me or you?' Spahr remained calm, saying, 'Of course, you are the commander and you can remain the commander as well, but in such an emergency you have got to react just a little bit faster.'

Just to make the point that the torpedo's steering mechanism had a fault that made it run in circles, this hair-raising moment was not the end of its reign of terror. It turned in a loop once more and came back towards U178, determined to sink something before dropping into the depths of the Indian Ocean, where it is probably lying to this day. The next torpedo did not do much better, but at least it had the courtesy not to come back to U178, although it also failed to hit the target.

The target was still at large. The ship was probably not in the least aware of U178's discomfort, and when the U-boat resurfaced, Ibbeken gave permission for an artillery attack, something the men had not tackled before during the voyage. This was not the easiest of undertakings, even when a little ready-to-use ammunition was stored inside water- and pressure-resistant containers near the gun. A trap door in the main corridor between the radio room and the commander's quarters had to be opened to get at the shells stored under the radio room. These were packed in special watertight tins, which kept them in such good condition that sealed containers fished out of wrecks some fifty years after the war were still shiny and in perfect condition. The shells were then manhandled through the small hatch into the central room, up the ladder into the conning tower control room and on up to the top of the bridge. There they had to be moved back onto the anti-aircraft gun platform, down a ladder on the outside and carried along the upper deck to the 105 mm gun forward of the conning tower. Once in position, Spahr, who was also torpedo and artillery officer as well as the first watch officer, asked for permission to fire but the commander for no apparent reason withheld this. The target was now no more than 300 metres away but despite the tense action, Ibbeken continued smoking as if putting on a firework display. This failed attack became the main subject of conversation and led the men to state openly that none of them would go to sea with Ibbeken again.

All this was taking place in almost unbearable temperatures, with the inside of the pressure hull usually being well over 30 degrees Celsius, so that everyone was permanently bathed in sweat. Yet, despite the incredibly hostile conditions, one day merged into the next as usual. The lookouts noticed that the albatrosses were appearing less frequently and at about the same time flying fish started darting over the hull. On 16 December 1942, the men celebrated their hundredth day at sea without too much ado. They had been heading north through the Atlantic for some time and people had started to focus on home. They had passed Ascension Island a few days earlier and were therefore making reasonable progress, but everyone was fully aware that the difficult passage closer to Gibraltar and up through the Bay of Biscay was still well ahead of them and that they would not be the first boat to be caught in this tricky area. A number of blockade breakers reached the Gironde Estuary, only to be caught by the RAF or by a lurking British submarine within sight of their goal. Yet, despite the dangers, U178 got back, arriving in Bordeaux at 10.45 hours on 10 January 1943 to be greeted by the FK Klaus Scholtz, commander of the Twelfth U-boat Flotilla. A group of Italian submariners even provided a crate of oranges as a welcome gift.

Much had happened while U178 had been at sea for 124 days since leaving Kiel on 8 August. A few days later, Admiral Karl Dönitz, was promoted to become Supreme Commander-in-Chief of the entire Germany Navy. Things

Above and below: U178 met an Italian U-boat in the Indian Ocean, but the planned refuelling had to be postponed due to bad weather.

were critical: Stalingrad had fallen and the entire German Army there had surrendered to Russian forces. The Allies had gained such a strong insight into German radio codes that they could now, without fear of retribution, confidently unleash the ruthless might of RAF Bomber Command.

U178's First Voyage: Ships Attacked		
Date	Target	Gross register tonnage
10.10.1942	British steamer *Duchess of Atholl*	20,119
01.11.1942	British steamer *Mendoza*	8,233
04.11.1942	Norwegian steamer *Hai Hing*	2,561
04.11.1942	British steamer *Trekieve*	5,244
13.11.1942	British steamer *Louise Moller*	3,764
15.11.1942	British steamer *Adviser* (damaged)	6,348
27.11.1942	US steamer *Jeremiah Wadsworth*	7,176

An intriguing incident took place in the Indian Ocean towards the end of November 1942 while U178 was a fair distance south of the Cape of Good Hope on its way home to France. It concerned U178's sister boat, U177 under Robert Gysae, a Berliner from Charlottenburg, who had already been awarded the Knight's Cross long before venturing into those distant seas.

During the morning of 28 November his lookouts spotted a smoke cloud. Gysae dived and eventually fired a salvo of three torpedoes at what looked like a British auxiliary cruiser. The passenger ship was painted to look like a warship and displayed a considerable array of armament. It must also have been carrying some highly volatile substances because it started burning incredibly fiercely immediately after the first detonation. The smoke was so thick that it was impossible to see what was going on through the periscope other than that the target had taken on such a severe list that the gunners could not hold themselves in their positions and had to abandon their weapons.

Raising the extendible rod aerial from periscope depth to listen for distress calls, the radio operator confirmed that the sinking ship was not using its radio, so Gysae took the opportunity to surface for a closer inspection, despite being close to the coast. To his surprise he saw that the decks of the ship were crowded with people. They were screaming wildly and others were splashing about in the water. Utter unexpected chaos. The fire had got an incredibly fast hold, shooting along the superstructure and even engulfing the bridge at such a speed that many people had no alternative but to jump into the water without lifeboats or rafts, although there were a good number of rescue aids bobbing about as well. It was an incredible inferno; something that Gysae had never experienced before.

Some 20 minutes had passed between the detonation and U177 surfacing, so there had been ample time for people to get away from the still floating wreck. Unsure of what to make of the frenzied scene, Gysae picked up two men drifting in the water. They told him he had sunk the 6,796 grt troop transport *Nova Scotia* with a crew of 200 British seamen, about eighty Africans and a thousand Italian civilian prisoners on board, who were being taken from Massawa in Eritrea on the Red Sea via Aden to Durban in South Africa. Gysae was already severely shocked by the chaos, the screams, the bedlam in the water and the general situation when he learned that the majority of the British crew had probably been incapacitated by the detonation and there appeared to be no one leading the evacuation of the sinking steamer. This was a shocking state of affairs to which he responded by first distancing himself from the scene. He was only a few miles east of South Africa and, despite the ship not having sent a distress call, the prominent black smoke could easily draw in quick retribution. It was too dangerous a place for a U-boat to be hanging around.

At the same time, Gysae sent a special urgent signal to U-boat HQ, asking for help. He saw U177 in a similar situation to the *Laconia* incident in which U156 under Werner Hartenstein had sunk a passenger ship two months earlier on 12 September 1942. The ship had already gone down by the time Hartenstein discovered that there were some 1,500 Italians on board and he mounted a by now famous rescue operation. U-boats, both German and Italian, converged on the spot and took on board a vast number of people in addition to towing those lifeboats that could be rounded up. After U156 broadcast a distress call in plain language for all to hear, the Americans, not taking heed of the masses in the water, responded by attacking this vast floating mass of humanity but failed to sink the U-boat. Despite there being so many people on board, the crew managed to dive and avoid the full force of the onslaught.

Seeing himself in a similar situation, Gysae could not decide what to do. Should he attempt a rescue operation? After all, the Italians and Germans were both fighting on same side. He was not too far from the coast, so the people stood a good chance of surviving if he did. However, doing so would go against what commanders had been told after the *Laconia* incident. The U-boat Chief had made it clear that rescue operations would not be recognised by the enemy, and U-boats picking up even British and American citizens were still liable to come under attack. U177 had left Kiel on 17 September 1942, heading for the area where the *Laconia* was sunk only a few days later. The entire chain of events was therefore followed closely by radio, and Gysae was well aware of what had gone on. He had taken a keen interest in the intricacies of the situation as it was reported, so the confusion he was now faced with placed him in an unexpected quandary.

The radio reply was so devastating that the men found it hard to obey. The U-boat Command confirmed what the men had been told earlier: 'CONTINUE OPERATIONS. WAR HAS PRIORITY. NO RESCUE OPERATION.' As a result, there was an enormous loss of life. War can be harsh and incidents like this hit hard across a far greater area than just the one U-boat in the centre of the incident. All those very long range boats listening in to the southern wavelengths were aware of what was going on. It made the men feel sick and gave them a deep and desperate resentment for conflict and authority around them.

This story has now settled so deeply in the sludge of history that it is almost forgotten, but it made a powerful impact on LzS Walter Schöppe and the rest of the crew. Schöppe was from the land-based Naval Artillery, but had become so fed up watching men polish large guns that he had volunteered to use his photographic skills to become a war correspondent. However, he was not on board and only got to know the rudiments of the incident at the time, the full details not coming to light until he researched the matter after the war.

CHAPTER 12

U178 – The Second Thrust to the Indian Ocean

The men of U178 did not need to be mind-readers to know that their next voyage would be as arduous as the first. There was no way in which Wilhelm Spahr was going to stay on board for another look at the Indian Ocean. Once back at base, he promptly resigned so that he could look forward to a new and more rewarding way of passing the best years of his life. However, in doing so he had not reckoned on the fact that a good number of the crew would not be going back for another long spell without him. An old-fashioned press gang was formed. Equipped with a good supply of beer, the 'lords' persuaded him not to abandon them. As a result, Spahr acquiesced and agreed to go out once more with the new commander – this time one with a Knight's Cross around his neck, but not one of the aggressive types. Wilhelm Dommes, born on 16 April 1907, was three years younger than Spahr, born on 4 April 1904, but both came from a similar mould, having joined the navy because they liked the sea. Dommes had carved out a merchant marine career for himself, starting his working life before the mast of a sailing ship. In 1932, he responded to a call from Admiral Erich Raeder (Commander-in-Chief of the German Navy) for the best merchant seamen to come forward to replace almost an entire year's intake of officer cadets who had been lost in the Fehmarn Belt when the sail training ship *Niobe* capsized in a sudden squall of heavy wind. The men who made the move were rewarded with incentives, including recognition of their seniority based on the time they had spent in the merchant marine. Hence people like Günther Prien, 'Ajax' Bleichrodt and Wilhelm Dommes had two crew numbers: one for when they joined to qualify as a naval officer and another (earlier) one for the time they had already spent at sea. (In this case 'crew' refers to the yearly intake of naval officers and is identified by the year the men joined.)

Dommes gained his Knight's Cross in the Mediterranean as commander of U431 from April 1941 until the last day of 1942. A man who had served

U178, with Wilhelm Dommes' 'Horrido' emblem on the conning tower.

U178's chief engineer, KL (Ing.) Karl-Heinz Wiebe after the second voyage when he was awarded the Knight's Cross.

under him said that Dommes was a grand chap with one weakness – his determination never to give up. He often drove himself much further than the men he commanded and as a result came very close to a mental breakdown. However, this could not have been terribly serious because it was only a matter of weeks before he accepted the post of commander of U178. It did not take him long to establish that some psychological changes were necessary and that there would be an entirely new set-up on the second voyage without the hang-ups created by the tensions of the first. The emblem of an aggressive white swan puffing up its feather for an attack was removed, to be replaced with the word 'Horrido', which had kept his first command safe under the most horrific conditions. Sailors do not meddle with a proven talisman.

There were a number of other new faces on board as well. Perhaps the most notable was the chief engineer, KL (Ing.) Karl-Heinz Wiebe as a replacement for Johannes Gottwald, who had moved on to become a flotilla engineer in the Mediterranean. Another new face was that of Walter Schöppe. He happened to have been in Bordeaux when the Cockleshell Heroes struck in December 1942, and was also sent out to cover the arrival of the first U-cruiser to return from the Indian Ocean. Although Schöppe left masses of papers with vast volumes of incredible first-hand research, none of them explained how or why he volunteered to sail with U178 on its second voyage to hell, especially as there were no guarantees of living long enough to make use of the return ticket.

On Sunday 28 March 1943, U178 left Bordeaux after a rousing speech from the flotilla commander, FK Klaus Scholtz, accompanied by grey skies and a persistent drizzle. It was not ideal for investigating the first signs of spring but brilliant for keeping RAF Coastal Command tucked up comfortably in bed. Yet, despite the poor flying conditions, U178 had a new toy on board, a box that buzzed, squeaked or whistled every time anyone with radar happened to be passing, and this suggested that there were people with aggressive intentions on the other side of the low clouds. Dommes was the type who never seemed to lose his temper, appearing to do everything at his own calm and steady pace, and avoiding aircraft and ships was nothing new to him. Anyone who had spent as much time in the dangerous Mediterranean as he had done would have found the run out of the Gironde Estuary to be a pleasant holiday. The slow-running ease of this almost relaxing atmosphere was brought to an abrupt end by a radio message at 22.00 hours on 30 March 1943, by which time U178 had already advanced the clocks by one hour to switch from

Wilhelm Dommes, commander of U178, on the left, with the medical officer, Joachim Wüstenberg on the right, questioning the senior navigator from the Greek freighter *Mary Livanos*, after having given him a cigar and some dry matches. The rest of the merchant seamen were provided with cigarettes, medical care and provisions before being given a course for the nearest coast.

German (or Mid-European) to Summer Time. 'FROM U-BOAT COMMAND TO RODLER, MOHR, RASCH AND DOMMES. ITALIAN SHIP SUNK BY ENEMY WARSHIP IN SQUARE BE9688. MAKE FOR SINKING AREA AT FAST CRUISING SPEED.' (U-boats were generally identified by the names of their commanders rather than by their numbers, and the above were U71 Hardo Rodler von Roithberg, U124 Johann Mohr, U106 Hermann Rasch, not to be confused with Heinrich Ratsch, who was killed in action as commander of U28 on 15 November 1941, or Eberhard Mohr of U133, who went down in the Mediterranean on 14 March 1942.)

Reaching the area of the sinking was considerably easier than finding survivors. Masses of empty life rafts and a few boats with their oars still in the rowlocks indicated that the ship that had attacked had also picked up survivors. The considerable damage to the floating wreckage looked as if it had occurred during the action and the life jackets in the water had not been closed, indicating that they had floated off the wreck rather than the people inside them having been killed in the water. The carnage was immense, with floating wreckage covering a large area. None of the recognition lights fired from signal pistols were answered, so in the end the men gave up and headed south to continue with their voyage. They were relatively close to Cape Finisterre, the north-west corner of Spain, so it was also possible that the survivors had set sails to make for land.

Much of the time was spent training rather than dealing with the war. There were enough new faces on board to make training a vital part of the operations, and both commander and chief engineer had to get used to the crew as well as the machinery. Dommes' previous boat, U431, was a very much smaller Type VIIC, and the huge size of U178 took some getting used to. Getting it to periscope depth was not the easiest of operations, and Dommes was not satisfied with the time it took to dive in an emergency. More drills were obviously called for. Surfacing from one such set of exercises the lookouts found themselves confronted with a forest of masts. They could see only the tips but there were enough of them for Dommes to send off an immediate sighting report. Not long afterwards came the reply prohibiting him from attacking. Instead he was to keep in touch and continue sending sighting reports so that a slightly smaller boat, U124 under KK Johannes Mohr, could make contact. This worked well. Mohr established contact with the convoy, leaving U178 to continue with its voyage into the Indian Ocean. Mohr then hit two ships (the 4,367 grt SS *Katha* and the 5,190 grt SS *Gogra*) from what was Convoy OS45. Immediately afterwards two escorts, HMS *Stonecrop* under Lt Cdr J. P. Smythe and HMS *Black Swan* under Cdr L. A. B. Majendie, depth charged U124 with the loss of everyone on board.

The men of U178 started to blame themselves for the loss, saying that the boat would have survived if they had not reported the convoy. Wiebe was an

Some of the crew of U124, under KL Wilhelm Schulz in May 1941, after the boat's fourth war cruise. Note that there is only one commissioned officer (wearing a greatcoat). The brilliant golden shoulder straps of the other men wearing peaked caps indicate that they are warrant officers.

old friend of the dead commander, so the loss hit him especially hard. To make matters worse, there was nothing other than the mandatory training to occupy the men's minds and the solemn atmosphere lasted for several days, with the men going around in a constant gloomy daze, while tests, training sessions and all manner of practices continued unabated whenever there was time to break off from the daily grind of steaming towards the Equator at the most economical speed of about 9 knots. The line was reached during the evening of 18 April 1943, and shortly afterwards there followed the 'Crossing the Line' ceremony. Such naval celebrations tended to be a bit on the rough side and the crew would have faced a court martial back home had they treated prisoners of war the way they dealt with their own comrades.

Dommes was itching for a look at the British dependency of St Helena, hoping there might be a target, but the waters around the lonely island were empty and there were no signs of radar transmissions either, so he stayed at a respectful distance of five miles or so, hoping to remain undetected. This was not particularly easy because the boat had been trailing a noticeable shimmer of oil for a little while. At first it was thought that something could have spilled out of somewhere, but the nuisance persisted long enough to indicate that there must be a permanent leak. This called for a hive of activity on the decks and while some of the men were searching for the cause, the gun crew were sent out to grease all the moving parts. This was indeed a major undertaking. The deck guns had some eighty greasing points and although these were painted bright red, it was still a major procedure to grease all of them in turn. There is such a gun in the German U-boat Museum and counting the red nipples is difficult enough without having to do it in total darkness, as was the case in the North Atlantic where aircraft could easily interfere with the process, making the retrieval of the crew problematic.

The general situation around South Africa had changed slightly since U178's first visit a few months earlier. There were now more U-boats in the area, providing some comfort for those who were thinking about being marooned as a result of mechanical failure. Now, at least, there was some support and some hope of getting a lift home if the machinery gave out. However, the additional hitting power also provided considerable disadvantages since there was not anything much south of South Africa and the merchant sea-lanes hugged the coast. The opposition did not appear to be idle either, despite being so far from the main theatres of war. Aircraft were seen so frequently that it was almost suicidal to stop in order to allow the crew to have a swim and wash in the refreshing sea. The U-boat did get a few clues about possible

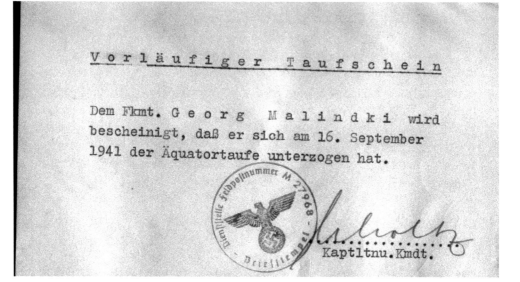

A provisional 'Crossing the Line' certificate officially issued by U108 and signed by the commander, Klaus Scholtz. Many boats produced highly elaborate certificates in addition to these small slips of paper.

Wilhelm Dommes wearing rain
gear during rough weather.

convoys reported by other boats, but finding these proved difficult and in the
first instance Dommes decided that hunting for any of the reported ships at
the normal fast cruising speed would consume too much fuel.

The general atmosphere within the boat was not good. It was the middle of
May by now and the men had been cooped up inside the tight confines of the
submarine since the end of March, which was plenty of time for everyone
to get on everyone else's nerves. One wonders whether Dommes had studied
the leadership technique of Horatio Nelson because he was conducting the
daily routines almost as if Nelson had trained him personally. Dommes had a
habit of thinking aloud, so the men he was working with could see what was
going on in his mind. That way the men knew what he was doing and they
could easily throw in their halfpenny's worth. In addition to giving sharp, crisp
orders, he was also a good listener, capable of absorbing the advice from the
men around him. The officers took it in turns to be the coward of the day, and
his task was to find fault with any decisions made by the other officers. One
wonders how old this process of leadership is. It resurfaced in management
training long after the war, with people claiming to have invented it then, but it
was nothing new for many of the men who sailed in U-boats on long voyages.

Yet all the leadership qualities did not bring any targets and that oil trace
was still there. Nothing too serious, but the faint shimmer on the surface of

the water was annoying and too much of an advert for the opposition. Trying to rectify the problem was difficult because no one could find where it was coming from. In the end the men resorted to sawing through several main oil pipes in order to give the inside a thorough scrub. This left the outside deck in such a mess that they dived fairly quickly to wash it clean again. Yet nothing seemed to get rid of the oil trace, or of the aircraft in the sky. At least the men assumed there to be aircraft. Often they heard only the signals from the irritating radar search device without waiting on the surface to meet the cause of the commotion. This was possible because the radar detector could 'hear' the opposition's radar long before the operator received an echo from the surfaced submarine. The men of U178 argued that had the radar sets been on board ships, then they should have got some indication on their highly sensitive sound detector after they had dived. So the assumption that the interference was created by aircraft remained. The weather was not particularly co-operative either, and the exploratory work for finding the oil leak had not gone too far when the waves became lively enough to make progress difficult.

Having eliminated all the obvious places where leaks might occur, the men crawled inside the fairing around the conning tower and into the space between the upper (outside) deck and the pressure hull. There was just about enough space there for a man to crawl through on all fours but this was not terribly comfortable, with knees taking quite a battering. The sights down there were rather surprising and shocking. Flaking rust was almost everywhere and some of the seals at the ends of some pipes and taps in the fuel and oil pipes were obviously leaking, much to the men's annoyance. The system of pipes the men had now reached was a set of dead ends, with special taps put there especially for emergencies when divers could come to the aid of a sunken crew. The idea was that a rescue ship could connect hoses to those dead ends to supply air to the crew or to blow the tanks. Assuming that the tanks might be damaged, there were also options of blowing air into fuel bunkers and lubricating oil tanks, and all these pipes came together in what looked like a plumber's knotty nightmare. In the end the men solved the problem by doing away with emergency connections ands merely sealing the pipes as dead ends, making it impossible for anything to leak out through faulty taps. Having done all this, and washed the upper deck again by submerging with considerable speed, the oil trace still remained. It was now becoming more than infuriating, almost as if some invisible force was making a hysterical impression on the men. It helped to make the atmosphere among the crew worse, especially when they heard that other boats around them were finding worthwhile targets.

Dommes was astute enough to know that every effort had now to be made to find a few targets so that some successes would wash away the atmosphere created by that persistent oil trace, and his argument was that no one was

Wilhelm Dommes, commander of U178, on the left.

likely to spot it in the dark. It was shortly after midnight on 24 May 1943 when the lighthouse at Bathurst (now Banjul) on St Mary's Island came into sight. The radar detector was working overtime, making it possible to dive before the aircraft carrying it came close enough to spot the U-boat. It was obvious that there was more than one plane in the vicinity, and in the end Dommes approached from below the surface. This paid dividends in that a couple of ships, as well as come escorts, were detected and he assumed that the radar detector had made it possible for them to dive before they were spotted by the opposition. So it looked as if they were on the way for a good surprise attack. However, it was not all that simple because the enemy was making life difficult instead of resting on its laurels. The first attack had to be abandoned because the target zigzagged into an unfavourable position. Dommes used the opportunity to tackle another ship with the stern tubes, but just at the critical moment when he ordered them to be made ready, the news came that the torpedo crew could not open the outside doors. It was infuriating. Now there was no more time to turn the boat for another attack with the bow tubes and all the men could do was to curse. To make matters even more infuriating, the targets were quite close but they were not be heard by the sensitive sound detector, making the men wonder whether this had broken as well.

The astonishing thing was that, despite everything, Dommes hardly cursed. He made the point that the training had been good, the men had done their jobs properly, and had the machinery functioned they would have had a couple of ships from this convoy to their credit. 'Convoy' was not really the right term; 'a small collection of ships sailing together' was a more apt description. Knowing that there were other boats in the vicinity that might make good use of the information, U178 shot to the surface to report the matter. Yet that short signal had hardly left when the radar detector went into its most irritating mode, suggesting an aircraft was approaching. The U-boat should have plunged back into the depths, but this time Dommes decided to take the aircraft on in a gun duel. This must have been quite a surprise for the aircraft crew, for they turned away, and with it being pretty dark, Dommes turned his back on this and then on another approaching aircraft while continuing to move away on the surface. (The anti-aircraft guns could fire only sideways or backwards but could not have been aimed at an aircraft approaching from the front.) It seems to have worked. Later, U178 did dive and on subsequently resurfacing was faced with the same problems as before: that of the radar detector indicating aggressive neighbours in the immediate vicinity. What was far more maddening than the presence of the aircraft was the persistent oil trail. In fact, it appeared to be more dominant than before. Dommes ordered the diesels to be shut down so that the boat could continue with pure electric drive but even that did not diminish the oil trace, so it was obviously not being ejected from the engines.

It was 04.00 hours on 27 May 1943 when U178 found itself in the main Cape Agulhas–St Francis shipping lane hoping for a juicy target, but the seas were empty. Again, the most annoying point was that the skies were once more full of radar impulses making life miserable. Then, at last, while submerged, the men heard an approaching ship, putting everyone on tenterhooks in the hope that Dommes was going to attack. The lookouts were still clambering up to the top of the conning tower when Dommes identified the intruder as a hospital ship. There was also a small fishing boat, and searchlights could be seen illuminating the sky in the distance. Once again there came that annoyingly frustrating squeak from the radar detector. It was an up-down-up process throughout the remaining hours of darkness, with the boat staying down in the depths for most of the time but nothing worth targeting coming into sight. It was infuriating. Then, when the batteries had run down and the interior needed urgent ventilation, came the surprise. Not a ship but an entire convoy. Despite all these targets, it was now too dangerous to start a chase, so U178 had to withdraw to charge the batteries and to fill compressed air tanks. All the men could contribute was a short radio signal with details of their find. Two boats, U198 under Werner Hartmann and U196 under Eitel-Friedrich Kentrat, were both in the vicinity and might well make good use of the information.

The problem for the men of U178 persisted. According to some historians, U-boats were manned by what they described as the 'killer Nazi' types of bloodthirsty and highly technical operators. Yet, in reality, the software in U-boats was made up of a group of highly superstitious characters who would by now have gone to the Temple of the Four Winds to provoke the oracle about the wisdom of being incarcerated inside this particular U-boat and whether there was a quick way out of it. Dommes knew full well that the men might follow him into the Indian Ocean, but once there they urgently needed some success if they were going to get home again without losing every ounce of sanity in the process. He had already told them on several occasions about the significance of targets, saying that a small ship sunk in distant waters might have far greater consequences for the enemy than a huge freighter lost on the doorstep of its main ports. In doing so he had pointed to some of the tiny, 20 ton targets sunk in the Mediterranean by U35 under the most successful submarine commander of all times, Lothar von Arnauld de la Perière. Of course, he was secretly hoping desperately for something more significant, and something along these lines did eventually cross U178's sights.

The weather was not particularly co-operative when this happened and it is quite likely that he would have abandoned the hunt had he not been in this most dire predicament of having to boost the crew's morale. It was early in the morning of 1 June 1943, but light enough to ensure that the only practical choice was a submerged attack. Although he could see only very little through the periscope due to the heavy seas, at 09.39 Dommes ordered, 'Tubes IV and V ready,' and a short time later, 'Fire.' By this time, word had got around the U-boat arm that pressing the triggers inside the conning tower might result in nothing happening due to some electrical fault further along the line, and the majority of commanders had given the standing order that the command 'Fire' be transmitted verbally through the boat so that the torpedo mechanics could also press the firing buttons by each tube to make doubly sure that the machinery got the message. It worked. As a result, the Dutch 6,586 grt freighter *Salabangka* went down at 31°08'S 31°18'E. This was a modest success but enough to break that almost hysterical curse which had been dominating everyone on board. There was not much else that Dommes could do at this stage. Once more he was in the dire predicament of urgently needing to recharge the batteries and therefore could not surface in such a situation where his presence might attract even mild retribution. They were only about 60 miles from Durban, so he argued that the sinking position was close enough to land for the opposition to come out and deal with the recovery of survivors. In any case, some minor repairs were also necessary, so U178 moved further away from the coast into a less frequented area.

Bearing in mind the failed attack of 24 May 1943, when the first target zigzagged out of the sights and then the rear torpedo tubes could not be opened in time, Dommes felt the deepest relief. Although no retribution came from the enemy, the weather did not want to play along with U178. The sky

The rear torpedo compartment of U178, looking towards the hatch by the electro-motor room. Spare torpedoes are stored under the floor and the iron derrick for lifting them and then pushing them into the tubes is clearly visible.

remained grey with such turbulent seas that the men were happy to spend some time in the cellar repairing one of the electric motors, topping up the batteries with distilled water and carrying out several other minor repairs, but none of this happened until after Dommes had a made a point of reporting his success back to base.

By this time it had been established that most of the traffic ran close to the coast and no ships at all were found in the established shipping routes running out from the main ports. This was somewhat disconcerting because the operations areas for U-boats had been allocated away from the coast. Bearing in mind that some of the boats were carrying a special autogyro type of kite, the Focke-Achgelis *Bachstelze*, for increasing the distance a lookout could see, there was not much scope for using such a contraption so close to land, with frequent enemy air patrols. Of course, there was also an advantage with shipping running parallel to the coast; it was much easier to get ahead of it without losing contact. The convoy's avoiding manoeuvres were severely limited, but many of the ships were reasonably fast and difficult to catch. In order to make use of such a situation, one really needed a team or pack of boats operating as one group in which one passed on the details of the convoy to another boat lying in wait near its destination, but although there were other boats in these southern waters, there was no planned co-operation between them.

With operations being comparatively close to the coast and the convoys being escorted by aircraft equipped with radar, much of the reconnaissance had to be carried out from under the water. This immediately identified a number of weaknesses as far as Dommes was concerned, having spent much of his time in a very much smaller Type VIIC. The first worrying point was that the batteries were no longer in a very good condition, having made two long distance voyages into the Indian Ocean, and there was not a great deal of power left in them for prolonged submerged hunting or, even more importantly, to evade a determined hunter. Whilst the underwater reconnaissance worked quite well, submerged attacks were virtually impossible unless conditions were perfect. Keeping the head lens of the periscope clear of the water without the bow and stern breaking through the surface was almost impossible and could only be carried out at speed when the hydrophones could get a better grip. Dommes was not afraid to commit his thoughts to paper in his log, adding that the old strategy of getting in to attack and sink ships was no longer working now that the opposition was approaching with radar. What was more, he and a number of other commanders made the point, which was also well known to Karl Dönitz, the U-boat Chief and now Supreme Commander-in-Chief of the Navy, that the opposition also appeared in remote locations where refuelling took place. So they must have had another way, in addition to radar, of finding such locations.

The reconnaissance continued. There was not much else to do. The radio did not supply any information about potential passing convoys and U178 was very much alone, although the men knew that U160 under Georg Lassen was also in the vicinity. There came a day when U178 remained at periscope depth close to Cape St Francis for the best part of daylight hours, cruising at a comparatively fast speed while also picking up a multitude of radio and radar signals. This made it possible to distinguish between airborne and land-based radar but did not help to bring any targets within torpedo range. The radar detector did not seem to like the continuous engagement either and gave up the ghost. The few radio messages that were sent back to U-boat HQ were enough to tell the Operations Room that not all was well in the Indian Ocean and something needed urgent attention. Dönitz therefore shuffled around the allocated operations areas, giving individual commanders more freedom to make on-the-spot decisions and to move into what they thought might be more profitable areas. At the same time, U177 under Robert Gysae was given permission to move away from the coastal routes into an area where it was thought safe for the deployment of their *Bachstelze*, the gliding helicopter or autogyro that had to be towed from the boat's gun platform.

Dommes and Schöppe remarked more than once that radar was making it exceedingly difficult to approach shipping without being detected and, on top of this, the finding of targets by searching from such a comparatively low

Peter-Ottmar Grau, the commander of U872, tries out the boat's gliding helicopter. He should not be confused with Peter Grau, who commanded U1191.

vantage point as the top of the conning tower was incredibly hard. The next step in this depressing situation was a meeting with a supply ship, and for that the boats had to leave the shipping routes to venture into lonelier parts of the ocean where they were less likely to be disturbed by the enemy. This might sound encouraging, but the 'lords' in U178 had already calculated that they were running out of basic essentials and therefore Dommes would soon have to start heading for home. The radio signal with details of the refuelling meeting came on 9 June 1943, and the men had left port towards the end of March, so they had been at sea for an incredibly long time and the majority of the men had never caught even a brief glimpse of the blue sky.

CHAPTER 13

U178 Reaches Penang in the Far East

Before continuing with U178's story, it is necessary to remember that there had already been considerable German surface ship activity in the Far East before U-boats ventured that far, and this makes it necessary to digress a little.

Shortly before the beginning of the war the High Command sent a warning to German ships at sea with instructions to run into a home port within four days or, if this was not possible, to make for a neutral harbour. The message emphasised that the United States was not to be considered as neutral. This left a large number of merchant ships scattered around the globe in remote locations, hoping the hostilities would not last too long. But by the spring of 1940, a number of German merchant ships had been fitted out with hidden armaments to be sent into remote waters with the principal aim of drawing both British and French naval units away from the main centres of action. Such raiders had already been employed during the First World War, and their significance was dramatically emphasised shortly afterwards when the official British history stated that some eighty ships had been sent out to hunt a single merchant raider, the light cruiser *Emden*. Thus merchant raiding in far-off waters had made a significant contribution to the war at sea with comparatively little cost.

The heyday for surface raiders of the Second World War was in 1940 and 1941. The last raider attempting to sail out of Europe, the *Komet* (KzS Ullrich Brocksien), was lost in the English Channel on 14 October 1942, at the start of her second voyage. That left only one ghost cruiser at large; the *Michel* (KzS Günther Gumprich) set out from Yokohama in Japan on 21 May 1943, to be sunk by the US submarine *Tarpon* on 17 October. Supply ships fared even worse; eight of them were sunk during one operation in June 1941, around the time of the *Bismarck*'s one and only war voyage. Just one supply ship (the *Spichern*) managed to escape that encounter, to return to St Nazaire. Although the German High Command had put considerable emphasis on specialised supply submarines long before the start of the war, the first dedicated U-tanker (U459 under Georg von Wilamowitz-Moellendorf) was not commissioned until 15 November 1941 and was then immediately engaged to prolong the fighting capacity of U-boats operating off the eastern seaboard of the United States. So these supply submarines did not play a role until later in the war. Japan's entry into the war at the end of 1941 made life a little easier for German ships stranded in Far Eastern ports because these could now seek direct help from the Japanese authorities. Up until then, Japan might have been keen to help Germany but also wanted to be seen to be maintaining strict neutrality and therefore at times made life quite difficult for marooned Germans.

One of the ships at sea shortly before the beginning of the war was the 7,747 grt motor tanker *Charlotte Schliemann* under *Kapitän* Rothe of the merchant marine. While on her way home from Curaçao with a full load of refined, and therefore useful, fuel oil she was ordered to make for Las Palmas in the Canary Islands instead of continuing her journey to Germany. There the ship was locked in a neutral harbour by the outbreak of war and for a couple of years it seemed as if both the ship and the crew were forgotten. The men were allowed ashore but only had a little money, so even the magical Canary Islands lost their attraction pretty quickly, especially for those who had families or girlfriends waiting at home. The *Charlotte Schliemann* had enough fuel on board, but ships stranded at sea required a good deal more than just oil. So clandestine changes had to be made before she could serve as a supply ship. Some items were secretly brought on board, and the crew had vague notions that they might be called upon to run the blockade into Europe, but for a long time there were no definite plans. The crew were also depleted when some men were released for other duties. The call to war eventually came on 20 February 1942, in the form of a radio signal. This was a couple of months after the first U-boat strike against the United States, at a time when Britain had been shut out of reading the U-boats' secret radio codes due to the introduction of the fourth rotor. As a result, refuelling operations in remote ocean areas were unhindered until the beginning of 1943, when Bletchley Park cracked the new coding system.

With the *Charlotte Schliemann* having been incarcerated in Las Palmas, where people spoke Spanish and not much German, the crew looked upon this signal to go to war as a means of bursting out of the monotony of daily life. Shore leave was cancelled immediately and in the dead of night the men cast off into the vast emptiness of the Atlantic. At that stage only a few of the officers knew where they were going and no doubt the crew of the *Charlotte Schliemann* might well have been under the impression that they were heading for home. They had no weapons and the crew consisted almost exclusively of men from the merchant marine with no military training. It was not the best of combinations for surviving on wild oceans during a wild war.

The strange thing about this entire undertaking was that it worked reasonably well, making a considerable contribution over a long and drawn out period of six months. The first ship to be supplied was the auxiliary cruiser *Michel*. It was also necessary to relieve the raider of a good number of prisoners of war and therefore the men had to construct secure accommodation inside the forward hold. This was neither desirable nor comfortable but was the best that could be provided under the harsh conditions. The crew were pleased when they learned that military specialists from the *Michel* would come on board to see to the guard duties in order to keep this mass of humanity under control. The *Michel* was not the *Charlotte Schliemann*'s only customer. The auxiliary cruiser *Stier* (KzS Horst Gerlach) also put in an appearance.

The length of time the ship had spent in Las Palmas and the six months at sea while acting as a supply ship for numerous other vessels put such an enormous strain on the men and machinery that complicated overhauls became necessary. So the men were pleased when their supplies ran out and they received orders to make for Singapore, which had by then been occupied by Japanese forces. The joy of arriving there was short-lived. Instead of being given permission to go ashore, the crew received orders to take on board a load of fuel oil for Yokohama in Japan. At that time the men did not know that German ships were waiting there to be refuelled in order to put to sea. Yet, despite the disappointment of not being allowed ashore, they were relatively contented that so far everything had run reasonably well and the admirals pushing paper ships around on tables in Berlin and in Tokyo seemed to have done their homework reasonably well.

It was 20 October 1942 when the crew received permission to go ashore in Tokyo. This was quite something, because the men received back pay for the last eight months since leaving Las Palmas. This ensured that even the low paid had no need to economise. Things got pretty hot in more ways than one. On 30 November, the port and the city beyond it were struck by an enormous explosion that shook the buildings almost like a mini-earthquake, followed by a huge black cloud rising high into the sky. Earthquakes were nothing new to the locals and they had even experienced fires with their associated smoke before, but this was rather unusual inasmuch that there was a loud band but relatively little movement of the earth. The reason for this was that it had been caused by the German fleet supply ship *Uckermark* blasting high into the air while transferring fuel and ammunition to the auxiliary cruiser *Thor*. Both were totally gutted and of no use for any further service. The *Uckermark* was known as the *Altmark* at the beginning of the war and was the ship that had an infamous brush with the Royal Navy destroyer *Cossack* in Norway during the autumn of 1939. The *Thor* had left Germany in June 1940 under KzS Otto Kähler and came under the command of KzS Günther Gumprich for her second voyage. The fire was so severe that it also set another supply ship, the *Leuthen*, (ex-*Nankin*) alight to burn with the other two.

U178's medical officer, Joachim Wüstenberg, wandering on Penang Hill. Sadly, he died a few days after this photo was taken.

The *Charlotte Schliemann* was far enough away to escape this destruction. She remained in dock until the spring of 1943 for a lengthy refit and considerable modification to make her more useful as a supply ship. Her crew of forty-two were supplemented with forty-eight soldiers led by an *Oberleutnant der Reserve* Wimmel, who had been prize officer aboard the auxiliary cruiser *Michel*. He was joined by a naval physician, Dr Schridde, and by LzS Steffens. It is necessary to bear in mind that all these characters had been living in foreign lands for rather a long time and were therefore completely out of touch with what was going on back in Europe. Obviously they had access to radios but not to newspapers or magazines, and many were blissfully ignorant of what was happening with the war. To some it came as a shock when they learned that U-boats had been operating in the Indian Ocean, but it did not take them long to deduce from what was being loaded that these were likely to be the *Charlotte Schliemann*'s next customers. In view of the lack of information trickling through into the Indian Ocean, it was necessary not only to supply U-boats but also to provide the means for everyone to exchange the latest news. Special meetings were arranged for medical staff, engineers, lookouts, officers and so forth. It is touching in many ways that several U-boat men who served in distant waters remarked on how well they were looked after and the great lengths to which these men from supply ships

Haircuts at sea.

went in order to make things comfortable for the U-boat crews.

Now to return to U178, where the boring daily routine continued unabated. From where the boat had entered the Indian Ocean, everyone on board knew that it was a case of either meeting a supply ship or starting the homeward voyage. The first refuelling attempts did not go as planned, so the rendezvous was pushed forward to 22 June 1943. That meant the boat had to withdraw to an isolated part of the ocean and wait. The daily checks revealed a chain of breakdowns, all needing attention but none of them occupying the majority of the crew. The men took to having a hair-cutting competition, and the old newspapers and magazines, which had been read several times by every person aboard, were cut up into small strips that were then glued together again to produce funny stories. This leisurely way of life in the Indian Ocean was going on at a time when Black May of 1943 was already history. U-boats had been temporarily withdrawn from vulnerable areas of the North Atlantic because Allied forces had sunk more than forty of them during that fateful month. The Eastern Front had collapsed around the beginning of the year, the entire army having surrendered at Stalingrad, and Russian forces had already started their offensive westwards. So things did not look good as the noose tightened around Germans everywhere.

The men of U178 knew full well that the refuelling would be fast and furious, with men on the upper deck working hard to make fuel, lubricating oil and water connections. Down below, the men had to clear space near the central control room to accommodate what they were hoping would be a good supply of fresh food. It was unlikely that the deck hatches could be opened and the men had to plan bringing everything down from the conning tower hatch. Supply submarines had a mechanical hoist there to help with the transfer of goods, but men in operational submarines had to manhandle everything that came through the hatch down a vertical ladder.

The crew were given the details of the supply ship only shortly before meeting it. There was little danger of anyone sinking it because U-boats were prohibited from attacking anything, except large transports, within a week or so of the planned meeting. The supply ship *Charlotte Schliemann* was quickly surrounded by a number of U-boats. Off duty watches were allowed on board her to take hot baths or showers, stretching their legs and finding new faces to swap news with. On this occasion the boats around the *Charlotte Schliemann* were U178 (Wilhelm Dommes), U196 (Eitel-Friedrich Kentrat), U197 (Robert Bartels), U198 (Werner Hartmann), and U181 (Wolfgang Lüth).

The refuelling process lasted for four days while several U-boats milled around the tanker. They would have been hopelessly exposed had they come under attack from aircraft, but the ring they formed would have done more than give any surface ship something to think about. It is quite likely that such hitting power could also have sunk the strongest attacker and even heavy cruisers such as those that approached the auxiliary cruisers *Atlantis* and *Kormoran* and the supply ship *Python* would have seen the end of their days. Yet the planning went well and there was no enemy intervention. Despite the heavy work and the constant worry of being surprised, everyone in U178 felt sad when they had to turn their back on the supply ship and once more head into the hunting grounds of the vast Indian Ocean.

Dommes was taking nothing for granted and told the men that he was hoping for some lucrative targets on the way. He therefore immediately instigated a series of drills to get the men back into their old routine. This worked well, except that the anticipated targets did not materialise as expected, and they had to wait a while before the 2,669 grt Norwegian *Breiviken* from Bergen came into sight. Sailing under the Allied flag, it fell foul of a torpedo. All this happened so quickly that there was not time even to send a distress call, leaving U178 in a good position to chase another set of mast tips spotted by the lookouts earlier. They were far enough away to warrant a spread of two torpedoes, one hitting fair and square while the other continued running on its own without impacting anything other than the bottom of the ocean. It took half an hour for the ship to fill with water and sink. Seeing no signs of imminent retribution, Dommes then closed in to find that he had sunk the 4,774 grt Greek ship *Michael Livanos* sailing from Aden to Lourenço Marques in ballast. Once again the radio had not been used to send a distress call, meaning that U178 refrained from reporting these successes to base in order not to reveal the boat's position.

Following these easy sinkings, things did not work out quite as expected.

Above and below: Survivors from the Norwegian freighter *Breiviken* alongside U178. Dealing with men in lifeboats and on rafts was such a traumatic experience that the majority of men were not allowed on deck when such exchanges took place.

Another ship came into sight, running so high in ballast that the top of the propeller lashed out above the surface of the water. It had depth charge throwers clearly visible on the stern and what looked like some guns covered with tarpaulin, suggesting that it could well have hostile intentions. This time Dommes started his run-in to attack so early that the target had ample time to yaw towards him, shortening the gap between the two and thus bringing the submarine a little too close to the target. At the same time it was impossible to turn to allow the stern tubes to be used. So it was a case of remaining submerged and waiting for another attack a few hours later when it was dark. Although the target did not look too impressive, the men aboard were certainly fully awake and two torpedoes had only just left the tubes when the ship stopped by going hard astern. As a result, both torpedoes missed. This put U178 in rather a dire predicament because the night was light enough for the lookouts to spot the U-boat, and remaining out of sight would entail firing over such a long distance that the torpedoes were likely to miss. This time U178 seemed to have the weather gods on its side. Suddenly and without warning, the men found themselves engulfed by a grey mist that gave them the ideal opportunity of creeping up on their target.

Several hours passed before Dommes managed to fire another spread of two torpedoes. He would have loved to shoot more but the bow tubes were now filled with two different types, each running at different speeds, making a bigger salvo impractical. Despite conditions having been good, the results were infuriating. One torpedo ran ahead of the target and the other passed behind it. The opposition had obviously been spending the past couple of hours polishing their lucky charms and must have noticed at least one of the torpedoes, probably the one running in front of their bow, for the ship stopped for a while before reversing. Then, when the next torpedo was running, the propeller started churning again to move the vessel out of the way. This put Dommes into a calamitous predicament because his lookouts had already reported a number of guns aboard the target being manned. If their shooting was as good as their avoiding manoeuvres then things might become rather awkward for U178. Dommes also considered another torpedo attack to be out of the question because the sea had now calmed to a mirror smooth surface with virtually no wind. So instead of taking on the old seadog aboard the freighter in a duel, he decided to play for time and withdraw to reload the torpedo tubes. After all, this little escapade had cost an entire load of six torpedoes.

This incident continued to vex both Dommes and Spahr, and it was discussed again when they met long after the war. Spahr was under the impression that the ship had wired an alarm bell to its sound detector. These devices had been developed to such an extent that there was no longer any need for anyone to listen to the monotonous tone continuously. Instead the microphones could be left on in such a manner that they responded to any change picked up by the sound receivers. Spahr maintained that with such a set-up one would need only to instruct the helmsman to ring down 'Full astern' while turning the rudder hard over as soon as the alarm went off, indicating something noisy was approaching the ship. Any fired torpedo would thus miss the target.

Dommes also made the most of the favourable weather conditions after having withdrawn to readjust the torpedoes. The four spares in the upper deck tubes were moved into the bow and stern compartments from where they could be fired. At best, a minimum of half an hour per torpedo was required to move one of them and usually, when conditions were good, commanders allowed considerably more time for such a cumbersome operation. The tenseness of the failed attack was relieved by a signal from HQ that gave both U178 and U196 (Eitel-Friedrich Kentrat) the freedom to do what they liked rather than following the orders issued earlier. Obviously the U-boat Operations Room had also come to the conclusion that changes had to be made if the boats were going to achieve any worthwhile results in those far-off waters. The conditions there were obviously different to what had been expected earlier.

The commander of U178 had not been too well for some time. This started with such a severe stomach cramp a few weeks earlier that the men close to Dommes were alarmed by his reaction, although they were not too concerned because the pain seemed to subside relatively quickly. However, it was obviously now getting worse, causing Dommes to hand over command for considerable periods to first watch officer Spahr. The crew were convinced that Dommes was in dire need of a prolonged holiday. After all, he had been in the bitterest of action without much rest since early 1941. His period as commander of U178 may not have been terribly exciting, but it had been far more stressful than average commanders were experiencing. Dommes also seemed to be suffering from bouts of depression, saying that there was no way they would ever get home again from this engagement. This could have proved fatal and damaged morale beyond repair had it not been for a powerful team supporting him. It was the chief engineer, Karl-Heinz Wiebe, who had strong words with him, saying that it was irresponsible to make such statements in the presence of the men. Dommes might have been down but he was definitely not out, responding by refraining from making such negative comments, but keeping the daily routine going was terribly difficult. It was the same every day and was just a matter of ensuring that everything, machinery and men, was running smoothly.

During the morning of Tuesday 13 July 1943, the men found themselves looking at the lighthouse on the island of Mafamede in the Mozambique Channel. Keeping a respectful distance of 14 miles, U178 prowled in what was thought to be the channel carrying merchant traffic along the coast and this effort was rewarded with the discovery of what appeared to be a lucrative, modern target. Following it until after the moon had set, Dommes got ready for a surface attack. This time the first torpedo hit just forward of the bridge, creating a massive explosion followed by such an intense fire that it looked as if a tanker had been hit. This subsided as rapidly as it had arisen, leaving the ship slightly lower in the water than it had been but otherwise with no apparent change. A *coup de grâce* was called for, but this proved quite hazardous. Dommes was still manoeuvring into a suitable position when the ship turned to expose its side to the U-boat and two large guns opened fire. A tricky situation. Dommes immediately dropped into the depths, not wanting to risk being damaged and possibly having the pressure hull holed. The next torpedo, again one of the fast type driven by an internal combustion engine, caused the target to settle deeper in the water without creating too much of a commotion. It appeared as if the hit had been in the engine room and the ship obviously had several watertight compartments, meaning that several of these could be flooded before it started sinking. The next torpedo did the trick, causing the stern to sink deeper and eventually disappear. After the war, it was possible to establish that this had been the 7,191 grt American freighter *Robert Bacon*, which went down at 15°25'S 41°13'E. Sinking ships had now become another part of the otherwise boring routine, and the most exciting event at this period of time was when one of the more intelligent men aboard calculated that they had enough fuel on board for only another sixty days and would then either be dead or have berthed in Bordeaux. This latter thought provided a great boost to the crew's sagging morale.

Unfortunately, things were not that easy, especially as the refuelling by the *Charlotte Schliemann* had brought a few unwanted guests on board. Despite every effort having been made to ensure that everything was clean, there must have been batches of tiny eggs among some of the provisions and these were now producing a second generation of cockroaches. Regarded as exotic nuisances at first, they became aggressive enough to chew off patches of skin while the men were sleeping, making life miserable. This pest provided the crew with a new sport of inventing all manner of traps to catch the offenders. However, the breeding capacity of cockroaches in the warm and damp air of the U-boat was greater than the traps, and the sport of hunting them soon turned into a painful plague. The creatures crawled into tiny nooks and crannies where the men could not get at them, and could go for days on end without feeding. They tended to come out only when it was dark, making them more than just a nuisance – they turned out to be a real nightmare. In the end, when the boat was fumigated in port, men collected more than thirty wheelbarrow loads of dead cockroaches from the submarines. The trouble was that while collecting the corpses the men saw other cockroaches that had obviously survived the gassing crawl away into tight hiding places.

It was 04.00 hours on 16 July 1943 when a few traces of smoke on the horizon caused Dommes to change course. Three hours later the mast tips came into sight, leaving an estimated distance to the target of about 15 nautical miles. Now able to work out approximately the ship's direction, Dommes increased speed to get in front but the ship also seemed to have zigzagged away, meaning that U178 was getting no nearer, and then a series of rain squalls decreased visibility considerably. Remaining on his general course, Dommes was later rewarded by an improvement in visibility and it was shortly after lunch when the lookouts sighted the tell-tale smoke cloud again. This time, when some 13 nautical miles away, Dommes dived for a submerged attack, shooting two electric torpedoes from the rear tubes at a range of about 10 miles. The approach was perfect, just as described in the training schedules, but the torpedoes seemed to malfunction. There was a thud followed by a dull explosion, making the men think that the batteries had blown up. Whatever had happened, there was no reaction from the target. It was also possible that vibrations caused by the boat running at fast speeds for prolonged periods on several previous occasions had damaged the torpedo mechanism. After all, the rear torpedo tubes were very close to the propellers, the shaft and main engines, all of which created such a din with violent vibrations that it was futile to talk or even shout near them. The scene in the film *Das Boot* in which the commander is talking to the diesel mechanic while the engines are running was an impossibility. There is no way in which any speech or even shouting could be heard under such conditions.

The target disappeared in another rain squall, giving Dommes the opportunity to position himself between it and the coast in the hope of getting a better view once visibility improved. Everything was perfect until the distance between the two had decreased to about 5 nautical miles when, infuriatingly, the target zigzagged away from U178. Eventually it was midnight of 16 July 1943 when two torpedoes detonated after a run of 132 seconds, indicating that they had travelled a distance of 2,700 metres. Just at the moment that the detonations were heard, the U-boat was hit by waves washing over the head lens of the periscope, making it impossible for Dommes to observe what was going on. Once the head lens was clear again he saw masses of smoke billowing out of the stern and the sound detector indicated that the engines had stopped. Dommes decided to take the risk of approaching the target because from his submerged position he could not determine what had happened and it could well be that the ship was only slightly damaged. This was a wise move. Other than the vessel having stopped and producing some smoke, there was nothing untoward visible and the crew would soon make headway again. As a result, another torpedo had to be sacrificed. This was a dramatic event for very much the wrong reasons. The torpedo was a G7a, commonly called an air torpedo because it was driven by an internal combustion engine that was fed fuel with a combination of steam and compressed air. These torpedoes were ejected in exactly the same way as the other, slower, electric torpedoes and differed only in that there was an automatic means of starting the engine at the same time as the eel was being pushed out of the tube by a piston. For some reason, this device failed to work on this occasion and all the men got was what they called a 'dead man' or *Grundläufer* (ground runner). Training torpedoes were adjusted so that they floated to the surface once they had done their job, and those with live warheads were supposed to sink at the end of their run if they missed their target.

The language coming from Dommes indicated that he was furious and there was no way that the target was going to get up enough steam to make headway again. Turning the boat, he shot another torpedo from the bow. This seemed to work. Surfacing, the men on the top of the conning tower noticed a number of lifeboats occupied by Asian sailors. Despite the darkness, Dommes spotted one white face among them. Guessing that this had to be an officer, U178 approached closer and took the man on board for questioning. This revealed the fact that they had just sunk the 6,692 grt freighter *City of Canton*. Exactly what happened next is now difficult to ascertain and we are not sure whether Dommes lost sight of the lifeboats in the darkness or whether he deliberately kept the second officer, Reginald Harry Broadbent, a Liverpudlian, as a prisoner of war. It was well known in Germany that the Allies were building ships faster than U-boats could sink them. Their biggest problem was not getting these ships to sea but filling them with trained men. So removing any of the officers would make a significant contribution to the enemy's ability to send ships to sea. Whatever happened, with only one torpedo left, there was no alternative but to turn round and make for home. The atmosphere inside the boat improved markedly as soon as the radio message with this intention was transmitted. Only Dommes' poor state of health gave the men considerable cause for concern, and Broadbent was not at all happy being cooped up inside a stinking submarine. He had been used to smoking forty cigarettes a day and was now lucky if he could smoke one or two at the top of the conning tower.

The next bombshell hit U178 on 22 July 1943, when a radio signal ordered Dommes to refuel an Italian U-boat (the *Torelli*) making for the Indian Ocean. The answer was short, saying he had only 48 metres of fire hose on board and therefore could transfer fuel only on an exceptionally calm day. This rendezvous, on 31 July at 15.30 hours, went quite well, making it possible to agree to meet early the following day to transfer the oil. It was considerably complicated because the German fittings did not match those on the Italian submarine, making it necessary for Wiebe to be transferred to the other boat to help out. The Italians had no hawsers on board and U178 carried only a few, all of them too weak for the job in hand. They kept breaking, making the whole process quite a difficult undertaking. The weather was not co-operative either. Nothing much had been achieved by lunchtime, but the waves increased in ferocity throughout the morning, making it increasingly difficult, and by mid-afternoon the two boats were so far apart that U178 had lost sight of the Italians. The following day was calmer and U178 was plodding around in the agreed meeting area when a freighter came into sight. Everything was perfect for an attack, except the torpedo, which failed to function. Luckily the steamer noticed neither torpedo nor U-boat and the sea was too rough for using artillery, so the day ended the same as the previous day.

The bombshell of having to refuel an Italian submarine on the high seas paled into insignificance when compared with what happened on 7 August 1943. While waiting for the Italian submarine still with U178's chief engineer, Wiebe, on board, another signal came from HQ asking for a simple of 'yes' or 'no' answer to the question of whether the machinery and the men of U178 were in a position to reach Malaya. The destination was identified by the reference LF65 from the naval grid chart. Owing to its considerable size and the length of the operation, U178 had a deputy chief engineer on board who doubled up as watch officer. So it fell to LzS Börner to make the decision on behalf of the machinery. It was at around midnight that Dommes gave the order to answer 'yes'. He added that one man had such a serious rupture that he needed an operation and that there were several other men with stomach complaints and rheumatism who would probably not be able to take part in the next voyage. Dommes also made the point that he hoped that the illness he was suffering from would not prevent him from remaining in command, but if he did get worse then he felt confident that the first watch officer, Spahr, could take command of the boat.

Following this, the general situation improved. The Italians came into sight again, U178 managed to retrieve the chief engineer, and the hosepipe connection was established. Only then did the waves start boiling again, so the connection did not last very long. Eventually it was the late afternoon of 12 August 1943 when some fuel was passed over to the Italians and the two commanders agreed to travel together to their Far Eastern destination.

In many ways, the idea of going to the Far East seemed far more attractive than attempting a run into Europe, and less dangerous, until it became apparent that the men were likely to face two enemies instead of one. It was necessary to avoid the Allies while at the same time making sure they were not sunk by over-zealous Japanese forces. There were no normal instructions, charts, handbooks or radio frequencies on board U178, so a wealth of information flooded through the ether, giving the cryptanalysts at Bletchley Park a field day in deciphering messages.

When both U178 and the Italian submarine reached the agreed rendezvous point off Malaya they found the seas empty, with no sign of any waiting patrol boats. In the end, one did turn up and to everyone's joy it was also obviously expecting the German U-boat. To make life even more enjoyable

U178, under Wilhelm Dommes, during its second operation to the Indian Ocean found that soon after arrival in the Far East there were a number of other German U-boats as well as several Japanese submarines moored at Swettenham Pier in Georgetown, Penang.

the Japanese brought two huge baskets piled high with fruit. There was so much that the baskets were left on deck for everyone to help themselves to as much as they wanted, and biting into something fresh after so long at sea was a great treat, especially as much of the fruit was almost unknown in Europe. Having followed the patrol boat, it was 07.50 hours on 27 August when U178 berthed at Swettenham Pier in Penang. Over the preceding 152 days, the U-boat had covered 24,038 nautical miles.

CHAPTER 14

An Unpretentious End and a Miraculous Journey

Having arrived in Penang on 27 August 1943, KK Wilhelm Dommes was appointed to set up U-boat bases in the Far East and his command of U178 was handed over to the first watch officer, KL Wilhelm Spahr. As the shipyard facilities in Penang were not good enough to provide the machinery with the thorough overhaul it required for the return journey to Europe, U178 sailed for Singapore on 9 October, underwent that overhaul, returned to Penang and then finally departed for another operation in the Indian Ocean on 27 November 1943.

It very much felt as if the Indian Ocean had decreased in size since U178 had operated there a year earlier. Aircraft were now flying further away from the coasts, making life in U-boats so much more difficult that many men had serious doubts whether they would ever get home again. It was now quite common to be hunted for two, three or four days after sinking a ship, driving the U-boat men and their machinery to extreme limits of endurance. Many of the crew were homesick for Europe, and remaining in the Far East did not appeal.

Following her successful employment in the Indian Ocean, the supply ship *Charlotte Schliemann* came into sight at 08.30 hours on 26 January 1944, the gentle sea and some clouds providing the ideal conditions for an immediate start to the refuelling process. The tanker crew were as helpful as they had been during the first meeting, only now there was a definite tension in the air. People talked openly about the increased patrols in even remote areas and it was obvious that the men were neither as happy nor as carefree as they had been when they first met. This time it was necessary to leave *Maschinenobergefreiter* Herbert Piekatz aboard the supply ship. He had developed a serious stomach complaint and also needed an operation for a rupture, something far beyond the primitive medical facilities aboard the submarine. In addition to the usual supplies, U178 took some 19 tons of raw rubber on board for stowing between

U178 brought a considerable load of raw rubber back from the Indian Ocean. This had been passed to the submarine by the supply ship *Charlotte Schliemann*.

the upper (outside) deck and the pressure hull, so it took a few days before the meeting came to an end.

It was 08.00 hours on 29 January when U178 headed back into the operations area. There was a mood of depression among the men on top of the conning tower, knowing that they had but a faint chance of getting home again whereas the tanker was doomed. The forty-two men from the original crew of the *Charlotte Schliemann* were still on board together with forty-eight military specialists picked up around the Indian Ocean. The ship had been disguised to look like the type of target U178 had been chasing, but it was obvious that even this was not going to be of great help once the enemy knew the location of the ship. Her days were numbered, and it was only a matter of time before the *Charlotte Schliemann* would be no more. It was not until U178 was far enough away that Spahr gave permission for the transmission of a vital message back to base in France: 'HAVE GOT PROVISIONS FOR 90 DAYS AND 19 TONS OF RAW RUBBER ON BOARD.' The message was a little longer than usual because he also added details about Piekatz being in the sick bay of the tanker and having taken *Maschinenobergefreiter* Johann Meyer as a replacement.

The *Charlotte Schliemann*'s days were indeed numbered. It was 11 February 1944 when she met U532 under FK Ottoheinrich Junker, but the refuelling had to be postponed because a radio signal from France warned that there was also an Allied destroyer in the vicinity. We now know that Bletchley Park was reading the U-boat code faster than the Germans, but at that time Walter Schöppe simply commented that it seemed strange that enemy forces always turned up in remote areas during refuelling. It is astonishing that no one in the Naval High Command noticed this, despite the U-boat Command pointing it out on more than one occasion. Incidentally, Bletchley Park never managed to break the earlier surface raider code, but some of these vessels were asked to supply submarines. The details of their positions were then broadcast on the U-boat code that had been decrypted in Britain, by which means it was possible to send out cruisers to sink them. Bletchley Park had also gained a significant insight into the coastal and Japanese codes, meaning that Britain had considerably more information about U-boat operations in the Far East than Germany. Many of the records kept by German forces in distant waters appeared to have vanished towards the end of the war. The breaking of the German radio code must have been difficult enough, and one wonders what type of brains were in Bletchley Park that they also managed to crack the more complicated Japanese code.

The *Charlotte Schliemann* was spotted by a long range Catalina flying boat. It kept at a respectful distance, far beyond the range of any anti-aircraft guns,

According to Walter Schöppe, this shows U532 coming alongside Swettenham Pier in Penang, but he did not say which of the two German boats was U532.

U532 (Otto-Heinrich Junker) and U183 (Heinrich Schäfer and then Fritz Schneewind) in the Far East on 5 November 1943. Both were standard ocean-going boats of Type IXC/40.

repeatedly asking for the recognition signal, which, of course, no one on the German side could supply. The end came quickly.

By that time Piekatz was reasonably comfortable in the tanker's medical centre, having been given a bunk on hinges so that it did not move as violently as the ship during rough weather. It was on 11 February 1944, a little over 12 hours after having exchanged recognition signals with U532, when the call came, 'Enemy cruiser in sight.' The men reacted automatically, engaging their avoiding manoeuvre, but there was no hope of escaping and the only orders that came were to launch the lifeboats, set scuttling charges and abandon ship. The cruiser turned out to be the destroyer HMS *Relentless*, capable of getting up to 34 knots, twice as fast as the *Charlotte Schliemann*. There was no point in any resistance. Every man on the bridge knew this was going to be the end and the most sensible action was to save as many lives as possible.

HMS *Relentless* came to within a couple of miles before opening fire and launching torpedoes. It is remarkable how, even in such hopeless situations, there are often men aboard ships who continue doing their duty rather than seeing to their own safety. Secret documents were thrown overboard, the radio operator tried sending a distress call, and all manner of little jobs were seen to. The men were keen to leave, to say the least, and the last few had just got far enough away not be sucked under by the sinking ship as the best part of a hundred tons of dynamite flew into the air with the most dramatic effect. Luckily for the men of the *Charlotte Schliemann*, they had been sunk by humanity and the destroyer stopped to pick up survivors. The Royal Navy did everything to enable them to clamber on board and every effort was made to help those struggling in the water. They even provided a tea service for those floundering on their decks. Forty men had been taken on board when something must have happened to upset the orderliness of the rescue. The destroyer's engines sprang to life and it sped from the scene, leaving another fifty or so men floating in the lifeboats.

Piekatz, who was only about 22 years of age, realising that this was a situation of every man for himself, grabbed his life jacket before jumping overboard, and this simple natural reaction became the trigger for a most horrific adventure in which he suffered pitiful treatment from his British captors. Unlike passenger ships, where there was always a good supply of life jackets, it was more common for naval personnel to be issued with their own life jackets. Although these technically belonged to the navy, they counted as each man's personal gear. As a result, one grew up with a powerful connection to one's life jacket and the one that Piekatz put on was a rather superior model, a Dräger lung. Originally developed at the beginning of the century for coalminers, it was further modified to provide an emergency breathing system for men in U-boats. At the same time it doubled up as escape apparatus, and when Piekatz was picked up from a floating raft this piece of equipment suggested that he was not part of the normal riff-raff. The Dräger lung vanished the instant he took it off aboard the destroyer. Someone probably grabbed it as souvenir.

It would seem that the British authorities had been badly hit by rumours or they somehow got hold of the wrong end of the stick and confused Piekatz with someone else. He had come out of school, completed a mechanical apprenticeship and was the type of lad who enjoyed dabbling with engines, but the British authorities must have assumed he was a key figure requiring detailed interrogation. The confusion around Piekatz resulted in him being taken with utmost speed to a special interrogation centre in London, and he must have been one of very few prisoners to have been moved so fast. Even the majority of high-ranking Allied service personnel had to endure a long sea voyage to get home. So obviously someone though this young German lad was somebody really special.

The survivors from the *Charlotte Schliemann* remained on board the destroyer for five days before being landed in Dar es Salaam. A Jeep took them to the railway station and from there they travelled by the Congo Express to Londiani to the east of Lake Victoria. Once there, Piekatz was separated from the other men and thrown into a hole in ground without light, measuring only about two metres by three. He was indeed in a rather tight corner. He could not see much out of it, other than that there was a guard standing at the top. Twice a day he was extracted from his prison for questioning by what he assumed was a German-speaking Jew. The threats Piekatz received were diabolical and he made things worse for himself by refusing to reveal details of his boat, although the Royal Navy probably already knew the answers to the questions they were now pressing on Piekatz. He realised that U178 was going to have enough problems getting home, and he was not going to add to those difficulties. Piekatz was told that he would be torn apart by wild dogs or left in the desert to die of thirst if he did not answer the questions, but he kept his cool.

The intensive interrogation came to end after about ten days when a Jeep took Piekatz to Khartoum, under guard of a lieutenant and another armed man. Flying with Piekatz from there to Alexandria, this lieutenant was considerably better natured than the earlier Gestapo imitators. He treated his prisoner well and provided the same food as he was eating. He even accompanied Piekatz to the heads, but this did not matter a great deal because U-boat men were used to having no privacy concerning such personal matters. Piekatz spent two days in an Egyptian prison before being taken by another aircraft to Gibraltar via Tobruk, Oran and Tunis. Here the lieutenant handed his charge over to a captain before the flight continued in a four-engine aircraft via Spain to London. There Piekatz found himself among other U-boat men and Luftwaffe personnel for about a fortnight in what appeared to be a reasonable interrogation camp. Eventually Piekatz was pushed into a van without windows and without light, taken to some other building and locked in a simple room with a bed but no mattress. This consisted of a metal frame supporting a coarse net made up of springs and interlocking hooks with sharp ends and the various components were of different thicknesses so that lying on the bed for any length of time was most painful. Every time he woke he found that he had the pattern of the springs and wires on his body. However, Piekatz remained silent, keeping the details of U178 to himself. He knew his comrades would still be at sea for several more weeks.

Finding information about Allied interrogation centres is not easy and even if records were kept, most of them were probably pulped after the war. It would seem that men were treated reasonably well, although some had to suffer the most horrendous tortures and this ill-treatment continued for many years after the end of the war. It was claimed that the treatment got considerably worse once there were no longer any Allied prisoners in Germany.

By the time Piekatz arrived in London, U178 had left the *Charlotte Schliemann* long behind and a knotty drama had been enacted in the Indian Ocean. The details of this vary slightly and it would appear that no one has yet published a definitive account. The reason for this is that many of the German records never got back to Europe, and even long after the war the Royal Navy was reticent in allowing non-naval officer access to its records.

The basic established facts are as follows. Sailing from Japan, the *Charlotte Schliemann* supplied the following boats from the first wave to travel to the Far East shortly after 21 June 1943, some 600 miles south of Mauritius: U177 (KK Robert Gysae), U178 (KK) Wilhelm Dommes, U181 (KzS Kurt Freiwald), U196 (KK Eitel-Friedrich Kentrat), U197 (KL Robert Bartels), and U198 (KzS Werner Hartmann). Some authors have included U195 (KK Heinz Buchholz), but I have been unable to find any records of her having been refuelled.

The *Charlotte Schliemann* then returned to Japan, where she received a thorough overhaul and the second wave of *Monsun* boats were supplied by her and by the supply ship *Brake* as follows:

- U168 (KL Helmuth Pich) met the *Brake* south of Mauritius on 11 September 1943; met the *Brake* 1,000 miles south-east of Mauritius on 11 March 1944;
- U178 (KL Wilhelm Spahr) met the *Charlotte Schliemann* 1,000 miles south-east of Mauritius on 27 January 1944. Refuelled U532 on 27 February 1944; Was ordered to supply UIT22, but the Italian boat was sunk before the meeting could take place;
- U188 (KL Siegfried Lüdden) met the *Brake* south of Mauritius on 11 September 1943;

Above and below: Men from U178 in Penang with their Japanese hosts. Wilhelm Dommes can be identified by the Knight's Cross around his neck.

USS *Altamaha* was an Attacker-class escort carrier that served during the Second World War as HMS *Battler* in the Royal Navy.

- U510 (KL Alfred Eick) 100 miles south-east of Mauritius on 27 January 1944;
- U532 (FK Ottoheinrich Junker) met the *Charlotte Schliemann* on 11 February 1944, bad weather preventing refuelling; picked up the *Charlotte Schliemann*'s crew and refuelled from U178 on 27 February 1944; met the *Brake* south-east of Mauritius on 11 March 1944;
- UIT24 refuelled from U532 on 19 March 1944 because the *Brake* had been sunk;
- U1062 (OLzS Karl Albrecht) from Bergen to Penang with a load of torpedoes was refuelled from U542 (OLzS Christian-Brandt Coester) on 10 April 1944.

The German decision to send U-boats to the Far East did not result in a significant shift of forces until after the battles of the convoy routes in the North Atlantic had been won by the Allies. Some authors have looked upon the sending of reinforcements to the British Eastern Fleet early in 1944 as more of a means of maintaining prestige than the urgent need to sink the German supply ships.

By early 1944, there was a considerable British force in the Indian Ocean. The problem was that the area to be covered was vast and tracking the German units was not easy. However, the cruiser HMS *Newcastle* and the destroyer HMS *Relentless* supported by seven land-based Catalina flying boats were attracted by a set of high frequency radio direction finder bearings (HF/DF) and HMS *Relentless* made contact with the *Charlotte Schliemann* during the night of 11/12 February 1944, resulting in the sinking of the tanker. The other supply ship, *Brake*, was found by aircraft from the escort carrier HMS *Battler* on 12 March and either sunk or scuttled later that day when the destroyer HMS *Roebuck* attacked her.

The sinking of these two supply ships resulted in dire consequences for a number of U-boats. Since there was no possibility of sending another tanker, and it would be a couple of months before a supply submarine could be sent from Europe, the only solution to this intractable problem was to curtail any action in distant waters. The only feasible alternative was to share out whatever fuel the submarines at sea had on board. This was neither easy nor welcomed by any of the men, but everyone could see that there was no other solution. The main difficulty with this plan was that the boats were spread over a considerable area and therefore had no easy way of making such a fuel exchange.

CHAPTER 15

Balloons and Autogyros

The summer of 1943 was dominated by stifling days with little wind, and amidst this heat the British and American air forces launched their massive bombing campaign against the bigger German cities. The firestorm in Hamburg took a severe toll, killing well over sixty thousand and injuring many more. The smoke cloud from this attack darkened the midday sky of the Baltic some 100 kilometres away. At around the same time the population of Berlin was decimated by ferocious attacks; cities were starting to become graveyards in which the survivors were left homeless without even life's basic necessities. Even the smaller town of Bremen was now coming under so much fire that an evening out was no longer a practical proposition. Yet the heavy industrial areas remained largely untouched and the few hits against machine shops were repaired within a day or so, meaning that U-boat production continued unabated, day and night. It is strange that Winston Churchill claimed U-boats were his most feared weapon but that hardly any effort was made to slow or halt their production until the last few months of the war.

During that hot summer, there were two virtually identical hulks lying in the fitting-out bays at the Deschimag AG Weser shipyard in Bremen. Today, the majority of historians would easily identify them as long range boats of Type IXD2, although at that time the particulars were so secret that even seasoned U-boat men would not have known much about them and snoopers would not have got close enough to view them. On the outside they looked like almost every other U-boat, and from a distance it would have been difficult to determine that they were larger than the average. No one would have guessed that they had been especially designed to make voyages to the Far East. Yet once they appeared in the Baltic ports they were often referred to as *Monsun* (monsoon) boats, making it obvious to all and sundry what their role would be.

The two new commanders commissioning these monsters, Jürgen Oesten and Heinrich Timm, found that they had both been allocated crews with a high proportion of men with serious sea-going experience. Aboard U863, for example, there was hardly anyone with a rank lower than leading seaman. This was not only a terrific advantage but also a great rarity in those harsh days of war. Oesten arrived at the shipyard with a Knight's Cross around his neck, making it obvious that he meant business, but neither of the two men had a reputation for recklessness. (Timm, incidentally, was awarded a Knight's Cross a few days after arriving in Penang on 9 September 1944.) Both men had commissioned boats before: Oesten U61 (a small coastal boat of Type IIC) just a few weeks before the outbreak of war and then the very much larger U106 (a Type IXB) a year later in September 1940; Timm had commanded U251 (a Type VIIC) since 20 September 1941. So there appeared to be nothing new to them as they prepared for war in Bremen during that sultry summer of 1943. However, their boats had a new and interesting innovation – an aircraft. This sounded good until one looked at the specifications and realised that this brilliant aid had no engine, being kept in the air by the forward motion of the U-boat and crashing down quite quickly if the cable connecting it to the boat snapped. Trying this out in the Baltic for the first time produced mixed reactions. The men specially trained to operate it were full of enthusiasm, while others wondered whether this raised lookout platform would ever bring any results. Retrieving the machine suggested that a lot more training would be necessary, and a life jacket would be an essential part of the outfit for the operator. The trials also suggested that only good swimmers should be allowed aloft, but no one had much choice in this matter. Only three or so of the crew were trained in flying the beast.

These gliding helicopters or autogyros, the Focke-Achgelis *Bachstelze*, were produced in large enough numbers and attracted enough hysteria that after the war they became sought-after acquisitions for museums. At least one of these, the Aeronauticum in Nordholz (Cuxhaven), has gone as far as rebuilding a flying model. Bearing in mind that this basic machine was designed many years before hang gliders, paragliders, microlights and the like, it represented a dinosaur-like stage in the development of flying and did not contribute greatly to the war. It would appear that only one ship was sunk with the aid of one of these cumbersome birds. This occurred on 5 August 1943, when U177 under KL Robert Gysae sighted and sunk the 4,195 grt Greek freighter *Efthalia Mari*. Yet, despite their poor results, they did provide a glimmer of hope during a time when successes were not just dwindling but plummeting into insignificance.

Despite both boats having relatively experienced crews, it was 20 April 1944 before they were ready to leave Kiel for their first operational cruises with Far Eastern destinations. Both had their own separate routes: U862 calling in at Narvik before heading south via the Azores, and U861 travelling via Brazil. Timm, in U862, had last been at sea a year earlier. He came back from northern waters during the Black May of 1943, but Oesten had not been at sea since the end of 1941 and there had been some extraordinarily significant changes while the two new boats were fitting out and training in the Baltic. The most troublesome of the new aids was a set of boxes capable of detecting enemy radar. The annoying effect of these was that they responded slightly differently depending on the strength of the signal they were picking up, and there was no way of finding out how far away the enemy radar set was or whether its operator was in a position to pick up an echo from the surfaced submarine. The boxes would remain silent for long periods and then, without warning, suddenly produce the most frightening squeaks and whistles. These would have been ideal for a horror film but not for maintaining sanity among an already tense crew. Oesten was fully aware that the opposition had taken to flying with their radar set switched on but with the aerial of the transmitter switched off. This meant that they could sight traces of the submarine and then approach it during the darkest night without any signal being received by the target's detector. Then, at the last moment, they would switch on the aerial to get a brilliant confirmation that they were heading straight for their target. The radar impulses were therefore picked up only seconds before guns opened up and there was very little the U-boat crew could do about it. If depth charges were accurate it was unlikely that anyone escaped, but a few did survive to report the matter back at base. Therefore everyone in the new U-boats knew they were heading into such difficult situations.

For much of the time, radar signals were detected long before the transmitter came close enough to obtain an echo, leaving plenty of time for the U-boat to dive out of the way. Max Schley of U861 explained how aircraft became a real threat when the boat entered the 'Rose Garden' to the north of Scotland. The plan was that the boat should remain submerged during daylight and surface at night to charge the batteries and to make more headway. Snorkels were already finding their way to the front, but neither U861 nor U862 had one fitted before leaving Kiel. Now the 'Rose Garden' had indeed become exceedingly prickly. With U861 having just settled on the surface during the first night, the radar detector indicated the presence of aircraft, causing the boat drop back into the depths. The same thing happened an hour later. The boat had only just settled on the surface again when the detector warned of another approaching aircraft. This repeated diving and surfacing procedure became so critical that the comparatively short night would soon be over and things eventually became so serious that Oesten ordered the anti-aircraft gun crews to get ready. At this time large, long range U-boats usually carried two twin 20 mm guns and a single- or double-barrelled 37 mm semi-automatic anti-aircraft gun, meaning that there were now so many people on the 'winter garden' or conservatory behind the conning tower that a fast alarm dive would no longer be possible. Thus it would a case of at least putting up such an

Towards the end of the war many boats carried two 20 mm anti-aircraft guns on the upper platform behind the conning tower. Although these weapons were not often used by very long range U-boats, they had to be fired occasionally in order to test that they were still working.

impressive show of retaliation that aircraft did not dare come too close. If this failed, then the firing would have to be intensive enough to blow the attacker out of the sky. This was by no means easy. The aircraft were huge monsters for such comparatively small guns and their vital components were armoured towards the front, making it difficult to inflict any serious damage. Aiming at them from a rolling and pitching U-boat was no easy matter.

With such a large number of men already on the bridge of the U-boat, one or two more would not make much difference so the Aphrodite crew were ordered up as well. This weapon was a float that was too heavy for a hydrogen-filled balloon to lift off the surface of the water. A length of string, to which several strips of metal foil were attached, connected the two. This invention was literally picked up from the debris left after the famous firestorm raid on Hamburg in July 1943, when so-called 'window' was used to confuse German radar. It worked exceedingly well at sea, and a series of such radar 'foxers' made life bearable in regions that were heavily patrolled by radar-equipped aircraft. The idea was to launch such a large number that any patrolling aircraft would have problems working out which of the many radar impulses was the real U-boat. Launching an Aphrodite was easy. A bottle containing hydrogen was strapped to the side of the conning tower and all the men had to do was to fill the balloon until it had a diameter of about 80 centimetres, unravel the cable and throw the float overboard. The foil reflectors were already attached to the cable.

Oesten was definitely in a bad mood while this was going, but no one recorded the vocabulary he used when ordering the radar detector to be switched off to prevent the audible warning signals from driving everybody berserk. So from then on it was a case of every available eye looking out for aircraft and lacing the ammunition so that the first shots would contain a higher proportion of tracers to put up a dramatic show at a time when the aircraft would still be a little too far away to hit. Hopefully the pilot would be put off his aim as he came close in order to drop depth charges. In the engine room men stood by ready to press instantly on the gas for full speed when it was required. The remarkable thing about this frightening exercise was that nothing happened. The men kept looking for aircraft, but there were none, so it looked as if the balloons with their silver foil strips were working. The following night the men started to launch balloons straight away while the anti-aircraft guns were manned and once again it worked. There was no interference. Yet progress was excruciatingly slow, with the boat managing not more than 2 knots during the hours of daylight, when it was necessary to remain submerged. This meant that in 10 hours they had covered only 20 nautical miles (23 land miles or 37 kilometres). If the boat had been fitted with a snorkel it could have covered at least twice that distance in the same time.

Slowly and painfully the general situation improved as the boat crept further away from the United Kingdom into the solitude of the Atlantic, and the men got used to the new routine of eating their lunch at midnight instead of the middle of the day. The boat felt, sounded and looked like a ghost ship when submerged, with the majority of men asleep. There was a couple on duty in the electro-motor room, and the helmsman, the hydroplane operators and the duty officer were awake but almost all the others were resting while the air in the boat slowly deteriorated. This stuffiness was laced with cooking smells and steam. Schley said that it would have been exceedingly boring had it not been for the medical officer and a war correspondent on board producing a regular newspaper. There was not much to connect the men with the outside world: the radio transmitter was switched off and the receiver picked up only a little of interest. None of the men ever saw the sun nor any ships or aircraft, and the only outside stimulation was that everyone noticed it was becoming warmer as they approached the Equator.

Having reached the fifteenth degree of latitude, it was thought safe to surface during daylight. So far there had been no aircraft in that part of the ocean and although it had become unbearably hot inside the U-boat, the men felt relatively safe and contented, hoping that they might run into rich pickings around the Rio de Janeiro area. However, they did not meet any significant targets. They had insufficient fuel to chase any either, and the journey was long enough without wanting to hang about waiting for targets to arrive. In the end, when one did come past, it did so during a period of such high natural luminescence that lookouts could see the torpedo speeding through the water. Obviously the people at the other end were not expecting an attack because no one took any notice and it was only a matter of minutes before the ship vanished from the surface. Two other attacks took place in the same area off Rio before U861 crossed the Atlantic to enter the Indian Ocean after rounding the Cape of Good Hope. All the action, including the evasion of countermeasures, was brief and occupied only the tiniest fraction of the whole voyage. The U-boat did run into another set of targets, and Oesten had the tenacity and skill to hit a couple of escorted ships.

Once far enough into the Indian Ocean, the designated operations area, Oesten decided it was time to try out the *Bachstelze*. Schley reported the matter with the statement, 'a change in routine at last'. The main problem with this was that the flying crew had not been particularly experienced the last time they tried this in March or early April and it was now mid-August. Yet despite the time lag, the men managed to put the set of aluminium tubes together, attach the rotors and get the bird ready for taking to the air. This was not the easiest of tasks because the parts were stored inside watertight containers and needed to be assembled on a small launching pad attached to the gun platform at the rear of the conning tower. This meant taking things out in the right order. The finished bird did not look too impressive, those on the upper deck being happy to watch rather than being detailed to have a go. It did not look safe. There were three possible pilots, all of them with the rank of leading seaman, indicating that the Naval High Command had not attached too much value to this new contraption. One of the men was required to be the pilot, while the other two controlled the 100 metre long cable and the winch inside the rear of the conning tower. Surprisingly it all went rather smoothly. The boat turned into the wind, the rotors started rotating and slowly the bird lifted off the small launching platform. Following this, the snag was that no one knew exactly how the pilot was going to get down again. Theoretically he should be pulled back to land on the launching pad, but in an emergency he could jump out with a parachute and if things got even more hectic there was a way of jettisoning the rotors and coming down quite fast. The problem with this was that the boat would have to dive without him if aircraft or warships surprised it. So the bird could be used only in areas where there were unlikely to be any interruptions, and a life jacket was an essential part of the pilot's equipment.

The cable holding the *Bachstelze* contained a set of telephone wires, and the device had not been up for very long on this occasion when U861 used it for the first time before the pilot reported a sighting. This sounded marvellous and immediately injected some urgency into the operation, with everything ready to head in the specified direction as soon as the pilot had been retrieved. Surprisingly this went far smoother than it had done the last time the men had tried the same trick in the Baltic. The boat turned to fast cruising speed towards the target as soon as the pilot was back on the landing pad. Then the bird was taken to pieces in order to fit it back into the containers while U861 was made ready for action.

Bearing in mind that nothing much had happened during the last few weeks of being incarcerated inside the confines of the submarine, this was indeed a red-letter day. Action at last, thanks to the naval air arm having come to the rescue by finding another ship. The euphoria did not last long though. It quickly became obvious that this was no ordinary target. There was no smoke coming from its funnel and it did not seem to be moving either. A stationary ship in these waters was likely to be accompanied by sentries, so the prospects looked rather ominous. Closing in at fast cruising speed, it quickly became obvious that it was not a ship but land. The boat was heading straight for the island of Aldabra, some 500 kilometres north of Madagascar. Oesten was not the type to get annoyed about such miscalculations; he merely shrugged his shoulders and made some cursory remark about the navigation department. No one appeared to be especially perturbed about the indifferent performance of the bird, and there were no untoward remarks when it became one of the first items to be discarded in the Far East to enable the watertight containers to be used for cargo. On U861 the space was used for storing earthenware bottles of iodine for hospitals back home.

Continuing northwards towards the Persian Gulf, U861 hoped for some worthwhile tankers before heading further east. There was no hope of being supplied with fuel at sea and there was only just enough in the bunkers to reach Penang. Chasing anything was out of the question, but in any case this subject was quickly forgotten when an operation to access the middle chamber of someone's ear became necessary. So far the medical officer had been regarded as no more than a tourist, although he had volunteered to stand watches with the other officers, but this intricate undertaking, whereby he used an especially sharpened woodworking chisel and a small hammer, became a talking point for some time. Even the commander, who was required to help, needed to sit down. It was a stomach-churning event, with many of the helpers feeling sick, yet everything worked out successfully. The whole process was carried out down in the depths to prevent any movement and the boat surfaced immediately afterwards to clear the oppressive air.

Following this, the arrival in Penang went without a hitch, a Japanese patrol boat appearing at the appointed time. This was not the display of power expected when running into harbour, but there did not appear to be too much

Johann Jebsen, while serving as first watch officer in U123. He later became commander of U565 (Type VIIC) and was subsequently killed in the Indian Ocean on 23 September 1944 while serving as commander of U859 (Type IXD2).

in the way of opposition either, and it was most welcome because a German officer came on board armed with several crates of fruit and some Japanese beer. The annoying thing was that U859 under KL Johann Jebsen had been due to run in with U861 but there was no sign of the other boat. Waiting for it had been more frustrating than sitting in an aircraft after a long flight because some strange regulation prevents it from reaching the terminal. The men had been at sea for 157 days and the wait had been irksome until a radio call had explained that U859 had made a navigation error and was not going to reach the rendezvous in time. Jebsen, from the small Friesian island of Pellworm, had suggested that U861 went on ahead and that he would find his own way into harbour in due course. This seems to have sealed his fate. The British submarine HMS *Trenchant* under Lt Cdr A. R. Hezlet was waiting nearby and torpedoed U859. The submarine surfaced to pick up a few survivors and a handful more were later spotted by a passing Japanese aircraft which called out a patrol boat to help the men in the water. However, the congenial Jebsen went down with his boat. He was one of the most remarkable characters of the U-boat arm, having joined the navy in 1935.

Penang received U861 with full military honours, even the commanding Japanese admiral turning out to greet the crew. Schley said that everything had been done at the base to prepare for the boat's arrival. The men were provided with an excellent meal followed by a welcome shower without the need to economise on water. Then everyone dropped into a bed with clean linen, with no pitching or rolling, no incessant engine noise, and no one coming to wake them for duty at midnight. It was like being in heaven. The men did not learn about the fate of U859 until the next day, but even this disaster was quickly forgotten. Life had to continue, and for the time being the men of U861 were going to take advantage of everything on offer in this incredible location with its lush accommodation.

The life of Riley did not last long. Boats arriving in the Far East had such a battering on the way that they needed a thorough overhaul and there were not enough mechanics on land to do all the jobs. Although relationships with locals were good by the time U861 and U862 arrived, the Germans did not allow foreign workers inside boats, so the crew had to work hard during the day to get their boat ready for the return journey. None of the German staff in the Far East had operational control; therefore plans for further operations had to be made by radio with the U-boat Command in Germany. This, of course, made life easy for the code-breakers at Bletchley Park and the secret Submarine Tracking Room in London, meaning that the limited resources could be employed where they were likely to be most effective. German communications had already become a serious handicap, often with commanders literally groping in the dark, unaware what was happening around them.

One of the plans hatched in the Far East was for three boats – U168 (Type IXC/40, KL Helmuth Pich), U537 (Type IXC/40, KL Peter Schrewe), and U862 (Type IXD2, KK Heinrich Timm) – to continue heading south towards Australia and New Zealand, but with no one in the Far East being in a position to give permission for such an undertaking it was necessary to radio the details to Germany. This was forthcoming, but communications remained in such chaos that no one in U862 was informed that U168 had been sunk on 6 October 1944. The route to be followed by U537 had also been advertised well enough for it also to have been sunk shortly afterwards, on 9 November, leaving U862 to continue alone into the southern oceans. The boat sailed around the west coast of Australia and circumnavigated New Zealand before returning to Batavia on 15 February 1945. It remained in the Far East, surrendering to Allied forces at the end of the war. When the surrender to end the war was signed, U861 under Oesten was in Norway and the boat was handed over to Allied forces in Trondheim.

Albert Schirrmann and Friedrich Peitl, both from U862, confirmed what British Intelligence had written about the poor Japanese-German co-operation. None of the German staff had any real idea as to where the best targets might be found, and the commander of U862, Timm, went as far as flying to several Japanese military centres for advice but returned without having made much progress. In the end, the men had nothing much more than some handbooks to determine where they should strike. Once under way they quickly discovered that much of information in these pre-war publications did not match reality. The German High Command answered the request to operate off New Zealand and Australia with the simple word 'Agreed' but did not provide any further details about where the most worthwhile targets might be found. On their way to the Far East the men had fished some British charts out of the water, but even these did not give enough information to determine the best course of action, and much of what went on was based on calculated guesswork rather than cool reasoning.

On 18 November 1944, U862 left Batavia with only twelve torpedoes on board and much of the available space packed with Japanese provisions. Batavia was one of the places where the navy did not have a great deal of control over the sources of its supplies and a high proportion of the provisions were far below the expected quality. Once the boat was far enough out at sea to make a return impractical, things became so bad that a high proportion of the crew suffered from dysentery. This is classified as a mild illness but can be devastating inside the narrow confines of a submarine. Men were running high temperatures and suffering severe stomach cramps, often not managing to get to the heads before they were overtaken by a powerful bout of diarrhoea. At one stage there were only two officers capable of going on duty and a man of petty officer rank had to take charge of the watch when these were sleeping. To make matters even worse, the southern oceans were showing the men in U862 that the waters there could be even more ferocious than the storms of the North Atlantic. Ballast pumps had to run continuously to discharge the water cascading down the hatch while the boat was cutting through 10 to 15 metre high waves. The noise was so deafening that even men shouting into each other's ears could not be easily understood. The general conditions inside U862 reduced morale to rock bottom, with everyone being pleased when the boat put back into Batavia on 15 February 1945.

By this time the news from Germany had become so chaotic that hardly anyone in the Far East was in a position to provide a genuine assessment of the war back home, so many of the crews started listening to British and American radio stations. Theoretically it was allowed for senior officers to listen to foreign broadcasts in order to gather intelligence and the men argued that since there was such a dire shortage of on-duty officers, anyone with a smattering of English should try to extract some news about the progress of the war. From this, it was not difficult to guess that it was going to be only a matter of time before Germany was totally defeated. Many Germans found it hard to accept that the Allies were not prepared to accept any alternative to unconditional surrender. The majority would have been happy to give up if an alternative face-saving move had been possible and, in a way, the men in the Far East were content to be away from the bloodshed in Europe and to put up with the difficulties imposed by Japanese forces at the end of the war.

Bibliography

Banks, Arthur, *Wings of the Dawning: The Battle for the Indian Ocean 1939–1945* (Malvern: Images Publishing, 1996.) (Deals with the RAF's fight against U-boats. Well written and most interesting.)

Brennecke, H. J., *The Hunters and the Hunted* (London: Burke, 1958.) (Translated from *Jäger-Gejagte*, Koehlers Jugendheim, 1956.)

Brennecke, H. J., *Haie im Paradies* (Munich: Wilhelm Heyne Verlag, 1978.)

Chapman, John W. M. (ed.), *The Price of Admiralty* Vols 1 & 2 (Lewes: University of Sussex Press, 1982.) (An annotated translation of the war diary of the German naval attaché in Japan.)

Giese, Otto and James Wise, *Shooting the War* (Annapolis: Naval Institute Press, 1994.) (Otto Giese served as an officer aboard the blockade breaker *Anneliese Essberger* and returned to the Far East towards the end of the war in U181; James Wise is a retired US Navy Captain.)

Hirschfeld, Wolfgang, *Feindfahrten* (Vienna: Neff, 1982.) (The secret diary of a U-boat radio operator, who served aboard two long distance U-boats, U67 and U109.)

Hirschfeld, Wolfgang and Geoffrey Brooks, *Hirschfeld: The Story of a U-boat NCO 1940–1946* (London: Leo Cooper, 1996.)

Pfefferle, Ernst (ed.), *Kameraden zur See* (Altmannstein: Ernst Pfefferle, from 1985.) (At least fifteen volumes were produced, describing life at sea during the war.)

Roskill, Capt. S. W., *The War at Sea 1939–1945* (London: HMSO, 1954.)

Wynn, K., *U-boat Operations of the Second World War* (London: Chatham Publishing, 1997.)

Index